D1273594

JIM BUTCHER'S

The DRESDEN FILES

WAR CRY

WAR CRY

A secret conflict is raging across the world, from the shadows of ancient Sicily to the nighttime streets of Chicago—a war between the vampires of the Red Court and Wizards of the White Council, protectors of the innocent.

The bad guys are winning.

In fact, the Council is so desperate to reinforce their decimated ranks that they've turned to someone they've long considered untrustworthy: Harry Dresden.

Now a Warden, Harry's been tasked with leading a team of young, inexperienced wizards—and their first mission will determine the outcome of the war with the Red Court...

written by **JIM BUTCHER** & **MARK POWERS**

pencils by **CARLOS GOMEZ**

colors by **MOHAN**

letters by **BILL TORTOLINI**

cover by **STJEPAN SEJIC**

consulting editor: RICH YOUNG

thematic consultants: PRISCILLA SPENCER, MICHAEL ASHLEIGH FINN & FRED HICKS

DYNAMITE®

Nick Barrucci, CEO / Publisher
Juan Collado, President / COO
Rich Young, Director Business Development
Keith Davidsen, Marketing Manager

Joe Rybandt, Senior Editor
Hannah Elder, Associate Editor
Molly Mahan, Associate Editor

Jason Ullmeyer, Design Director
Katie Hidalgo, Graphic Designer
Chris Caniano, Production Assistant

STANDARD EDITION ISBN-10: 1-60690-574-0
STANDARD EDITION ISBN-13: 978-1-60690-574-6
SIGNED EDITION ISBN-10: 1-60690-575-9
SIGNED EDITION ISBN-13: 978-1-60690-575-3

First Printing   10 9 8 7 6 5 4 3 2 1

Visit us online at **www.DYNAMITE.com**
Follow us on Twitter **@dynamitecomics**
Like us on Facebook **/Dynamitecomics**
Watch us on YouTube **/Dynamitecomics**

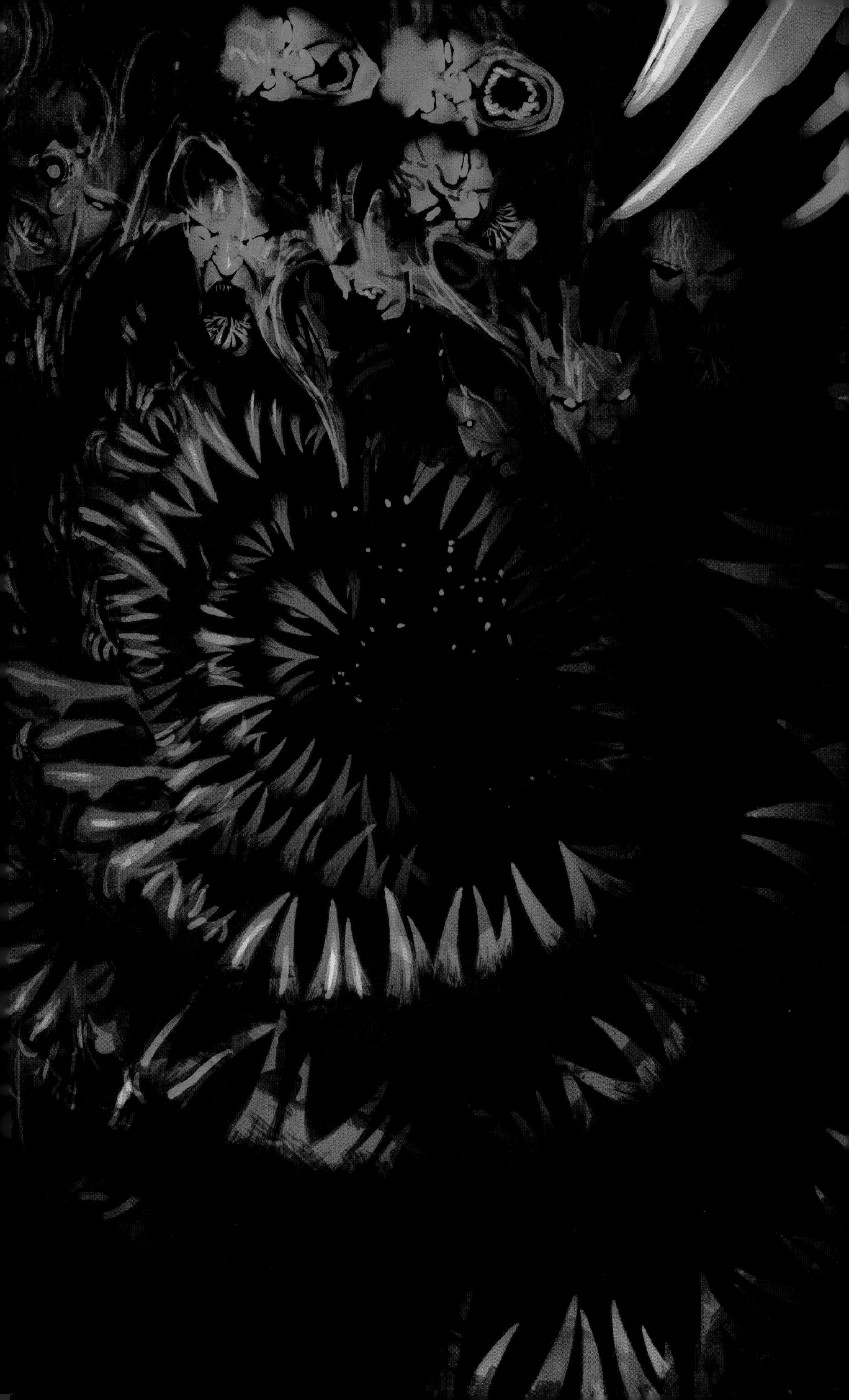

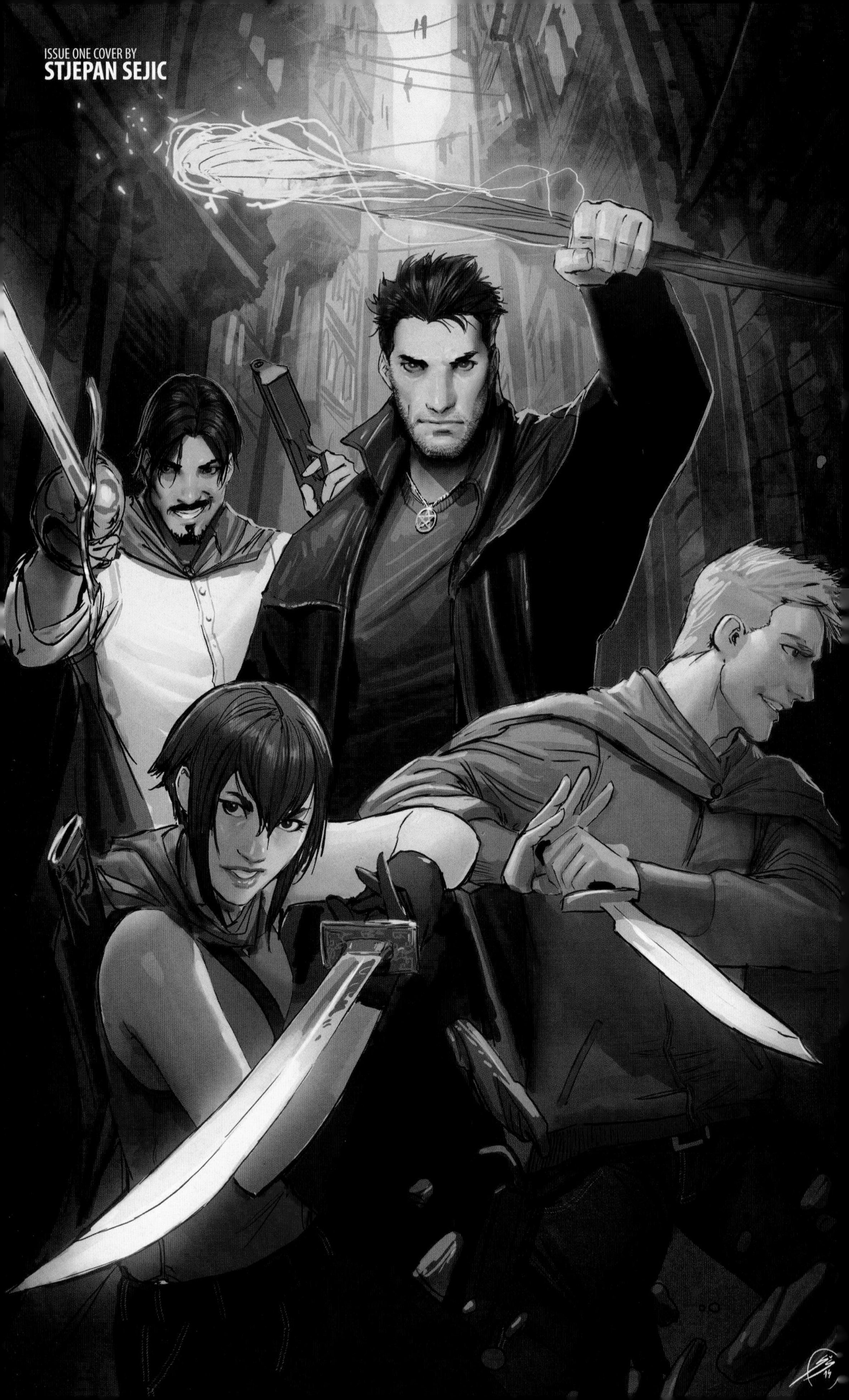

ISSUE ONE COVER BY
STJEPAN SEJIC

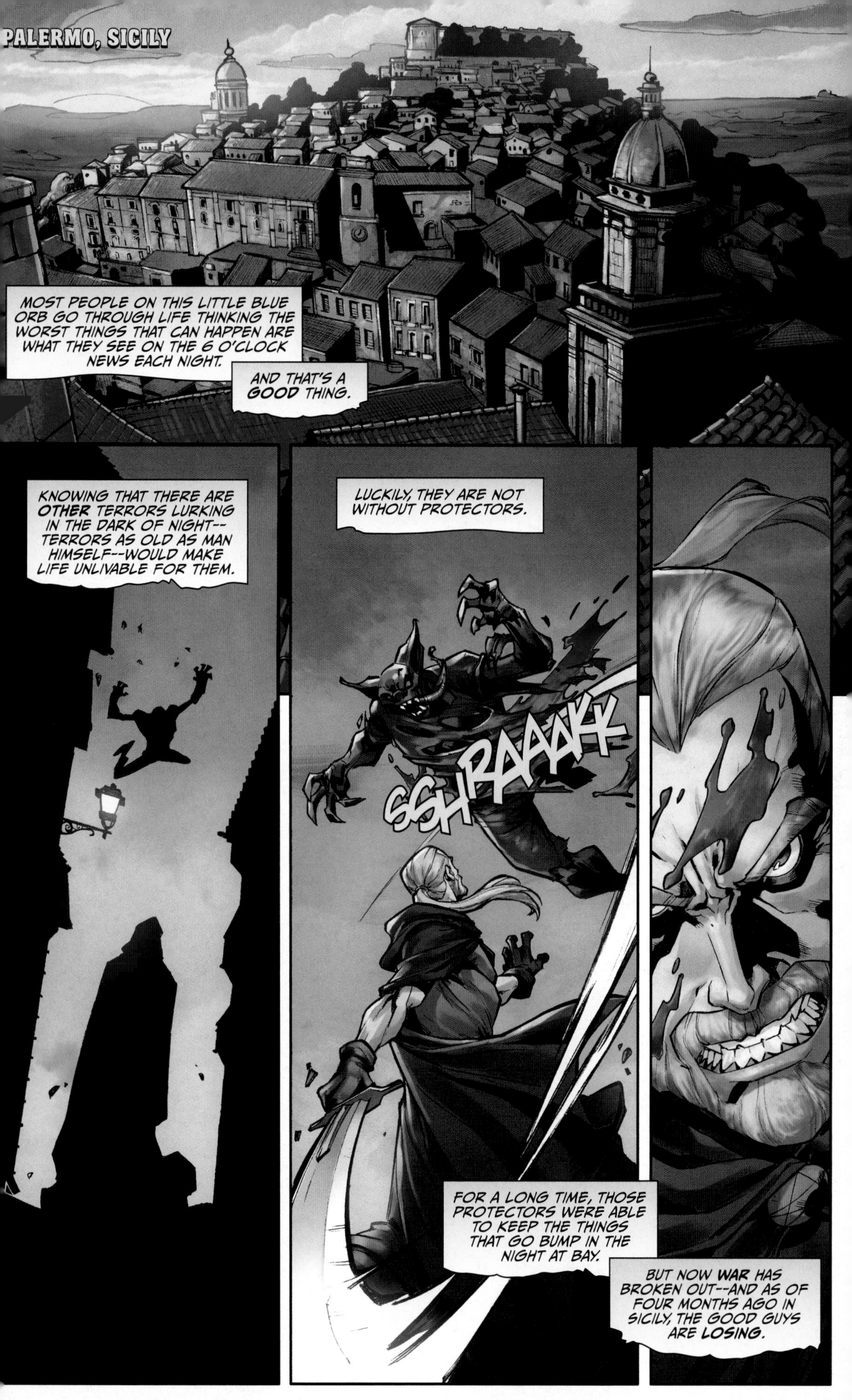

PALERMO, SICILY
MOST PEOPLE ON THIS LITTLE BLUE ORB GO THROUGH LIFE THINKING THE WORST THINGS THAT CAN HAPPEN ARE WHAT THEY SEE ON THE 6 O'CLOCK NEWS EACH NIGHT.
AND THAT'S A GOOD THING.
KNOWING THAT THERE ARE OTHER TERRORS LURKING IN THE DARK OF NIGHT--TERRORS AS OLD AS MAN HIMSELF--WOULD MAKE LIFE UNLIVABLE FOR THEM.
LUCKILY, THEY ARE NOT WITHOUT PROTECTORS.
SSHRAAAKK
FOR A LONG TIME, THOSE PROTECTORS WERE ABLE TO KEEP THE THINGS THAT GO BUMP IN THE NIGHT AT BAY.
BUT NOW WAR HAS BROKEN OUT--AND AS OF FOUR MONTHS AGO IN SICILY, THE GOOD GUYS ARE LOSING.

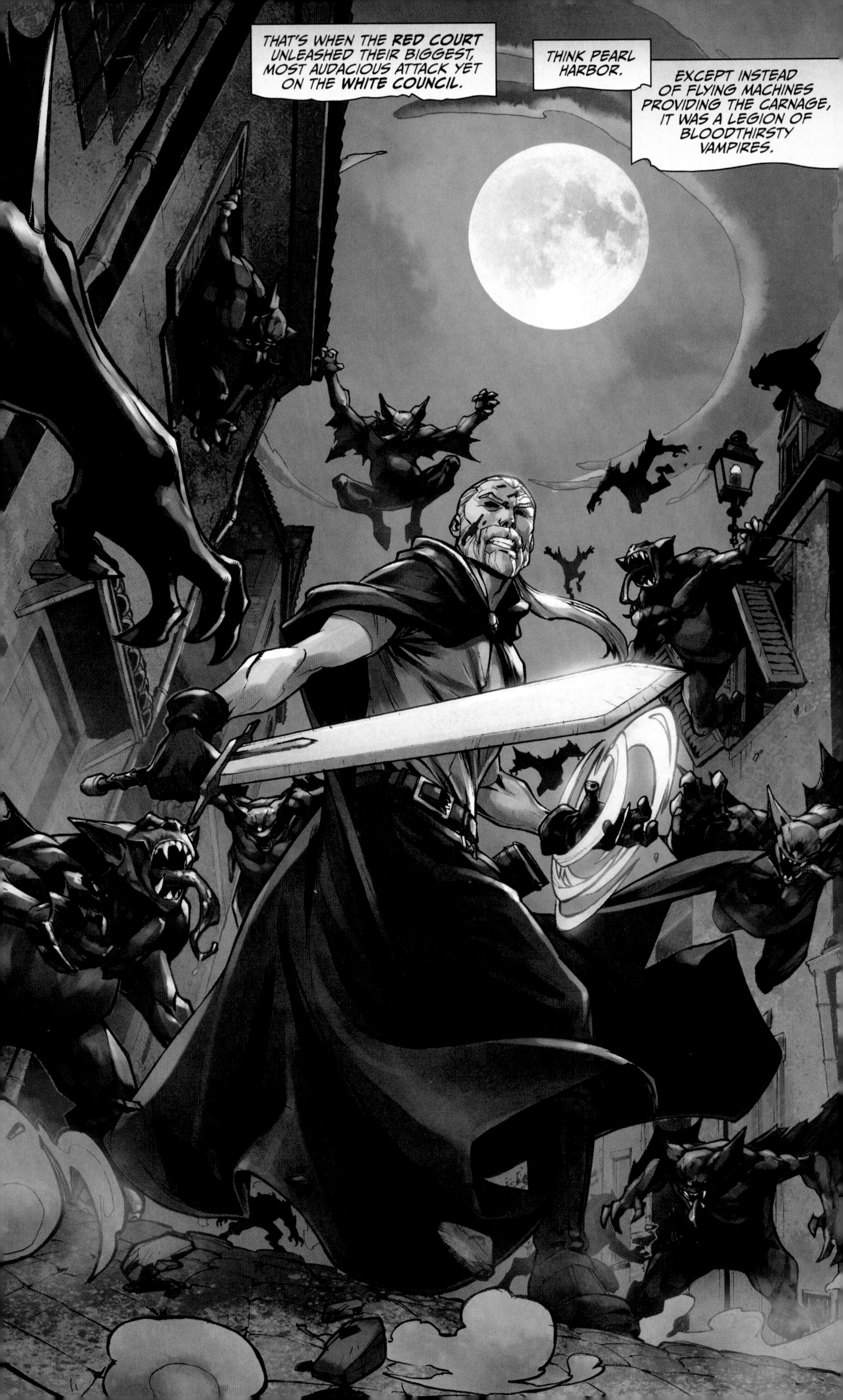
THAT'S WHEN THE **RED COURT** UNLEASHED THEIR BIGGEST, MOST AUDACIOUS ATTACK YET ON THE **WHITE COUNCIL**.
THINK PEARL HARBOR.
EXCEPT INSTEAD OF FLYING MACHINES PROVIDING THE CARNAGE, IT WAS A LEGION OF BLOODTHIRSTY VAMPIRES.

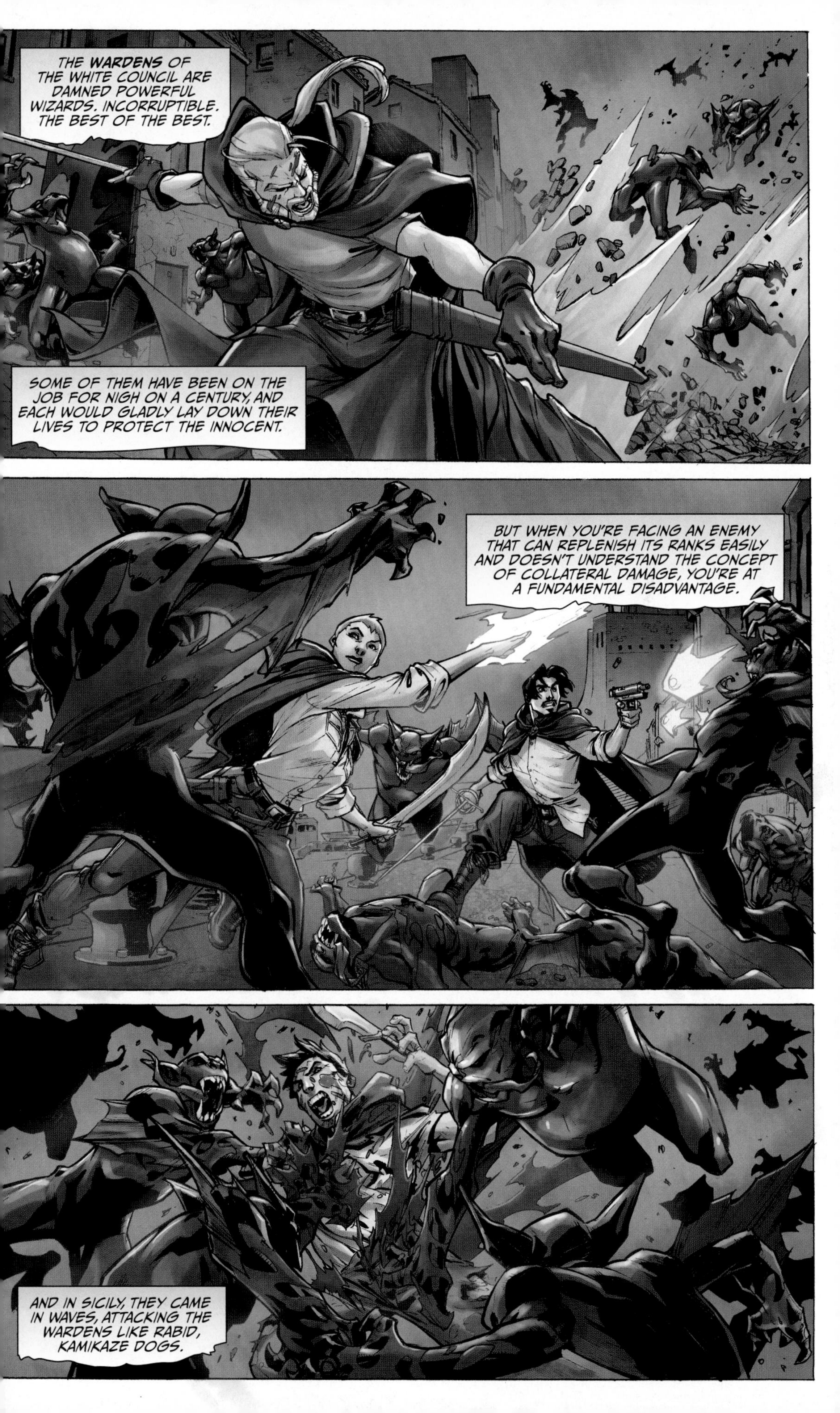
THE WARDENS OF THE WHITE COUNCIL ARE DAMNED POWERFUL WIZARDS. INCORRUPTIBLE. THE BEST OF THE BEST.
SOME OF THEM HAVE BEEN ON THE JOB FOR NIGH ON A CENTURY, AND EACH WOULD GLADLY LAY DOWN THEIR LIVES TO PROTECT THE INNOCENT.
BUT WHEN YOU'RE FACING AN ENEMY THAT CAN REPLENISH ITS RANKS EASILY AND DOESN'T UNDERSTAND THE CONCEPT OF COLLATERAL DAMAGE, YOU'RE AT A FUNDAMENTAL DISADVANTAGE.
AND IN SICILY, THEY CAME IN WAVES, ATTACKING THE WARDENS LIKE RABID, KAMIKAZE DOGS.

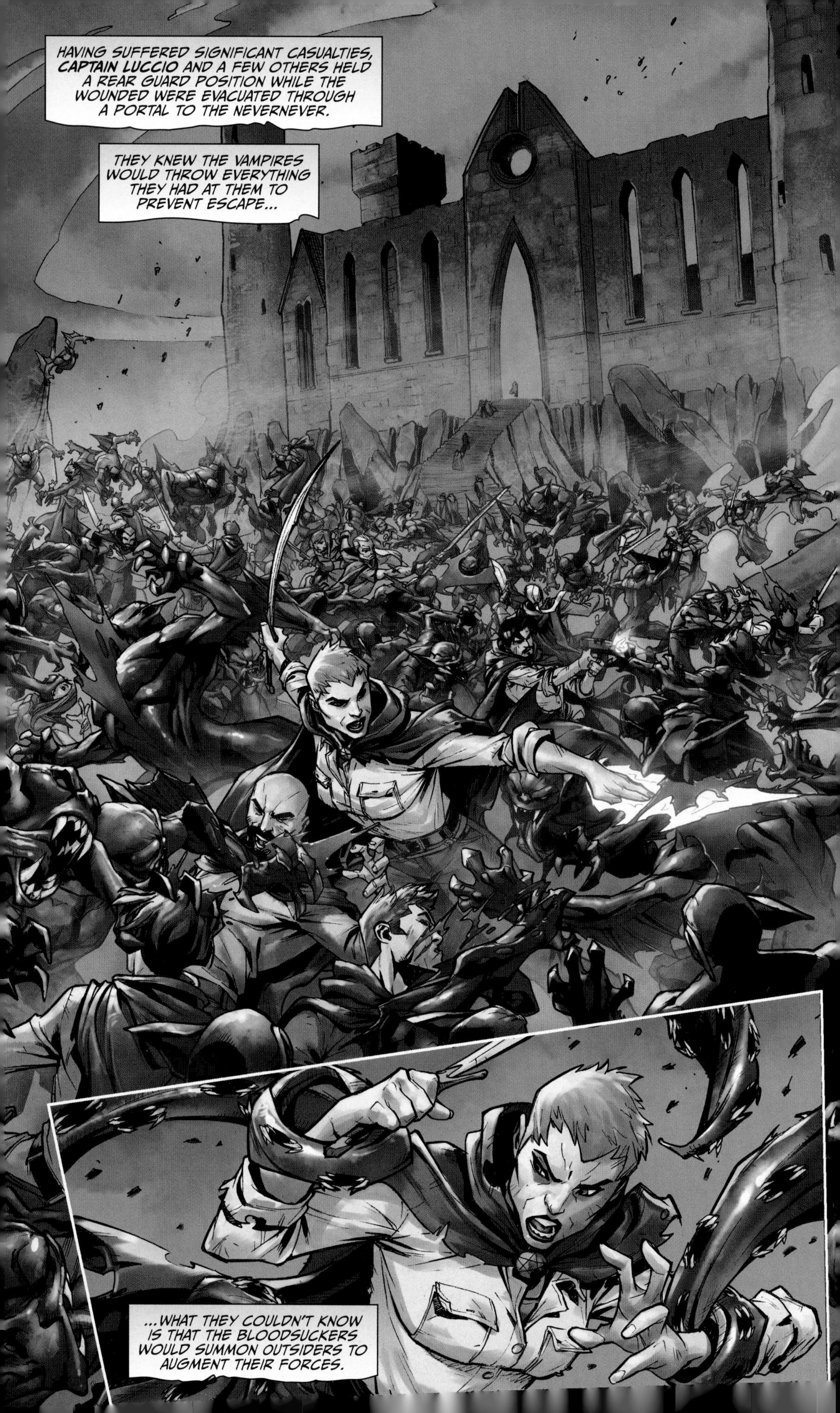
HAVING SUFFERED SIGNIFICANT CASUALTIES, **CAPTAIN LUCCIO** AND A FEW OTHERS HELD A REAR GUARD POSITION WHILE THE WOUNDED WERE EVACUATED THROUGH A PORTAL TO THE NEVERNEVER.
THEY KNEW THE VAMPIRES WOULD THROW EVERYTHING THEY HAD AT THEM TO PREVENT ESCAPE...
...WHAT THEY COULDN'T KNOW IS THAT THE BLOODSUCKERS WOULD SUMMON OUTSIDERS TO AUGMENT THEIR FORCES.

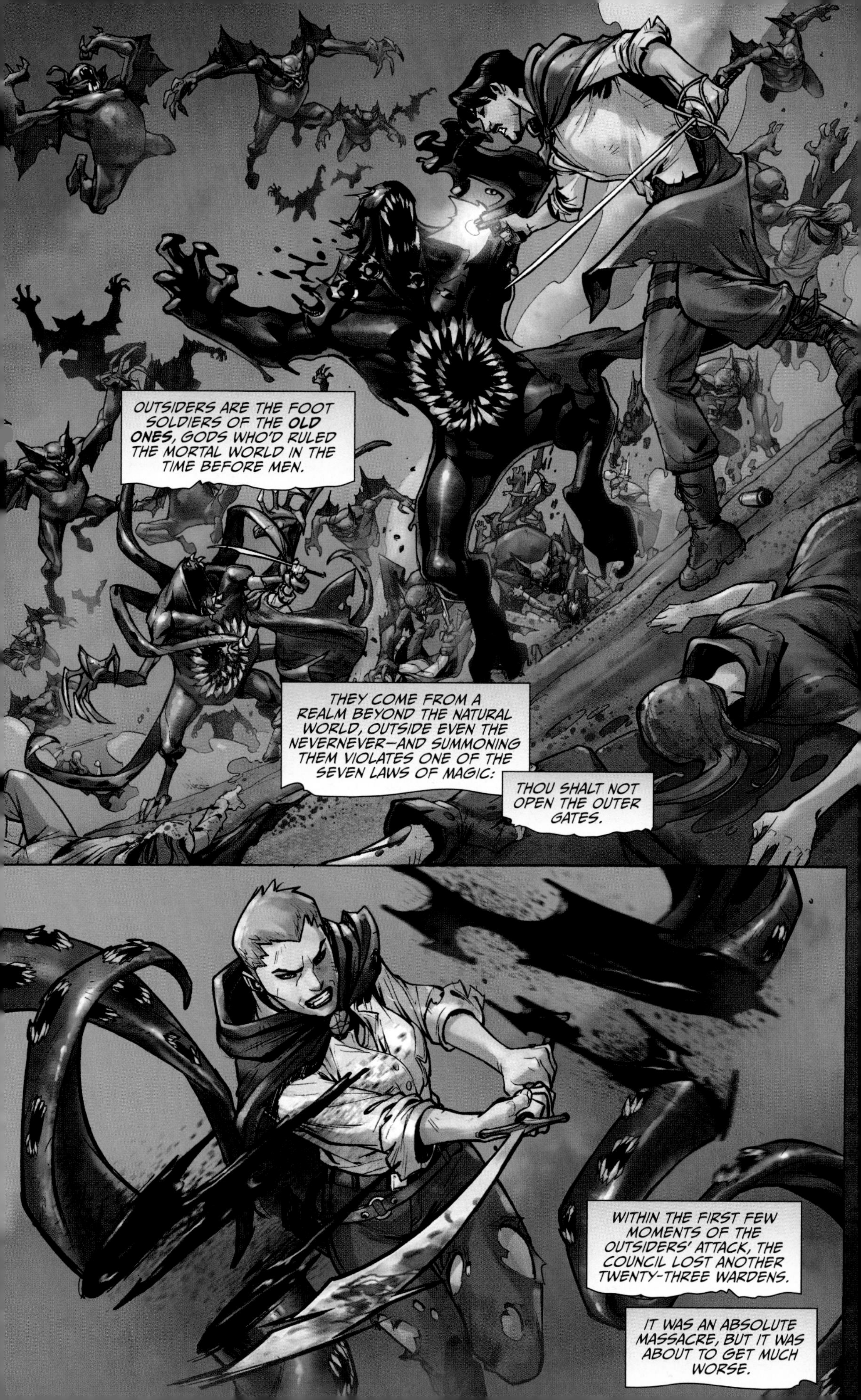
OUTSIDERS ARE THE FOOT SOLDIERS OF THE **OLD ONES**, GODS WHO'D RULED THE MORTAL WORLD IN THE TIME BEFORE MEN.
THEY COME FROM A REALM BEYOND THE NATURAL WORLD, OUTSIDE EVEN THE NEVERNEVER—AND SUMMONING THEM VIOLATES ONE OF THE SEVEN LAWS OF MAGIC:
THOU SHALT NOT OPEN THE OUTER GATES.
WITHIN THE FIRST FEW MOMENTS OF THE OUTSIDERS' ATTACK, THE COUNCIL LOST ANOTHER TWENTY-THREE WARDENS.
IT WAS AN ABSOLUTE MASSACRE, BUT IT WAS ABOUT TO GET MUCH WORSE.

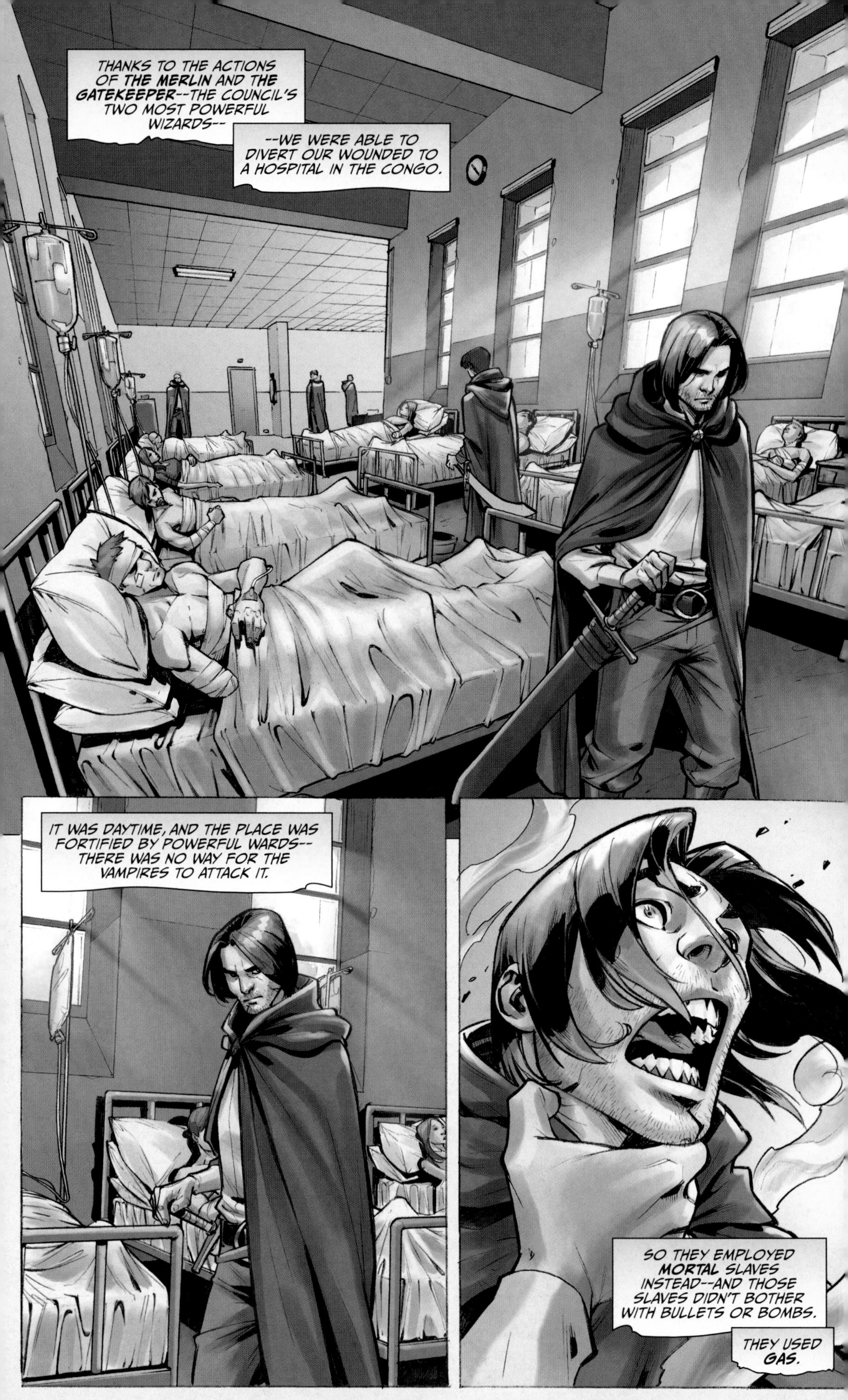
THANKS TO THE ACTIONS OF THE MERLIN AND THE GATEKEEPER--THE COUNCIL'S TWO MOST POWERFUL WIZARDS--
--WE WERE ABLE TO DIVERT OUR WOUNDED TO A HOSPITAL IN THE CONGO.
IT WAS DAYTIME, AND THE PLACE WAS FORTIFIED BY POWERFUL WARDS--THERE WAS NO WAY FOR THE VAMPIRES TO ATTACK IT.
SO THEY EMPLOYED MORTAL SLAVES INSTEAD--AND THOSE SLAVES DIDN'T BOTHER WITH BULLETS OR BOMBS.
THEY USED GAS.

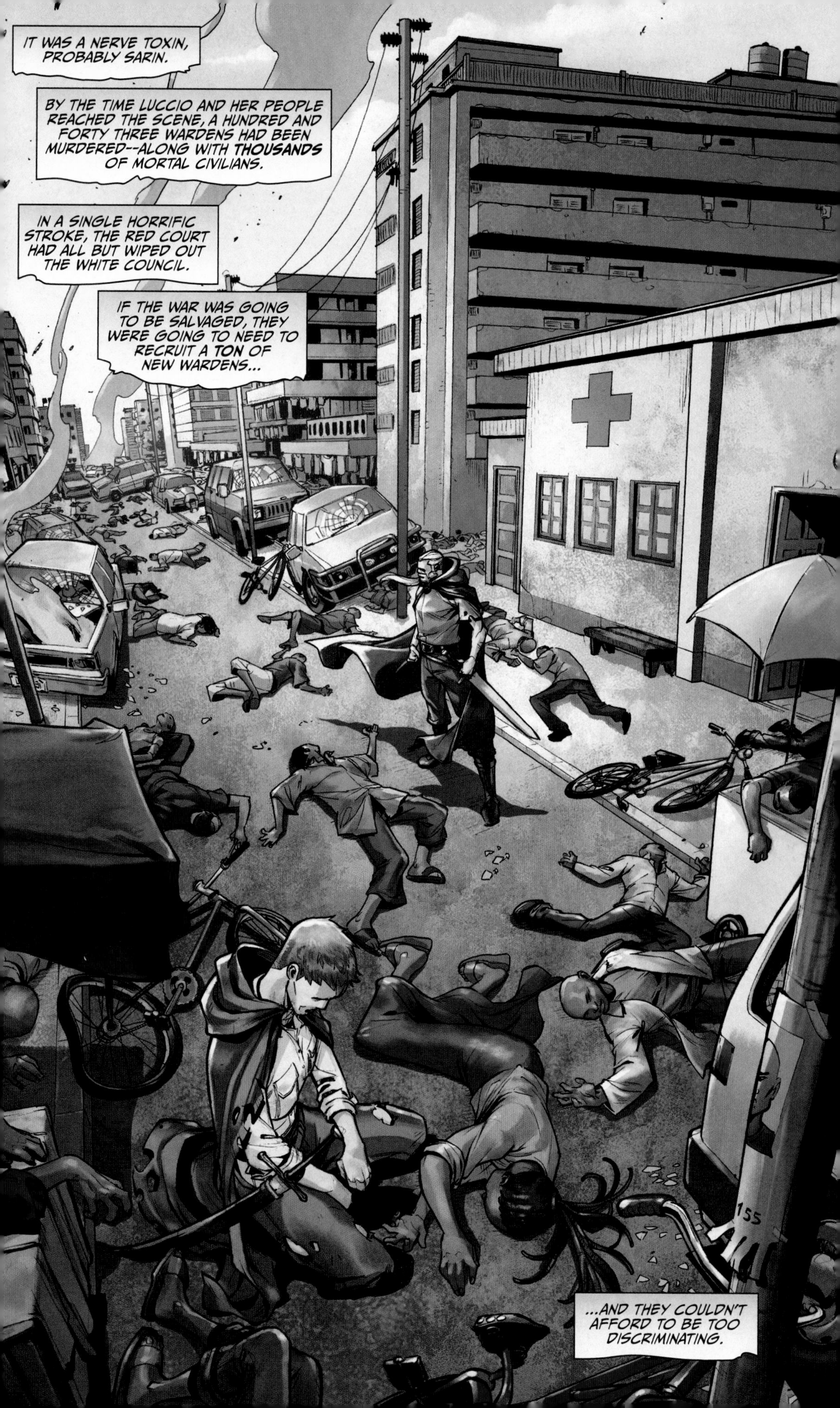
IT WAS A NERVE TOXIN, PROBABLY SARIN.
BY THE TIME LUCCIO AND HER PEOPLE REACHED THE SCENE, A HUNDRED AND FORTY THREE WARDENS HAD BEEN MURDERED--ALONG WITH **THOUSANDS** OF MORTAL CIVILIANS.
IN A SINGLE HORRIFIC STROKE, THE RED COURT HAD ALL BUT WIPED OUT THE WHITE COUNCIL.
IF THE WAR WAS GOING TO BE SALVAGED, THEY WERE GOING TO NEED TO RECRUIT A **TON** OF NEW WARDENS...
...AND THEY COULDN'T AFFORD TO BE TOO DISCRIMINATING.

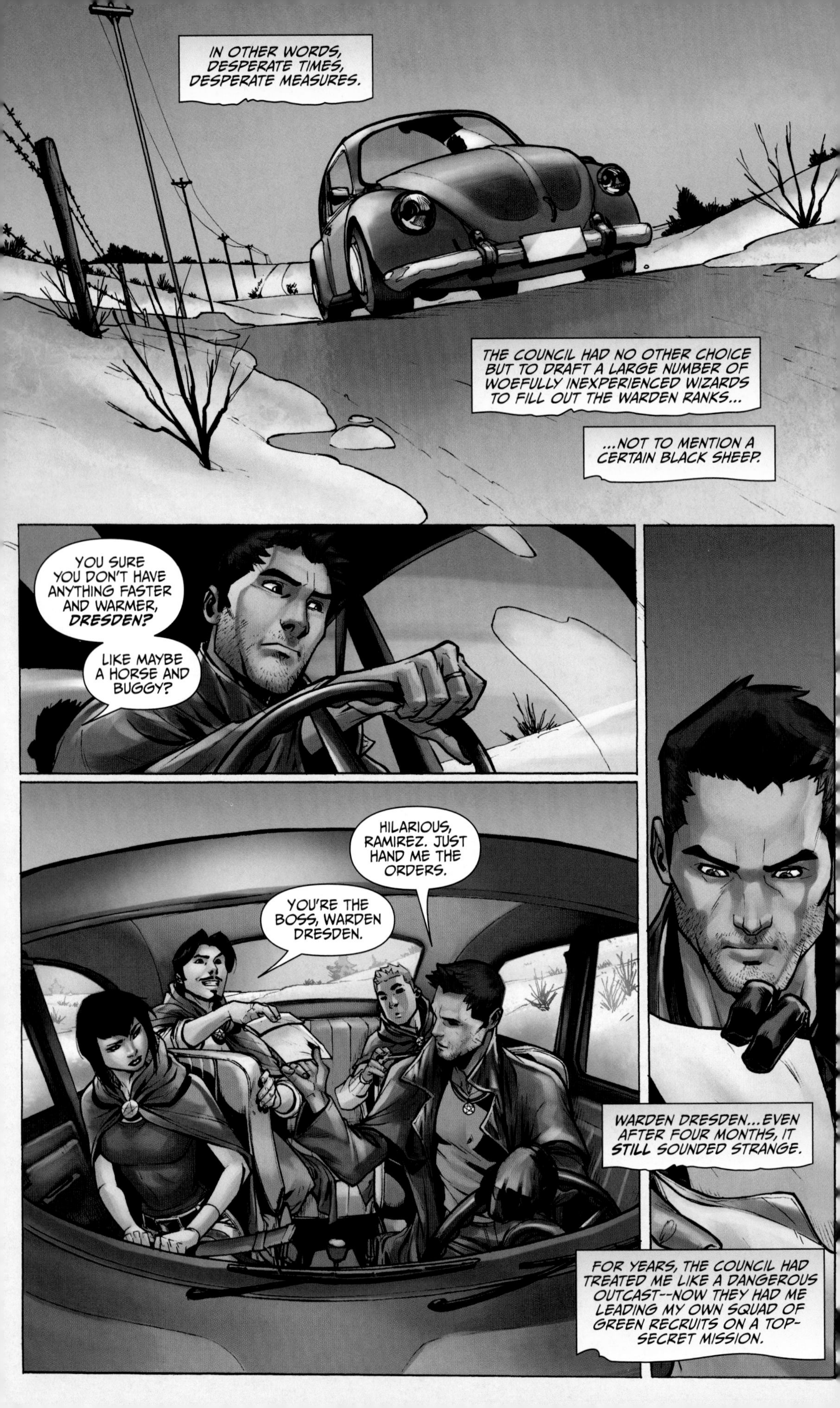
IN OTHER WORDS, DESPERATE TIMES, DESPERATE MEASURES.
THE COUNCIL HAD NO OTHER CHOICE BUT TO DRAFT A LARGE NUMBER OF WOEFULLY INEXPERIENCED WIZARDS TO FILL OUT THE WARDEN RANKS...
...NOT TO MENTION A CERTAIN BLACK SHEEP.
YOU SURE YOU DON'T HAVE ANYTHING FASTER AND WARMER, DRESDEN?
LIKE MAYBE A HORSE AND BUGGY?
HILARIOUS, RAMIREZ. JUST HAND ME THE ORDERS.
YOU'RE THE BOSS, WARDEN DRESDEN.
WARDEN DRESDEN...EVEN AFTER FOUR MONTHS, IT STILL SOUNDED STRANGE.
FOR YEARS, THE COUNCIL HAD TREATED ME LIKE A DANGEROUS OUTCAST--NOW THEY HAD ME LEADING MY OWN SQUAD OF GREEN RECRUITS ON A TOP-SECRET MISSION.

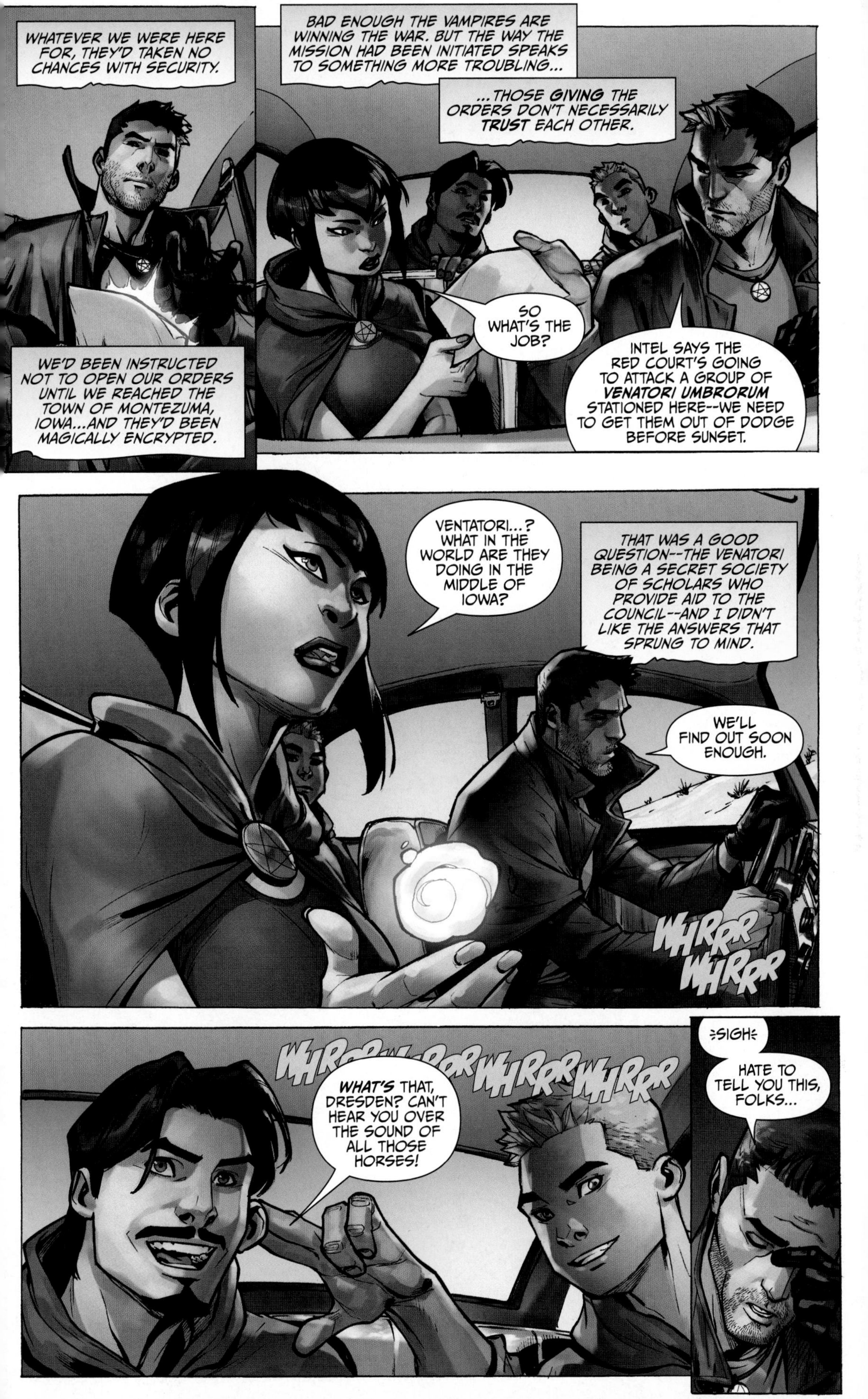
WHATEVER WE WERE HERE FOR, THEY'D TAKEN NO CHANCES WITH SECURITY.
WE'D BEEN INSTRUCTED NOT TO OPEN OUR ORDERS UNTIL WE REACHED THE TOWN OF MONTEZUMA, IOWA...AND THEY'D BEEN MAGICALLY ENCRYPTED.
BAD ENOUGH THE VAMPIRES ARE WINNING THE WAR. BUT THE WAY THE MISSION HAD BEEN INITIATED SPEAKS TO SOMETHING MORE TROUBLING...
...THOSE GIVING THE ORDERS DON'T NECESSARILY TRUST EACH OTHER.
SO WHAT'S THE JOB?
INTEL SAYS THE RED COURT'S GOING TO ATTACK A GROUP OF VENATORI UMBRORUM STATIONED HERE--WE NEED TO GET THEM OUT OF DODGE BEFORE SUNSET.
VENTATORI...? WHAT IN THE WORLD ARE THEY DOING IN THE MIDDLE OF IOWA?
THAT WAS A GOOD QUESTION--THE VENATORI BEING A SECRET SOCIETY OF SCHOLARS WHO PROVIDE AID TO THE COUNCIL--AND I DIDN'T LIKE THE ANSWERS THAT SPRUNG TO MIND.
WE'LL FIND OUT SOON ENOUGH.
WHRRR WHRRR
WHRRR WHRRR WHRRR WHRRR
WHAT'S THAT, DRESDEN? CAN'T HEAR YOU OVER THE SOUND OF ALL THOSE HORSES!
SIGH
HATE TO TELL YOU THIS, FOLKS...

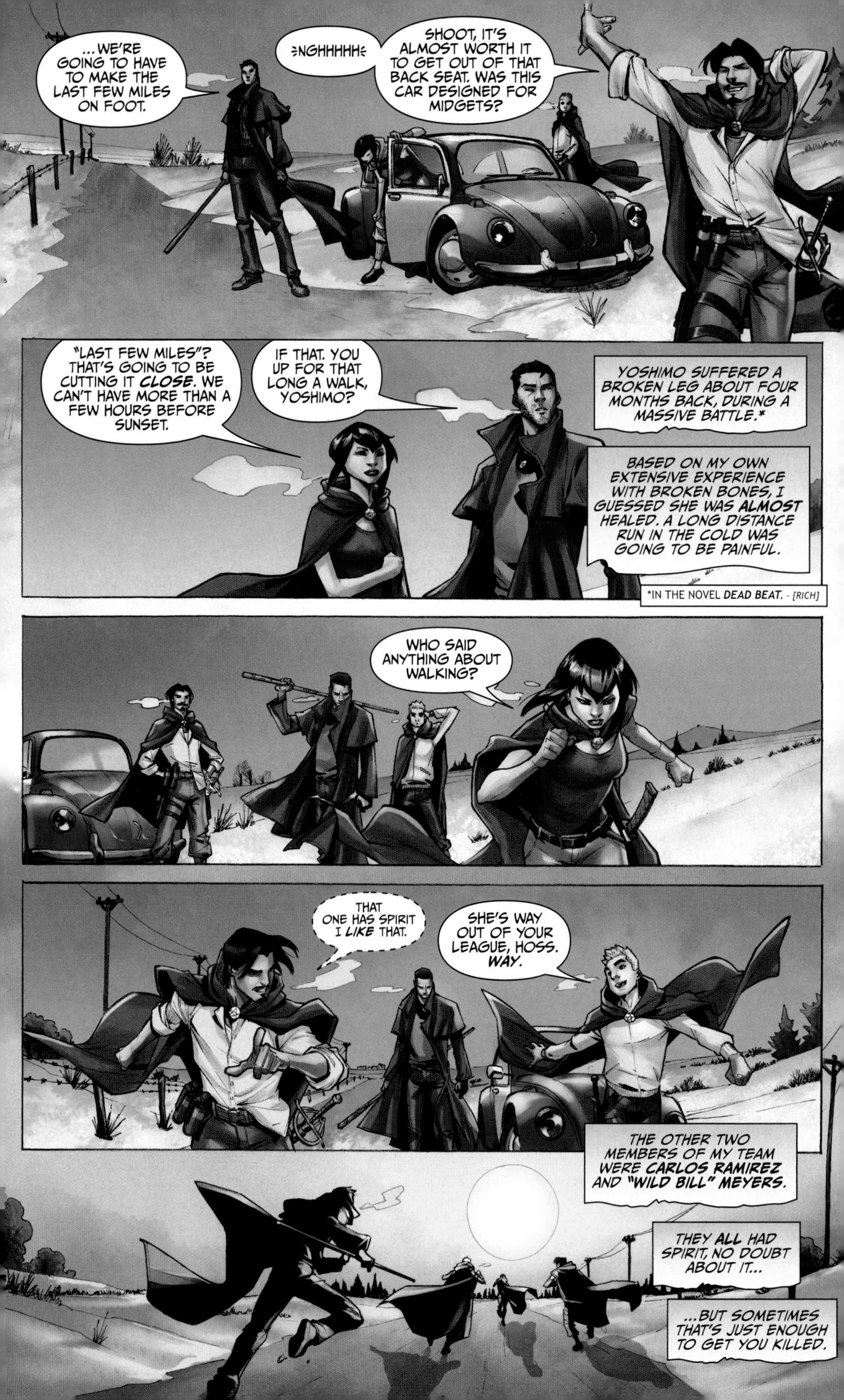
...WE'RE GOING TO HAVE TO MAKE THE LAST FEW MILES ON FOOT.
NGHHHHH
SHOOT, IT'S ALMOST WORTH IT TO GET OUT OF THAT BACK SEAT. WAS THIS CAR DESIGNED FOR MIDGETS?
"LAST FEW MILES"? THAT'S GOING TO BE CUTTING IT CLOSE. WE CAN'T HAVE MORE THAN A FEW HOURS BEFORE SUNSET.
IF THAT. YOU UP FOR THAT LONG A WALK, YOSHIMO?
YOSHIMO SUFFERED A BROKEN LEG ABOUT FOUR MONTHS BACK, DURING A MASSIVE BATTLE.*
BASED ON MY OWN EXTENSIVE EXPERIENCE WITH BROKEN BONES, I GUESSED SHE WAS ALMOST HEALED. A LONG DISTANCE RUN IN THE COLD WAS GOING TO BE PAINFUL.
*IN THE NOVEL DEAD BEAT. - [RICH]
WHO SAID ANYTHING ABOUT WALKING?
THAT ONE HAS SPIRIT I LIKE THAT.
SHE'S WAY OUT OF YOUR LEAGUE, HOSS. WAY.
THE OTHER TWO MEMBERS OF MY TEAM WERE CARLOS RAMIREZ AND "WILD BILL" MEYERS.
THEY ALL HAD SPIRIT, NO DOUBT ABOUT IT...
...BUT SOMETIMES THAT'S JUST ENOUGH TO GET YOU KILLED.

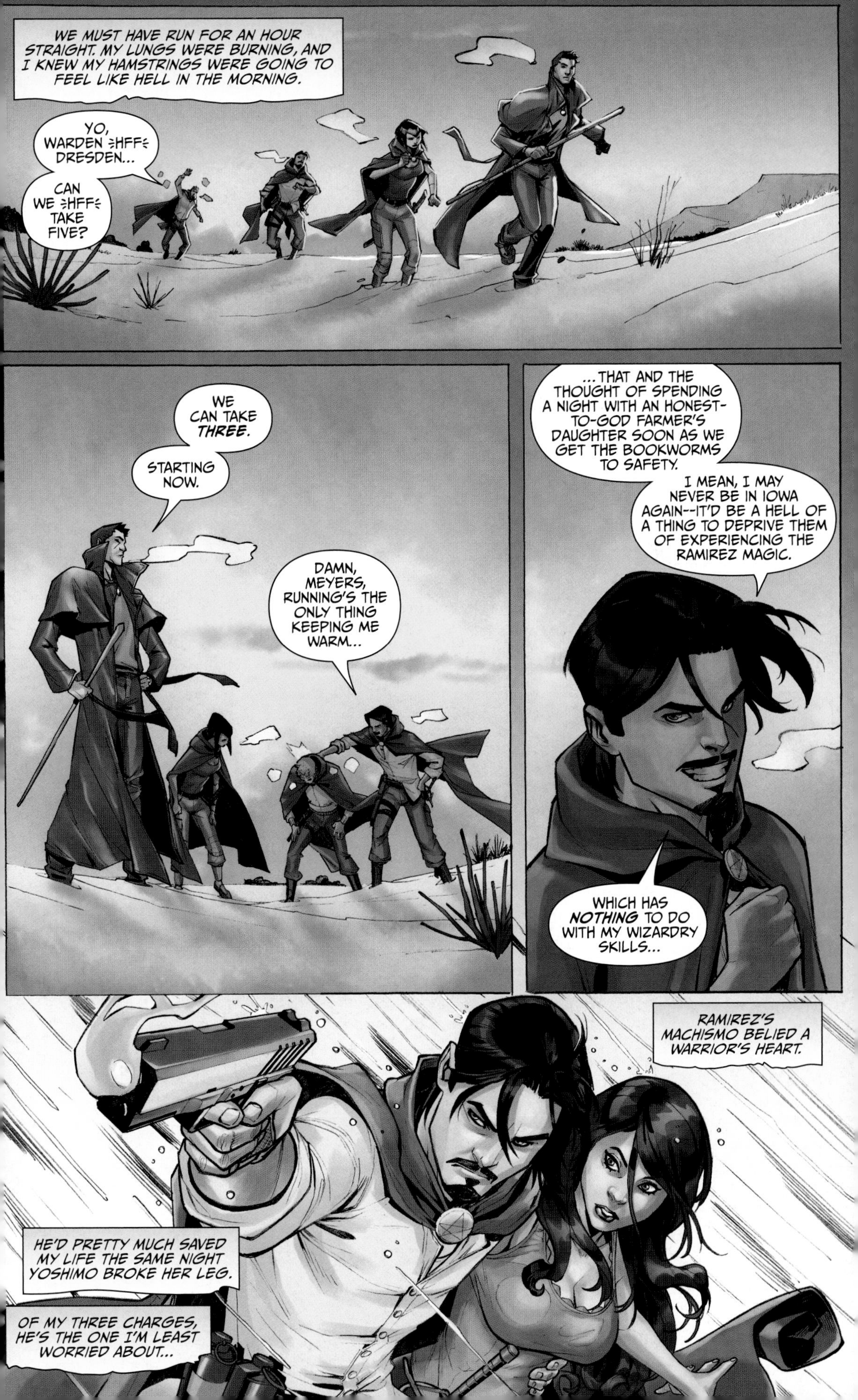

WE MUST HAVE RUN FOR AN HOUR STRAIGHT. MY LUNGS WERE BURNING, AND I KNEW MY HAMSTRINGS WERE GOING TO FEEL LIKE HELL IN THE MORNING.
YO, WARDEN HFF DRESDEN...
CAN WE HFF TAKE FIVE?
WE CAN TAKE THREE.
STARTING NOW.
DAMN, MEYERS, RUNNING'S THE ONLY THING KEEPING ME WARM...
...THAT AND THE THOUGHT OF SPENDING A NIGHT WITH AN HONEST-TO-GOD FARMER'S DAUGHTER SOON AS WE GET THE BOOKWORMS TO SAFETY.
I MEAN, I MAY NEVER BE IN IOWA AGAIN--IT'D BE A HELL OF A THING TO DEPRIVE THEM OF EXPERIENCING THE RAMIREZ MAGIC.
WHICH HAS NOTHING TO DO WITH MY WIZARDRY SKILLS...
RAMIREZ'S MACHISMO BELIED A WARRIOR'S HEART.
HE'D PRETTY MUCH SAVED MY LIFE THE SAME NIGHT YOSHIMO BROKE HER LEG.
OF MY THREE CHARGES, HE'S THE ONE I'M LEAST WORRIED ABOUT...

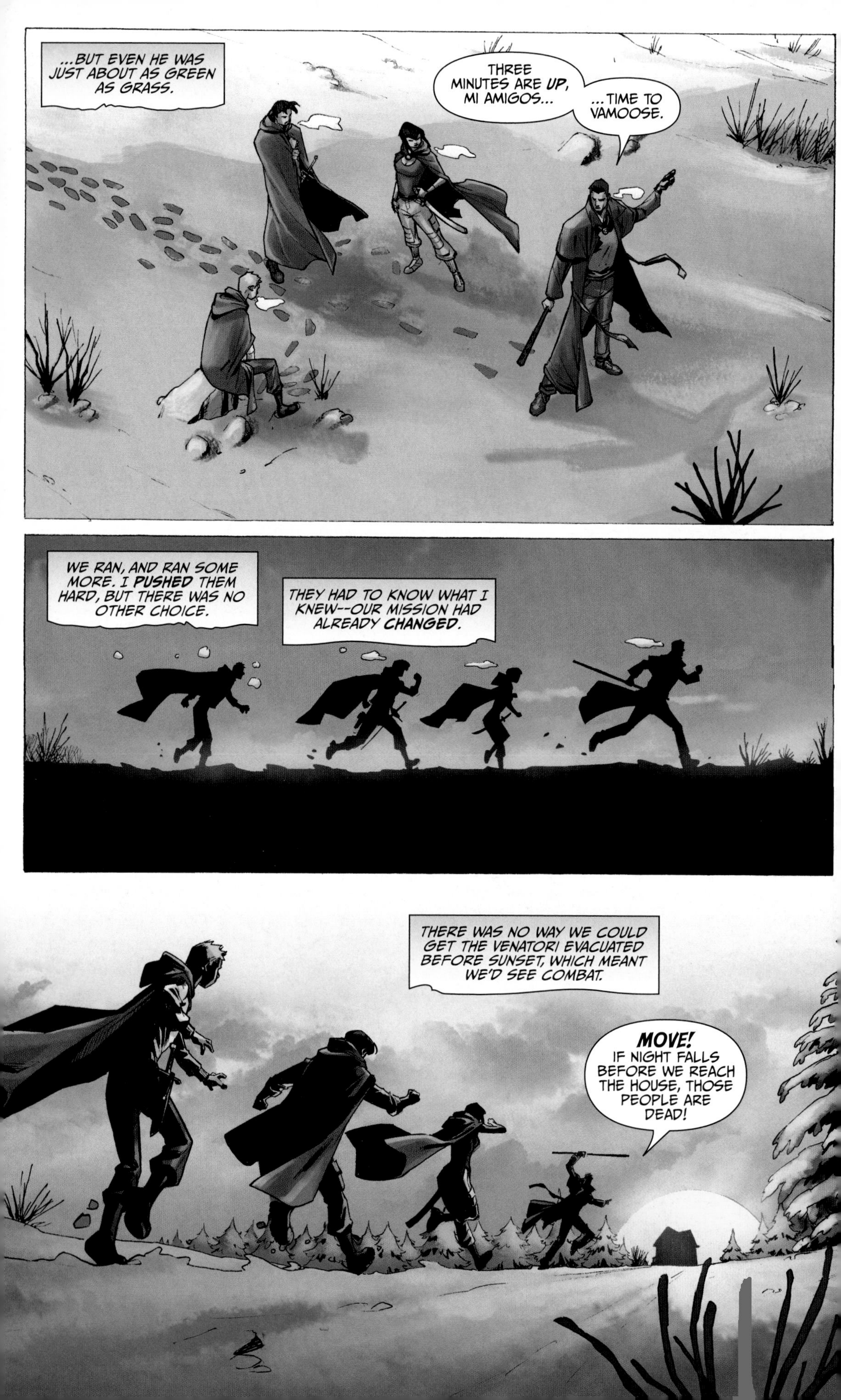

...BUT EVEN HE WAS JUST ABOUT AS GREEN AS GRASS.
THREE MINUTES ARE UP, MI AMIGOS...
...TIME TO VAMOOSE.
WE RAN, AND RAN SOME MORE. I PUSHED THEM HARD, BUT THERE WAS NO OTHER CHOICE.
THEY HAD TO KNOW WHAT I KNEW--OUR MISSION HAD ALREADY CHANGED.
THERE WAS NO WAY WE COULD GET THE VENATORI EVACUATED BEFORE SUNSET, WHICH MEANT WE'D SEE COMBAT.
MOVE! IF NIGHT FALLS BEFORE WE REACH THE HOUSE, THOSE PEOPLE ARE DEAD!

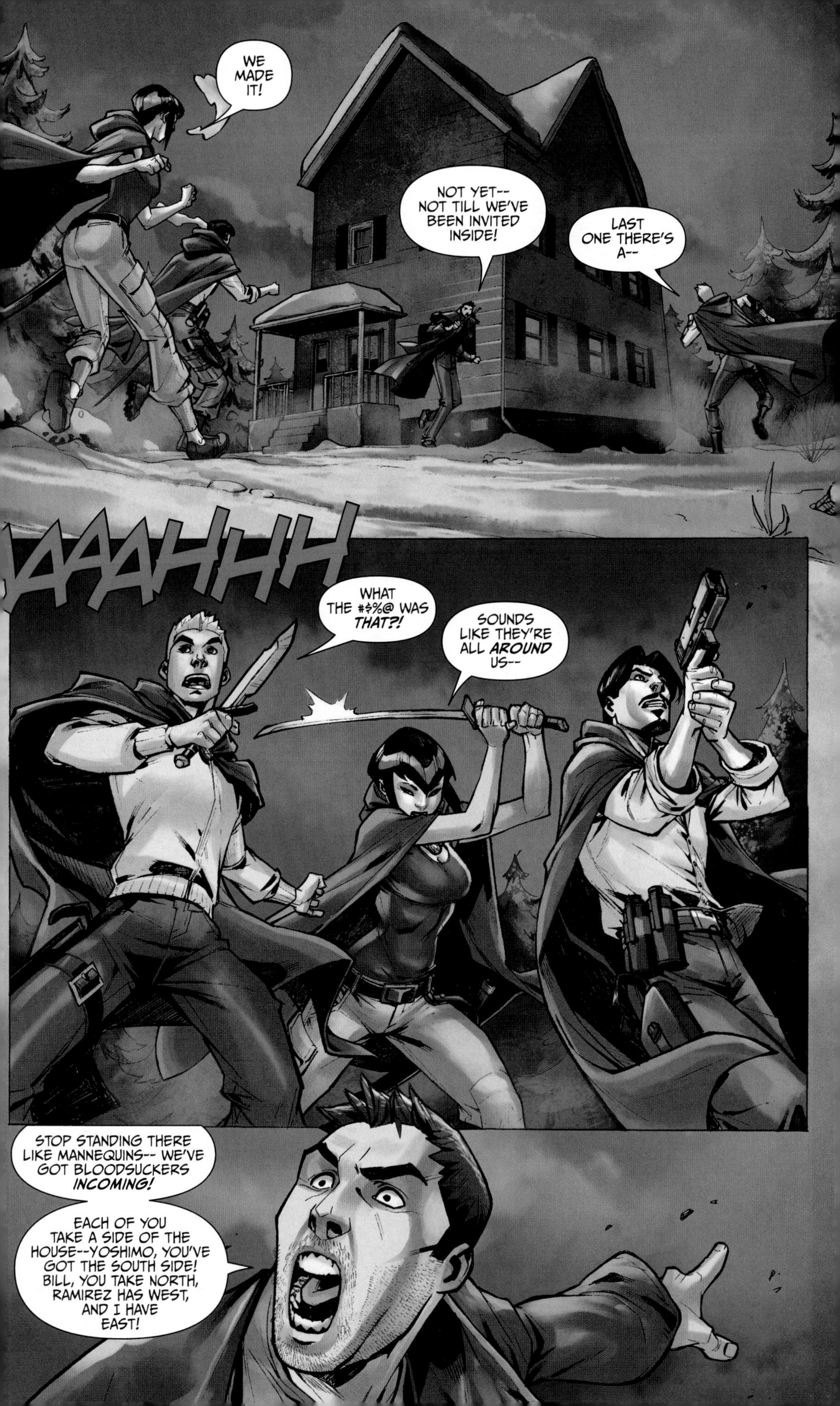
WE MADE IT!
NOT YET-- NOT TILL WE'VE BEEN INVITED INSIDE!
LAST ONE THERE'S A--
AAAHHH
WHAT THE #$%@ WAS THAT?!
SOUNDS LIKE THEY'RE ALL AROUND US--
STOP STANDING THERE LIKE MANNEQUINS-- WE'VE GOT BLOODSUCKERS INCOMING!
EACH OF YOU TAKE A SIDE OF THE HOUSE--YOSHIMO, YOU'VE GOT THE SOUTH SIDE! BILL, YOU TAKE NORTH, RAMIREZ HAS WEST, AND I HAVE EAST!

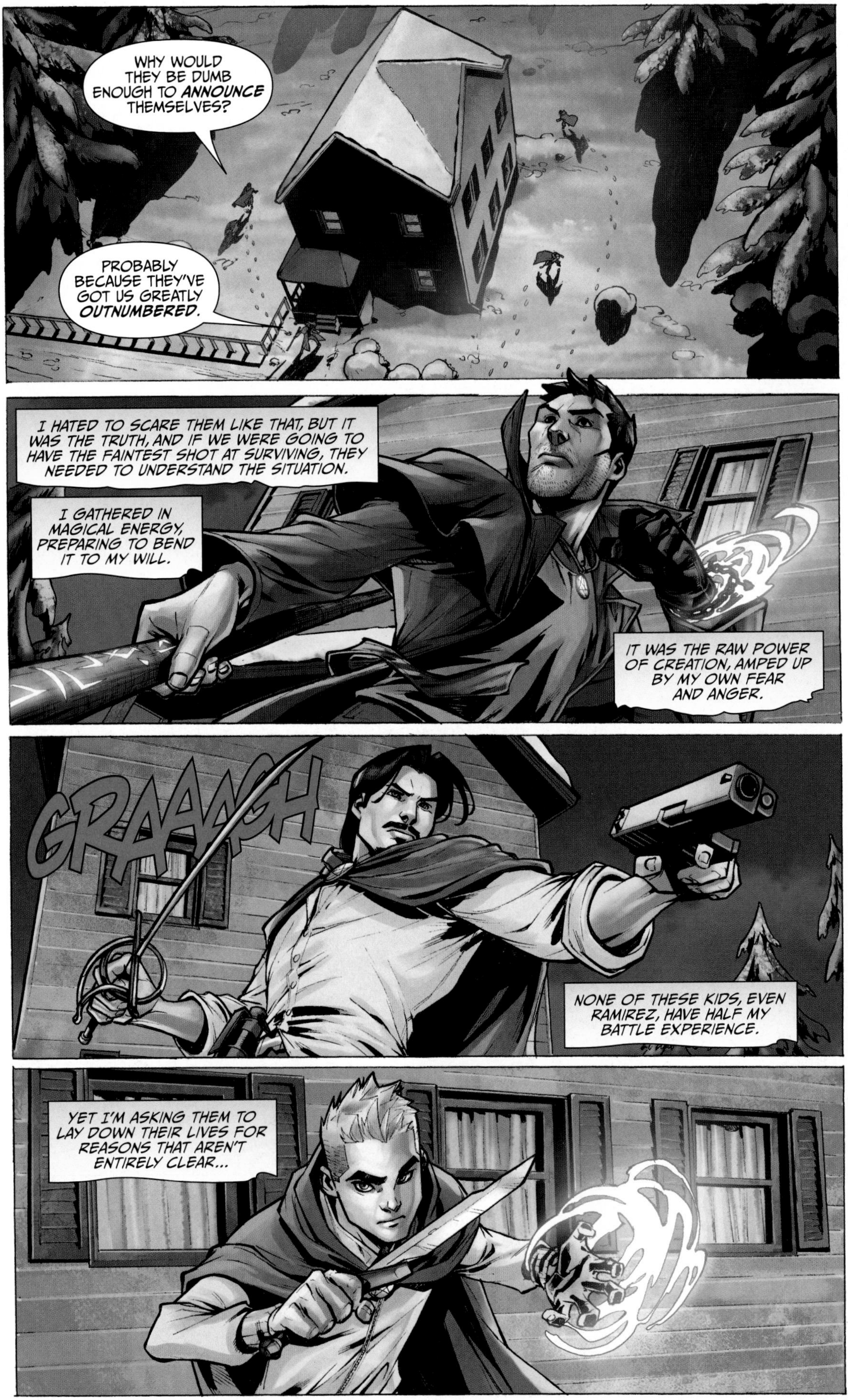
WHY WOULD THEY BE DUMB ENOUGH TO ANNOUNCE THEMSELVES?
PROBABLY BECAUSE THEY'VE GOT US GREATLY OUTNUMBERED.
I HATED TO SCARE THEM LIKE THAT, BUT IT WAS THE TRUTH, AND IF WE WERE GOING TO HAVE THE FAINTEST SHOT AT SURVIVING, THEY NEEDED TO UNDERSTAND THE SITUATION.
I GATHERED IN MAGICAL ENERGY, PREPARING TO BEND IT TO MY WILL.
IT WAS THE RAW POWER OF CREATION, AMPED UP BY MY OWN FEAR AND ANGER.
GRAAAGH
NONE OF THESE KIDS, EVEN RAMIREZ, HAVE HALF MY BATTLE EXPERIENCE.
YET I'M ASKING THEM TO LAY DOWN THEIR LIVES FOR REASONS THAT AREN'T ENTIRELY CLEAR...

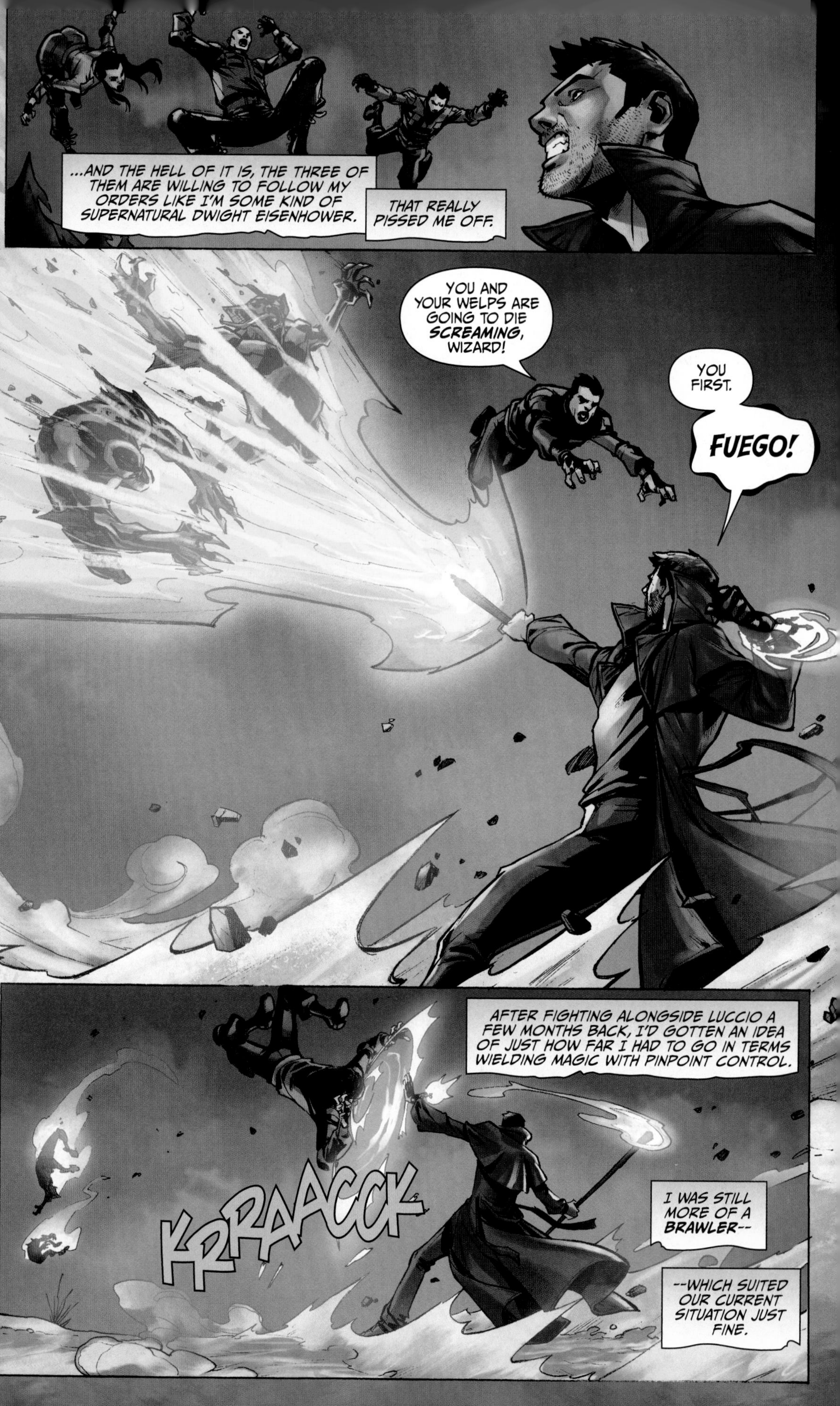
...AND THE HELL OF IT IS, THE THREE OF THEM ARE WILLING TO FOLLOW MY ORDERS LIKE I'M SOME KIND OF SUPERNATURAL DWIGHT EISENHOWER.
THAT REALLY PISSED ME OFF.
YOU AND YOUR WELPS ARE GOING TO DIE SCREAMING, WIZARD!
YOU FIRST.
FUEGO!
AFTER FIGHTING ALONGSIDE LUCCIO A FEW MONTHS BACK, I'D GOTTEN AN IDEA OF JUST HOW FAR I HAD TO GO IN TERMS WIELDING MAGIC WITH PINPOINT CONTROL.
KRRAACCK
I WAS STILL MORE OF A BRAWLER--
--WHICH SUITED OUR CURRENT SITUATION JUST FINE.

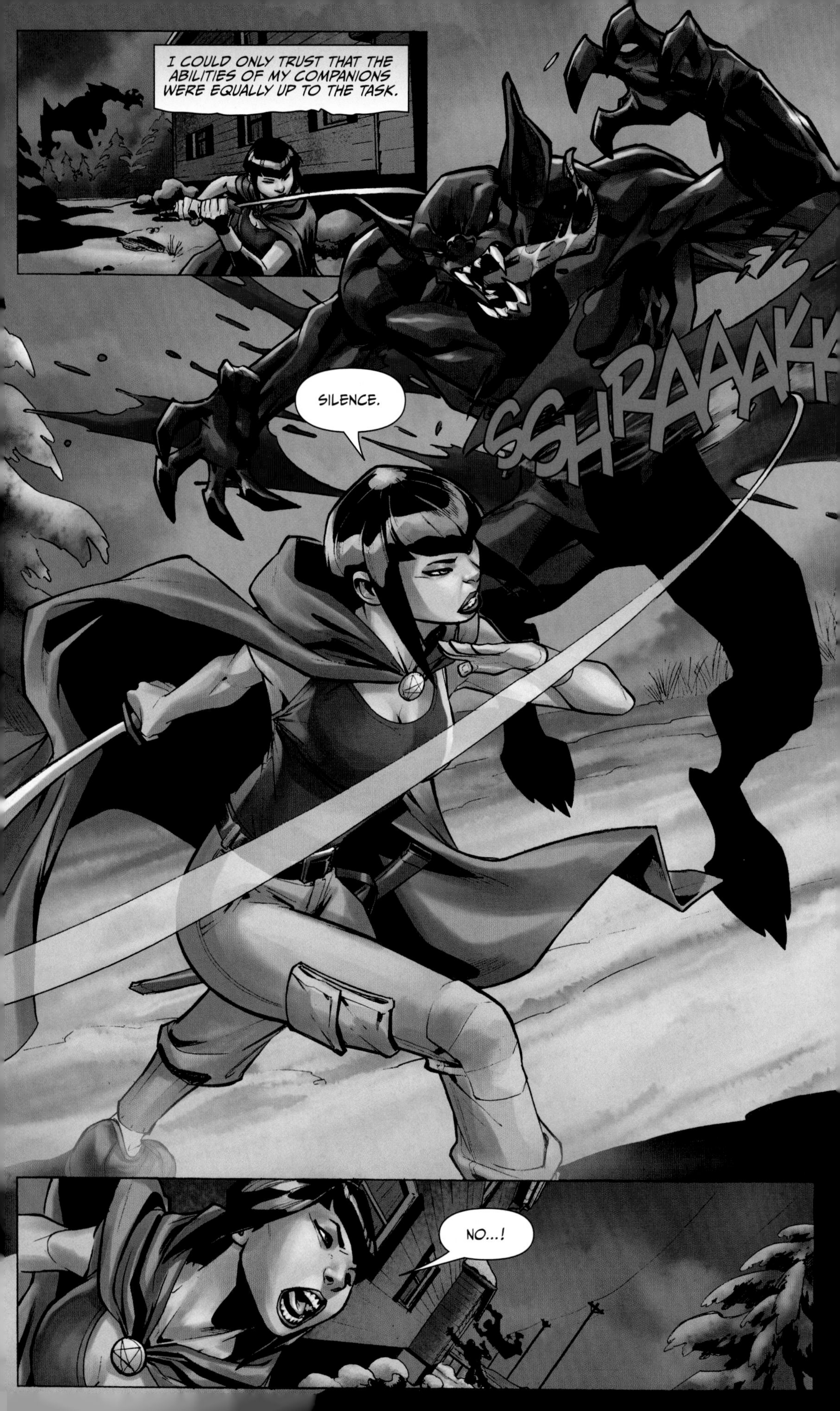
I COULD ONLY TRUST THAT THE ABILITIES OF MY COMPANIONS WERE EQUALLY UP TO THE TASK.
SILENCE.
SSHRAAAKK
NO...!

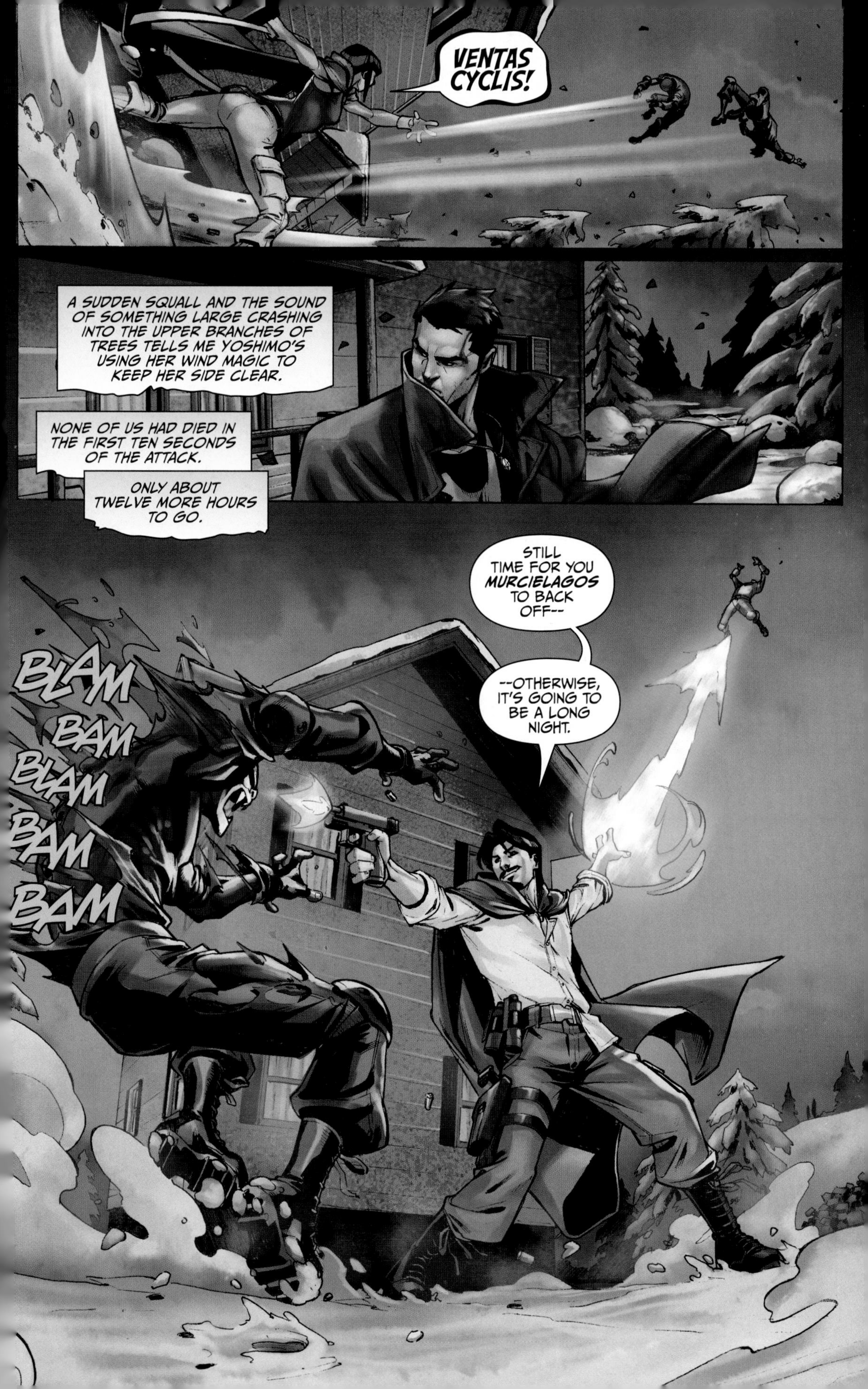

VENTAS CYCLIS!
A SUDDEN SQUALL AND THE SOUND OF SOMETHING LARGE CRASHING INTO THE UPPER BRANCHES OF TREES TELLS ME YOSHIMO'S USING HER WIND MAGIC TO KEEP HER SIDE CLEAR.
NONE OF US HAD DIED IN THE FIRST TEN SECONDS OF THE ATTACK.
ONLY ABOUT TWELVE MORE HOURS TO GO.
STILL TIME FOR YOU *MURCIELAGOS* TO BACK OFF--
--OTHERWISE, IT'S GOING TO BE A LONG NIGHT.
BLAM
BAM
BLAM
BAM
BAM

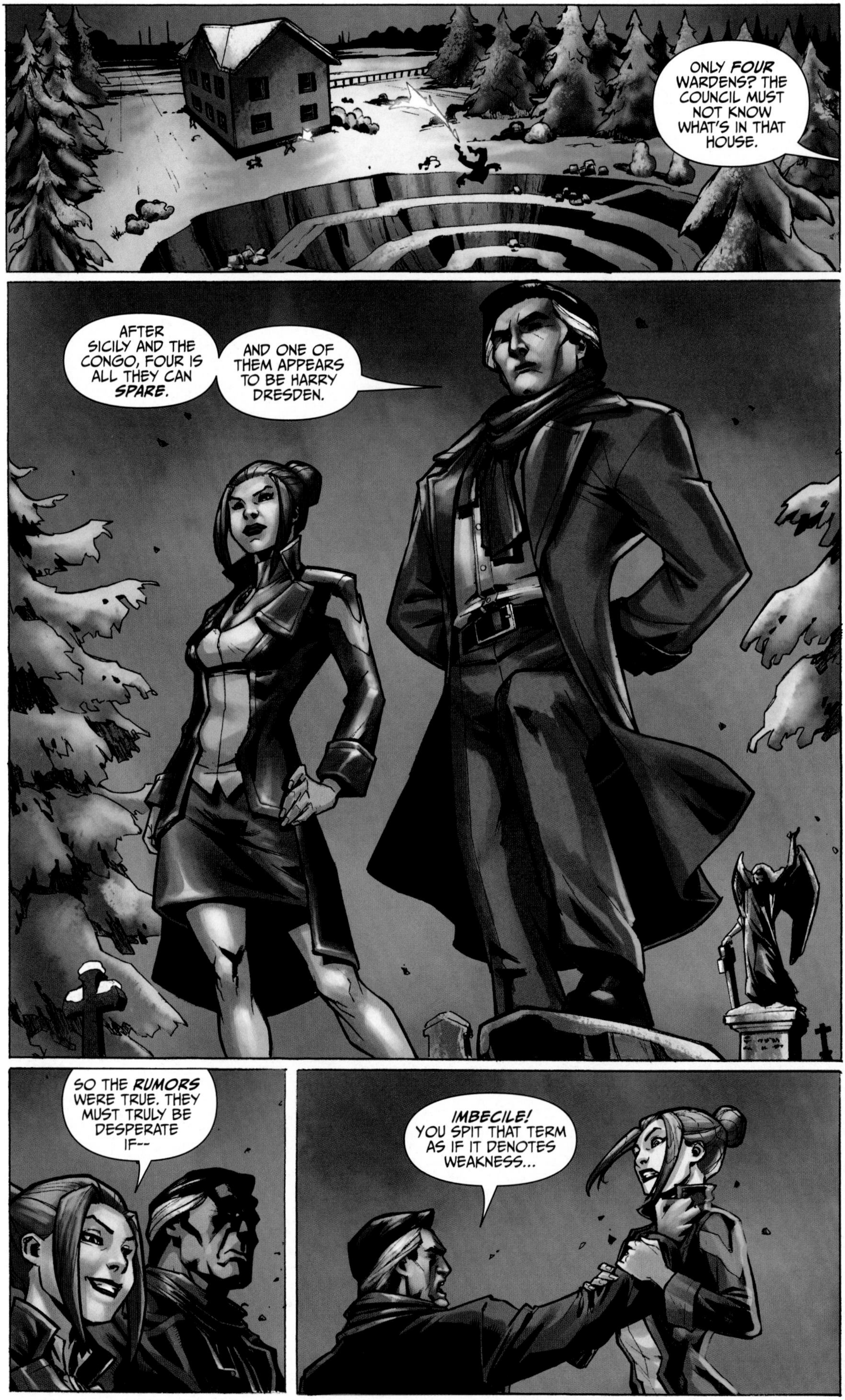
ONLY *FOUR* WARDENS? THE COUNCIL MUST NOT KNOW WHAT'S IN THAT HOUSE.
AFTER SICILY AND THE CONGO, FOUR IS ALL THEY CAN *SPARE*.
AND ONE OF THEM APPEARS TO BE HARRY DRESDEN.
SO THE *RUMORS* WERE TRUE. THEY MUST TRULY BE DESPERATE IF--
IMBECILE! YOU SPIT THAT TERM AS IF IT DENOTES WEAKNESS...

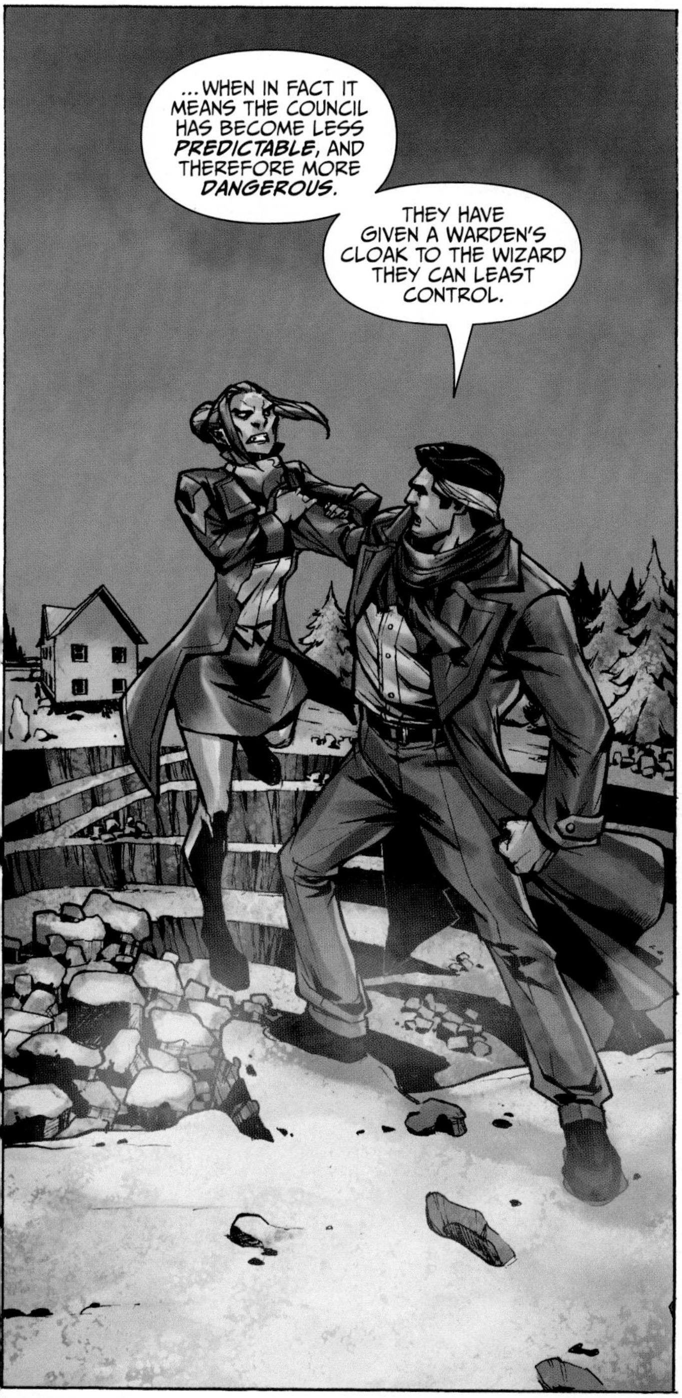
...WHEN IN FACT IT MEANS THE COUNCIL HAS BECOME LESS *PREDICTABLE*, AND THEREFORE MORE *DANGEROUS*.
THEY HAVE GIVEN A WARDEN'S CLOAK TO THE WIZARD THEY CAN LEAST CONTROL.

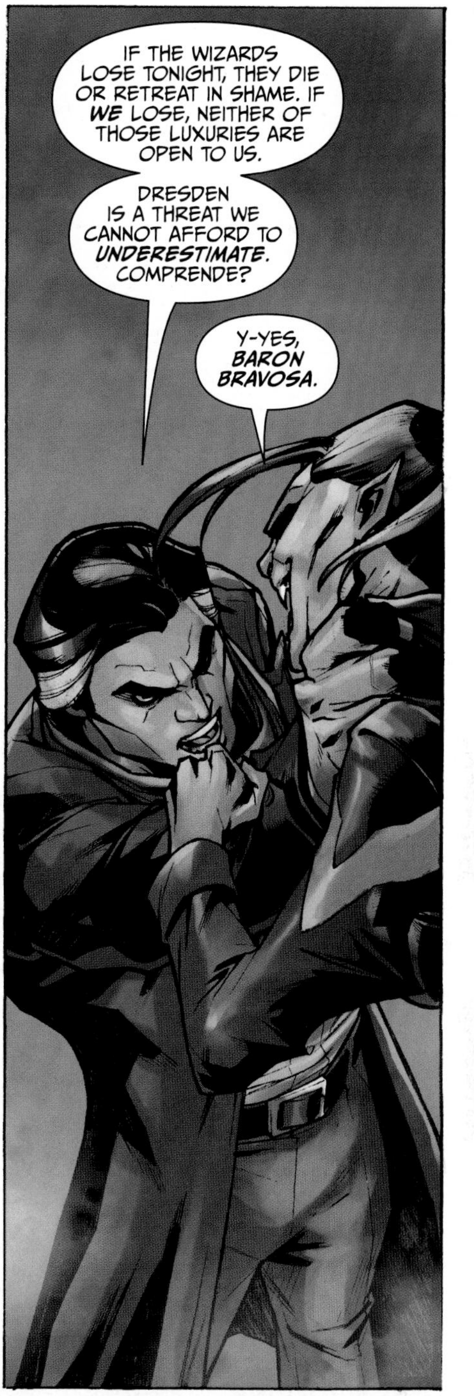
IF THE WIZARDS LOSE TONIGHT, THEY DIE OR RETREAT IN SHAME. IF *WE* LOSE, NEITHER OF THOSE LUXURIES ARE OPEN TO US.
DRESDEN IS A THREAT WE CANNOT AFFORD TO *UNDERESTIMATE*. COMPRENDE?
Y-YES, *BARON BRAVOSA*.

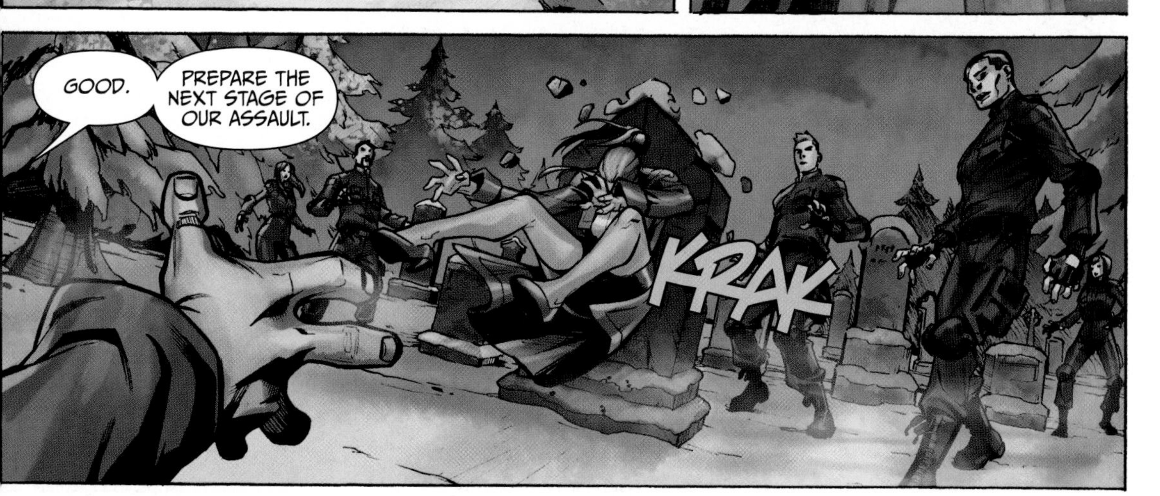
GOOD.
PREPARE THE NEXT STAGE OF OUR ASSAULT.
KRAK

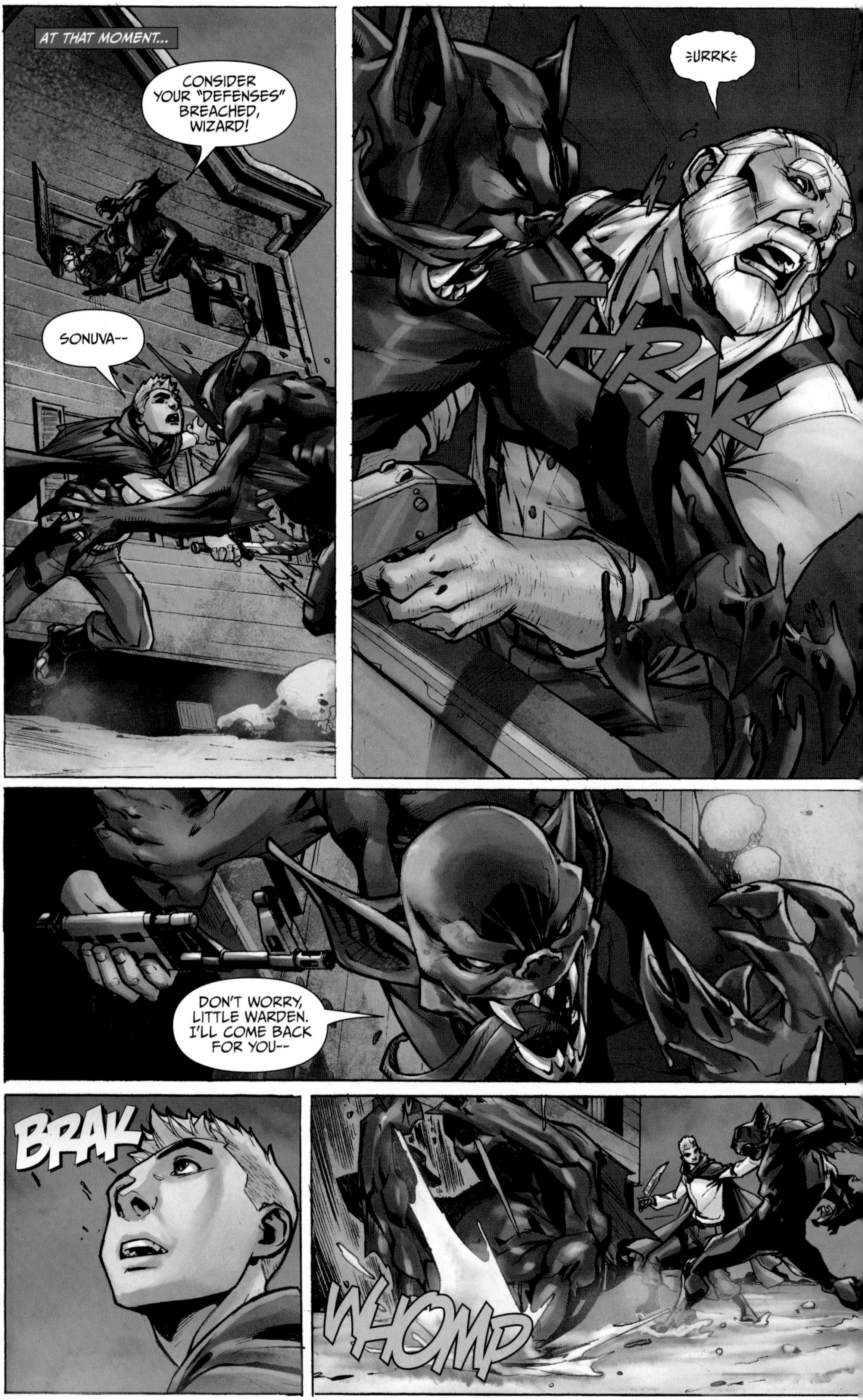

AT THAT MOMENT...
CONSIDER YOUR "DEFENSES" BREACHED, WIZARD!
SONUVA--
URRK
THRAK
DON'T WORRY, LITTLE WARDEN. I'LL COME BACK FOR YOU--
BRAK
WHOMP

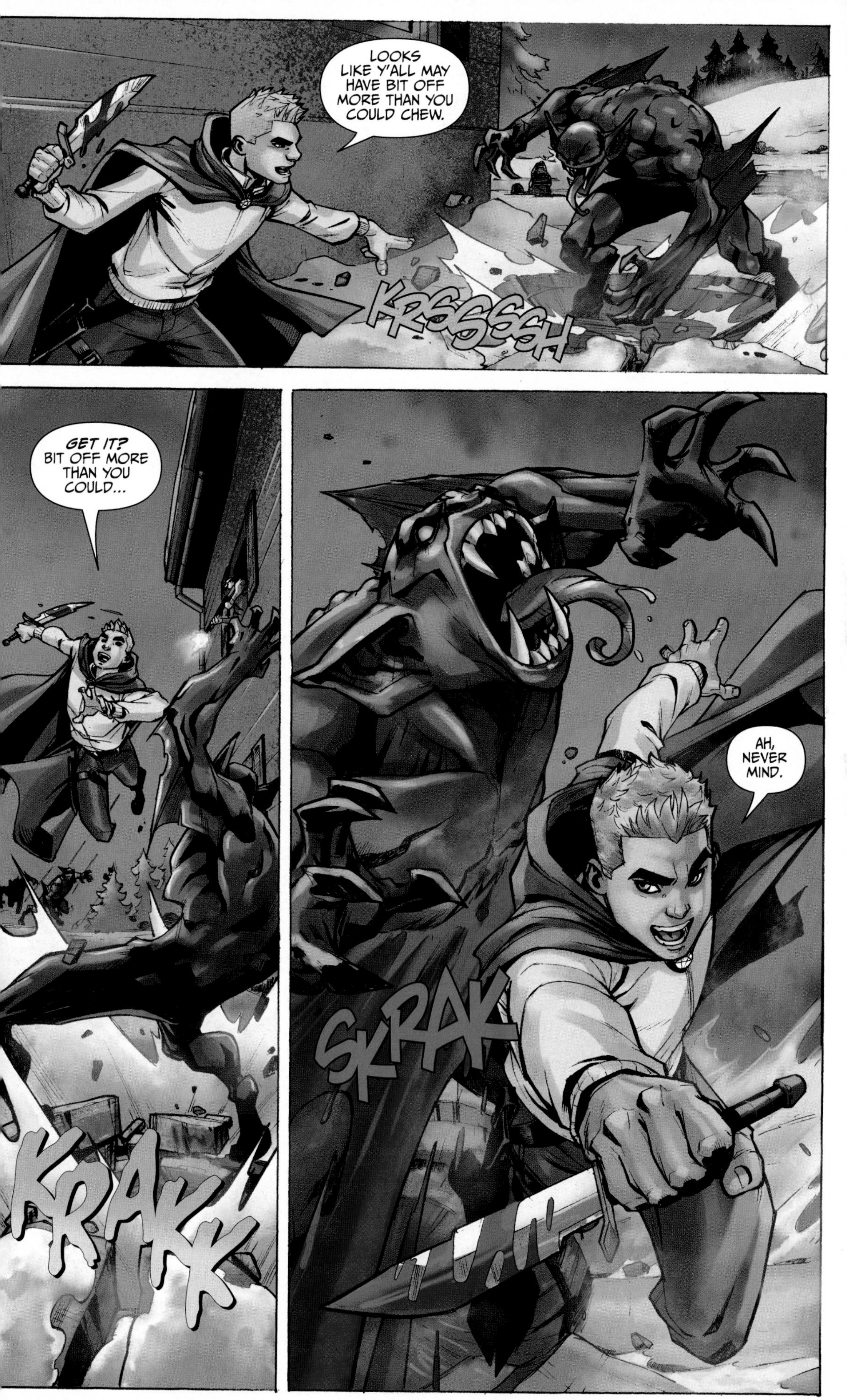
LOOKS LIKE Y'ALL MAY HAVE BIT OFF MORE THAN YOU COULD CHEW.
KRSSSSH
GET IT? BIT OFF MORE THAN YOU COULD...
KRAKK
SKRAK
AH, NEVER MIND.

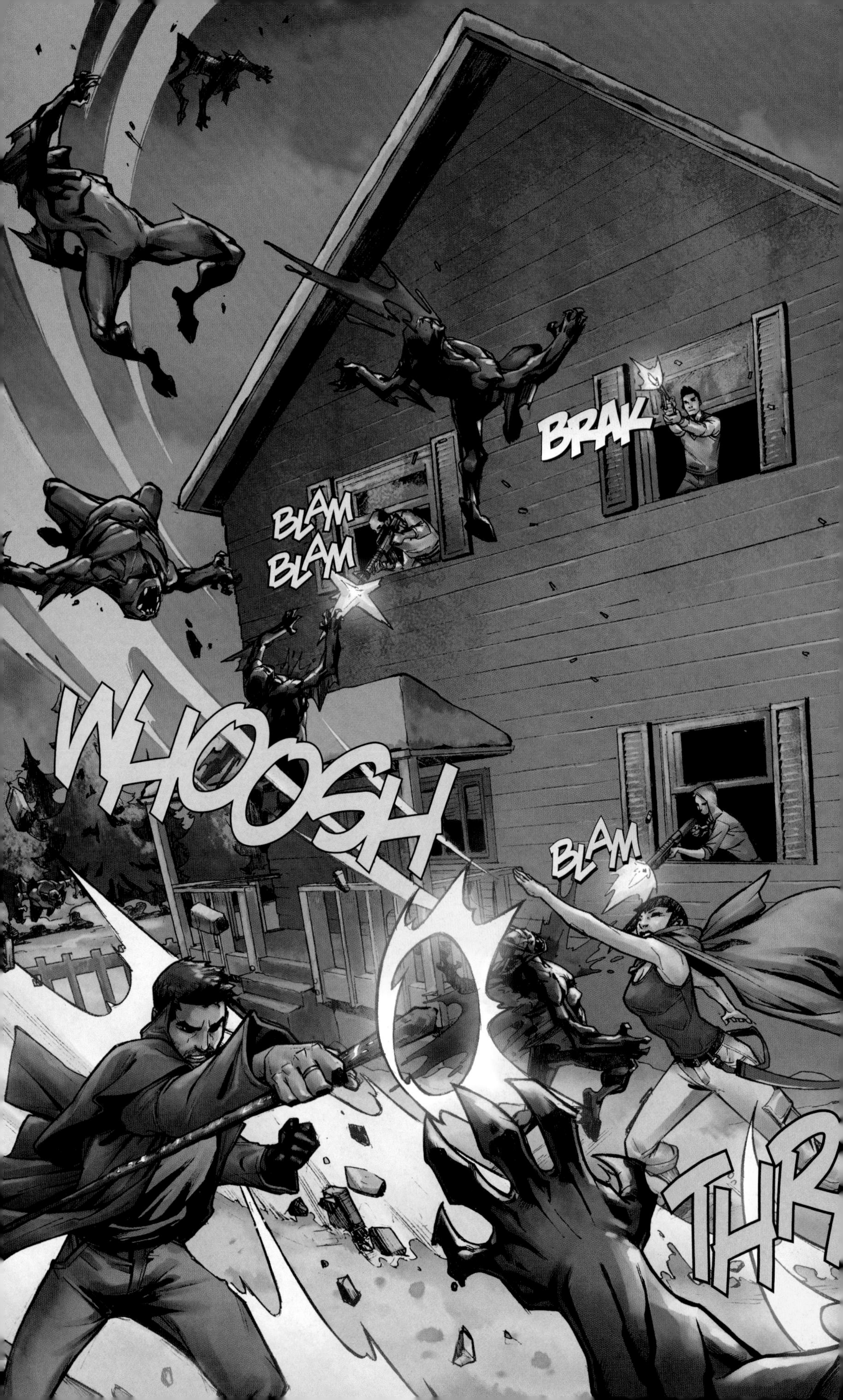
BRAK
BLAM
BLAM
WHOOSH
BLAM
THR

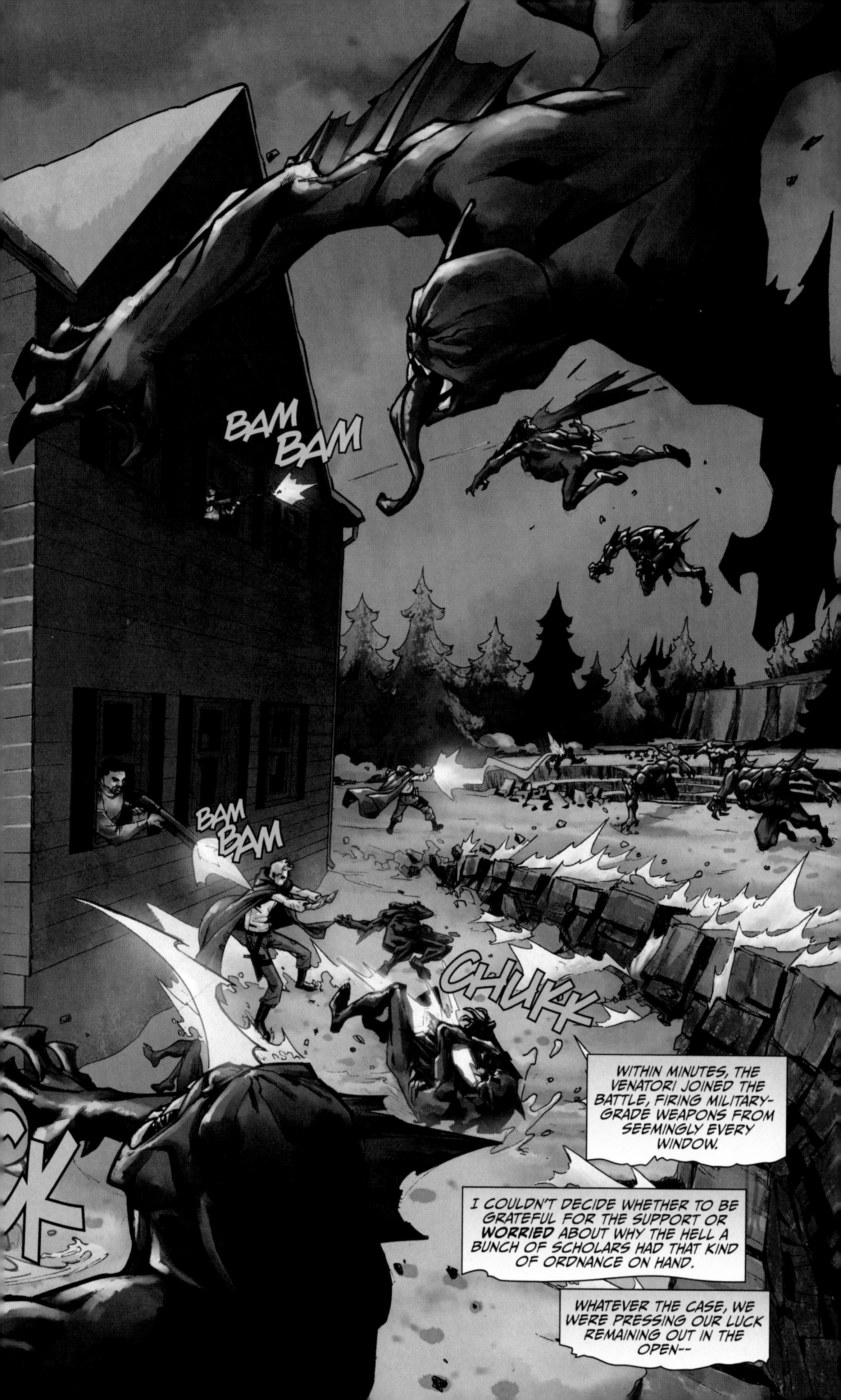

BAM BAM
BAM BAM
CHUKK
WITHIN MINUTES, THE VENATORI JOINED THE BATTLE, FIRING MILITARY-GRADE WEAPONS FROM SEEMINGLY EVERY WINDOW.
I COULDN'T DECIDE WHETHER TO BE GRATEFUL FOR THE SUPPORT OR WORRIED ABOUT WHY THE HELL A BUNCH OF SCHOLARS HAD THAT KIND OF ORDNANCE ON HAND.
WHATEVER THE CASE, WE WERE PRESSING OUR LUCK REMAINING OUT IN THE OPEN--

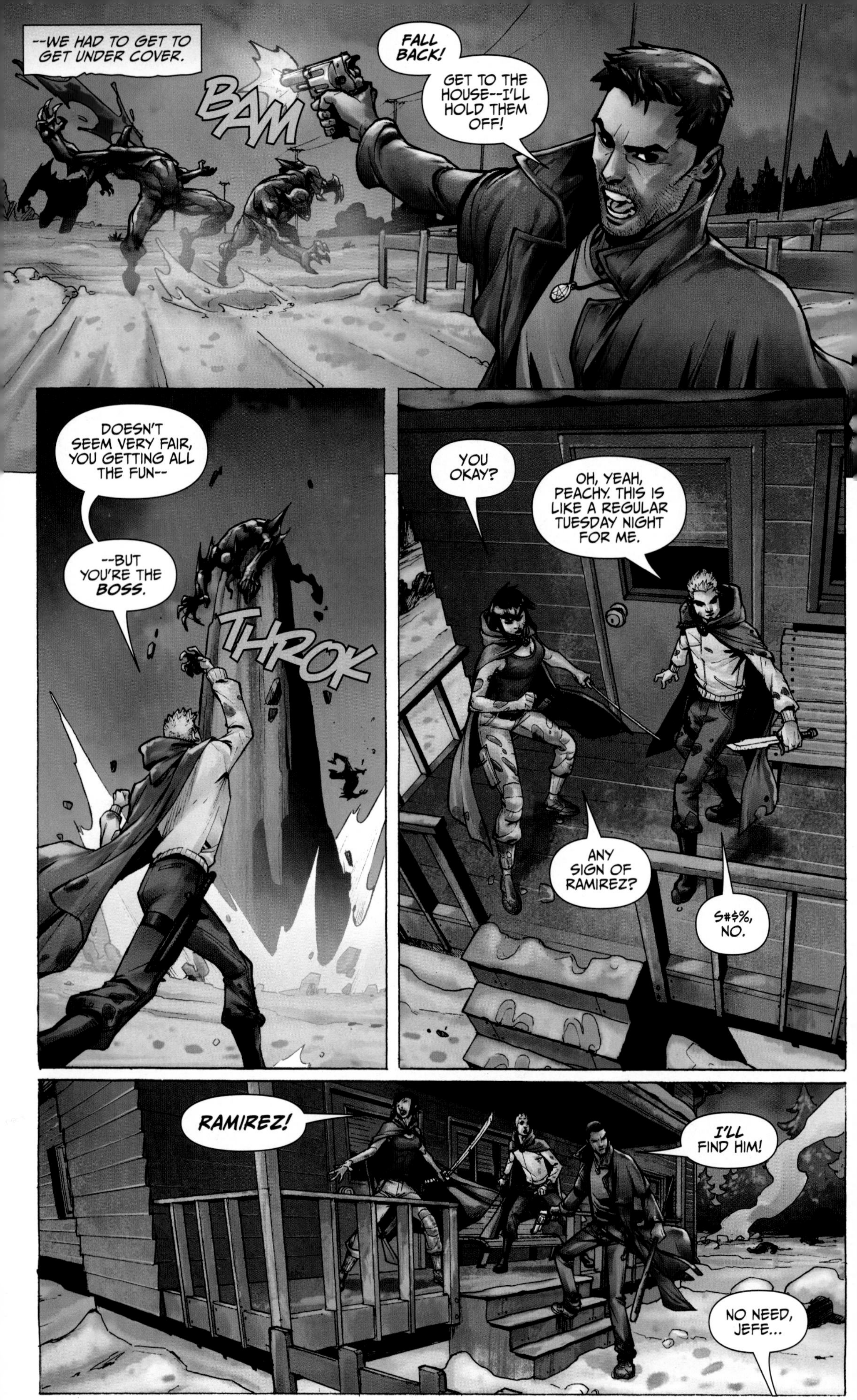
--WE HAD TO GET TO GET UNDER COVER.
BAM
FALL BACK!
GET TO THE HOUSE--I'LL HOLD THEM OFF!
DOESN'T SEEM VERY FAIR, YOU GETTING ALL THE FUN--
--BUT YOU'RE THE BOSS.
THROK
YOU OKAY?
OH, YEAH, PEACHY. THIS IS LIKE A REGULAR TUESDAY NIGHT FOR ME.
ANY SIGN OF RAMIREZ?
S#$%, NO.
RAMIREZ!
I'LL FIND HIM!
NO NEED, JEFE...

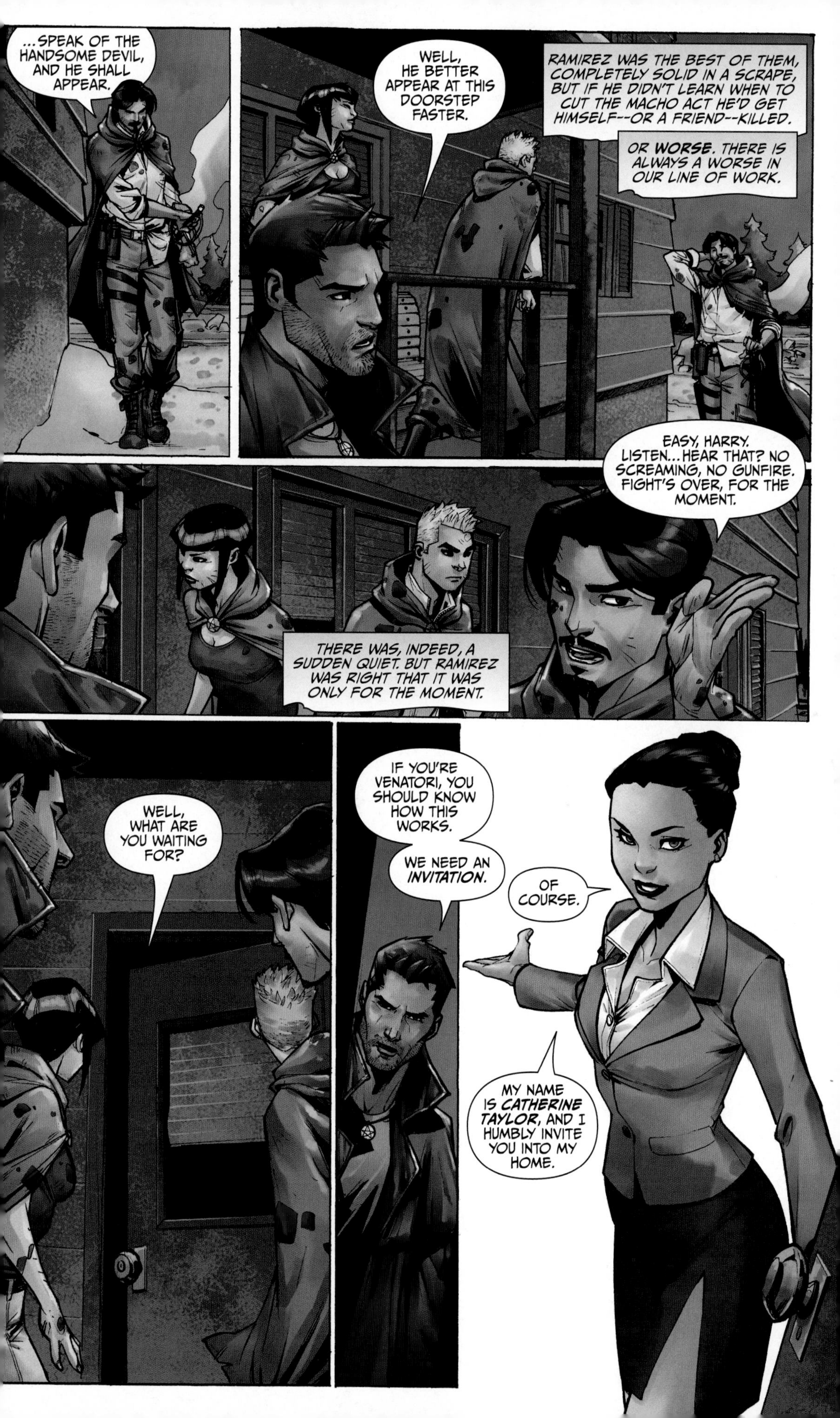
...SPEAK OF THE HANDSOME DEVIL, AND HE SHALL APPEAR.
WELL, HE BETTER APPEAR AT THIS DOORSTEP FASTER.
RAMIREZ WAS THE BEST OF THEM, COMPLETELY SOLID IN A SCRAPE, BUT IF HE DIDN'T LEARN WHEN TO CUT THE MACHO ACT HE'D GET HIMSELF--OR A FRIEND--KILLED.
OR WORSE. THERE IS ALWAYS A WORSE IN OUR LINE OF WORK.
EASY, HARRY. LISTEN...HEAR THAT? NO SCREAMING, NO GUNFIRE. FIGHT'S OVER, FOR THE MOMENT.
THERE WAS, INDEED, A SUDDEN QUIET. BUT RAMIREZ WAS RIGHT THAT IT WAS ONLY FOR THE MOMENT.
WELL, WHAT ARE YOU WAITING FOR?
IF YOU'RE VENATORI, YOU SHOULD KNOW HOW THIS WORKS.
WE NEED AN INVITATION.
OF COURSE.
MY NAME IS CATHERINE TAYLOR, AND I HUMBLY INVITE YOU INTO MY HOME.

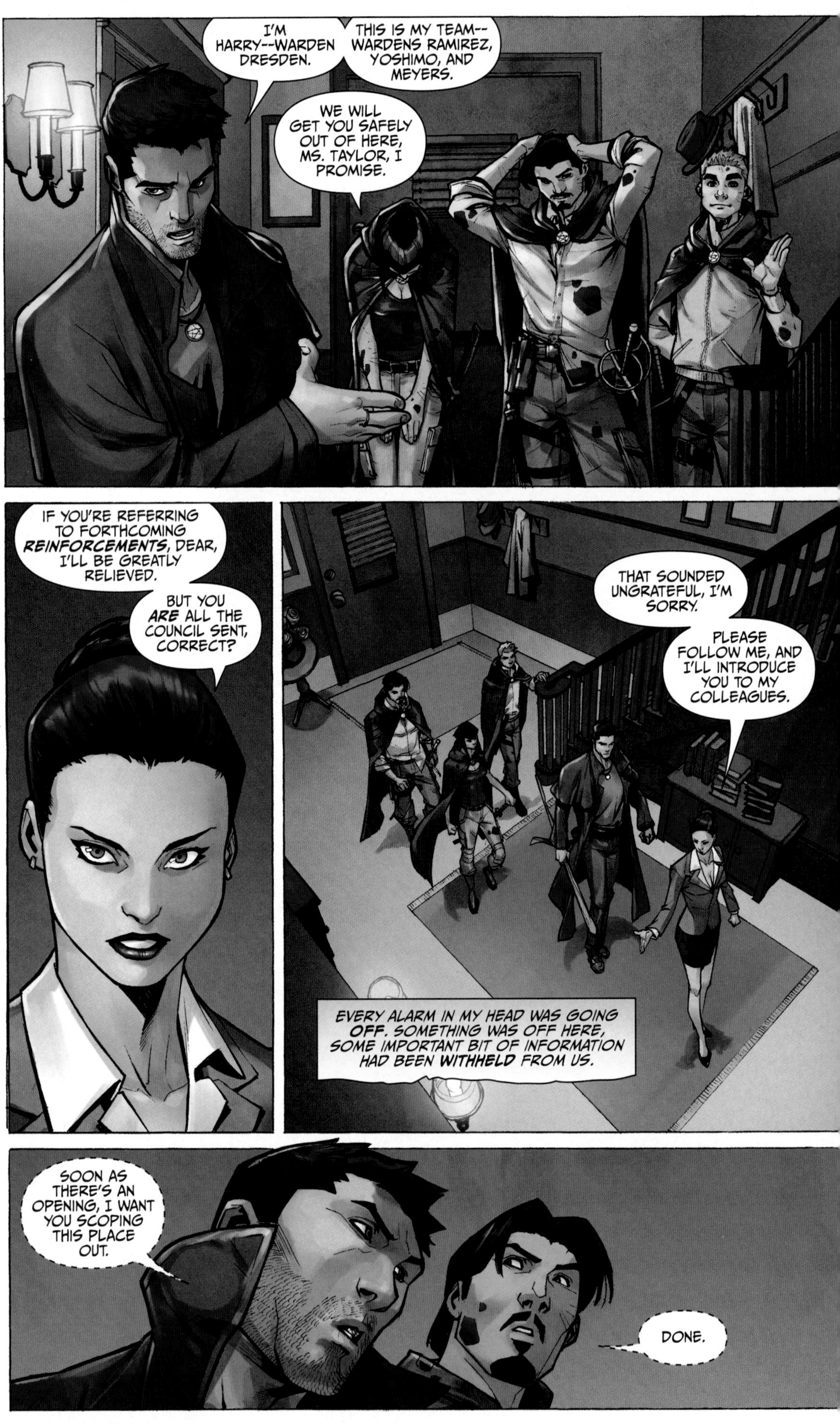
I'M HARRY--WARDEN DRESDEN.
THIS IS MY TEAM--WARDENS RAMIREZ, YOSHIMO, AND MEYERS.
WE WILL GET YOU SAFELY OUT OF HERE, MS. TAYLOR, I PROMISE.
IF YOU'RE REFERRING TO FORTHCOMING REINFORCEMENTS, DEAR, I'LL BE GREATLY RELIEVED.
BUT YOU ARE ALL THE COUNCIL SENT, CORRECT?
THAT SOUNDED UNGRATEFUL, I'M SORRY.
PLEASE FOLLOW ME, AND I'LL INTRODUCE YOU TO MY COLLEAGUES.
EVERY ALARM IN MY HEAD WAS GOING OFF. SOMETHING WAS OFF HERE, SOME IMPORTANT BIT OF INFORMATION HAD BEEN WITHHELD FROM US.
SOON AS THERE'S AN OPENING, I WANT YOU SCOPING THIS PLACE OUT.
DONE.

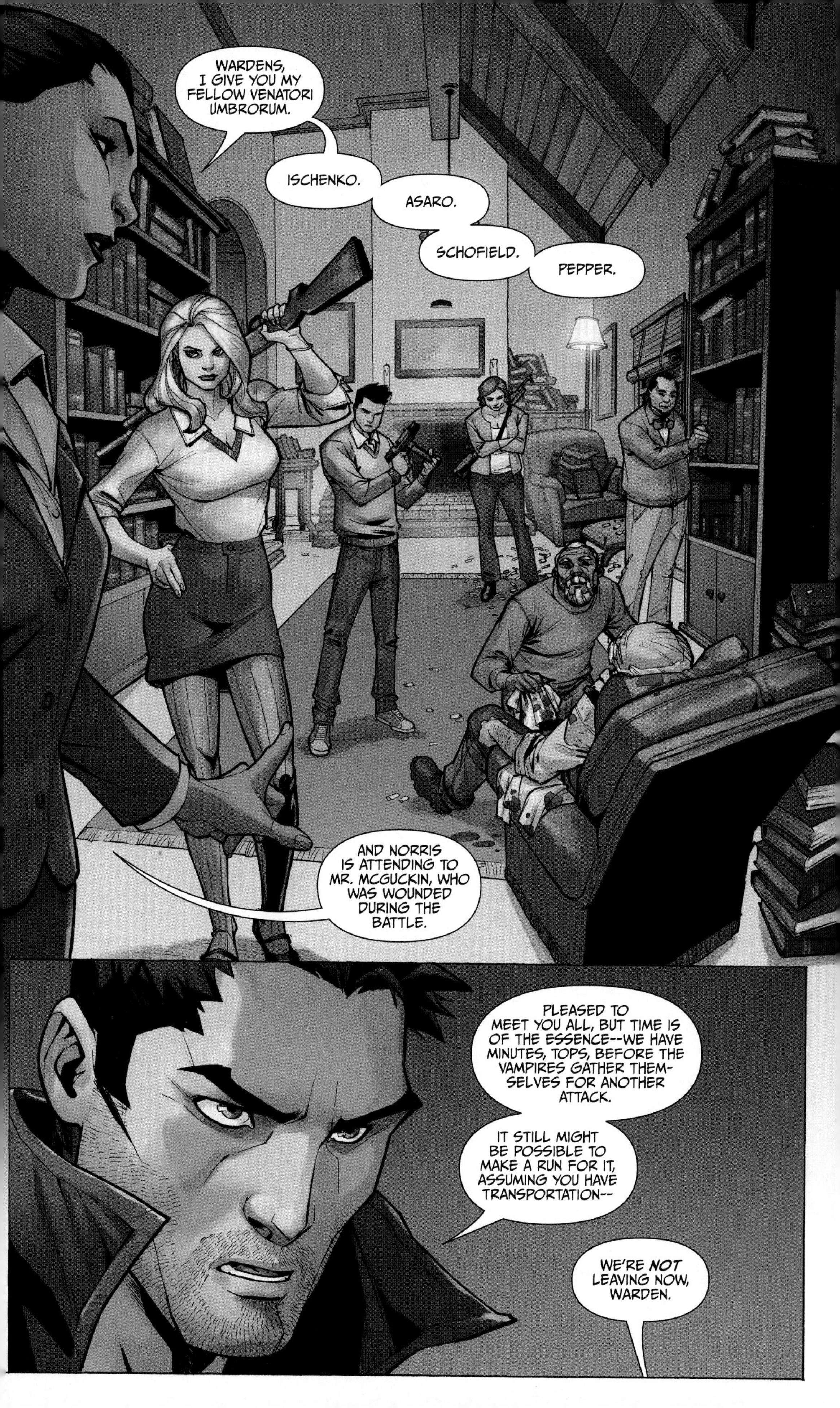

WARDENS, I GIVE YOU MY FELLOW VENATORI UMBRORUM.
ISCHENKO.
ASARO.
SCHOFIELD.
PEPPER.
AND NORRIS IS ATTENDING TO MR. MCGUCKIN, WHO WAS WOUNDED DURING THE BATTLE.
PLEASED TO MEET YOU ALL, BUT TIME IS OF THE ESSENCE--WE HAVE MINUTES, TOPS, BEFORE THE VAMPIRES GATHER THEMSELVES FOR ANOTHER ATTACK.
IT STILL MIGHT BE POSSIBLE TO MAKE A RUN FOR IT, ASSUMING YOU HAVE TRANSPORTATION--
WE'RE *NOT* LEAVING NOW, WARDEN.

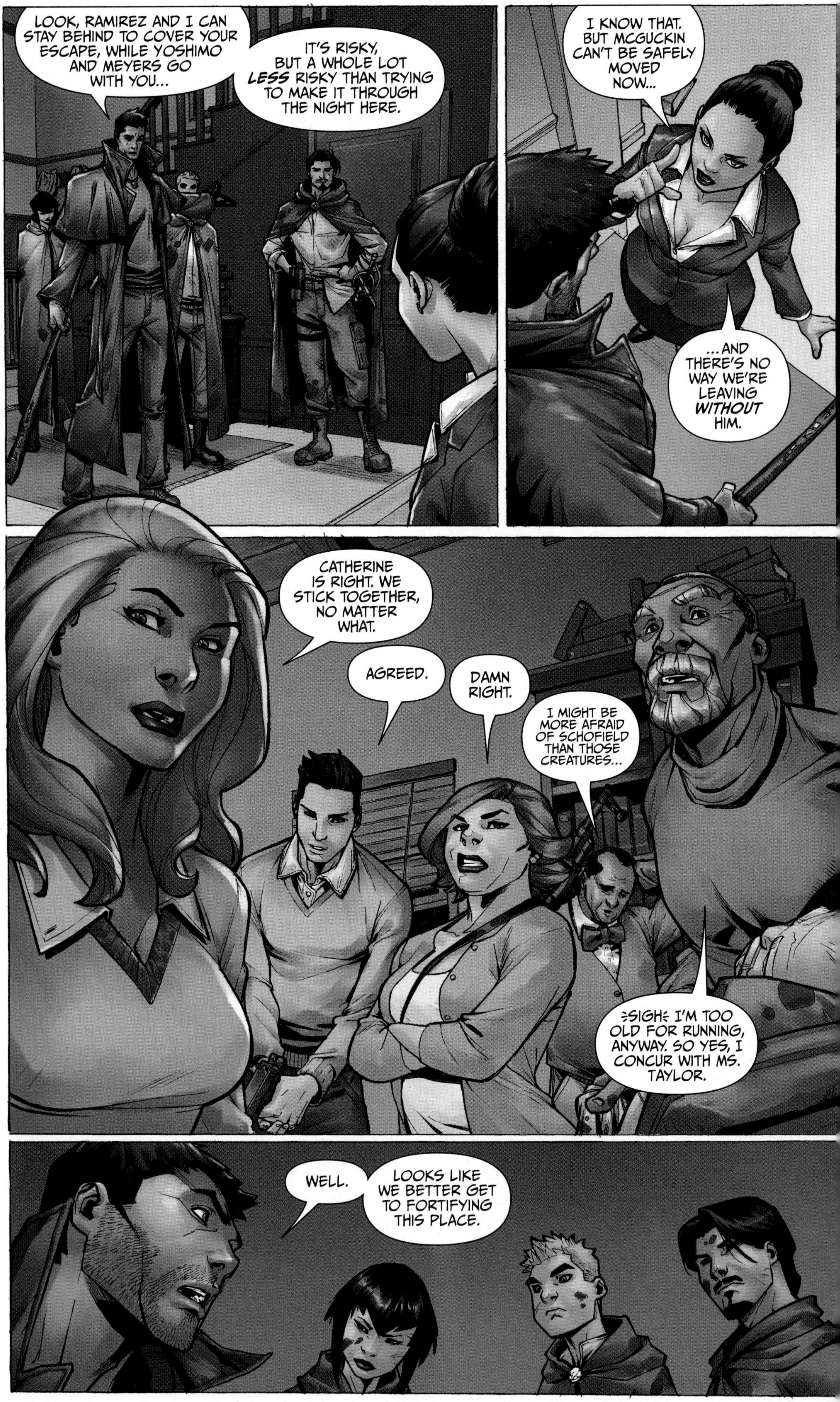
LOOK, RAMIREZ AND I CAN STAY BEHIND TO COVER YOUR ESCAPE, WHILE YOSHIMO AND MEYERS GO WITH YOU...
IT'S RISKY, BUT A WHOLE LOT LESS RISKY THAN TRYING TO MAKE IT THROUGH THE NIGHT HERE.
I KNOW THAT. BUT MCGUCKIN CAN'T BE SAFELY MOVED NOW...
...AND THERE'S NO WAY WE'RE LEAVING WITHOUT HIM.
CATHERINE IS RIGHT. WE STICK TOGETHER, NO MATTER WHAT.
AGREED.
DAMN RIGHT.
I MIGHT BE MORE AFRAID OF SCHOFIELD THAN THOSE CREATURES...
SIGH I'M TOO OLD FOR RUNNING, ANYWAY. SO YES, I CONCUR WITH MS. TAYLOR.
WELL.
LOOKS LIKE WE BETTER GET TO FORTIFYING THIS PLACE.

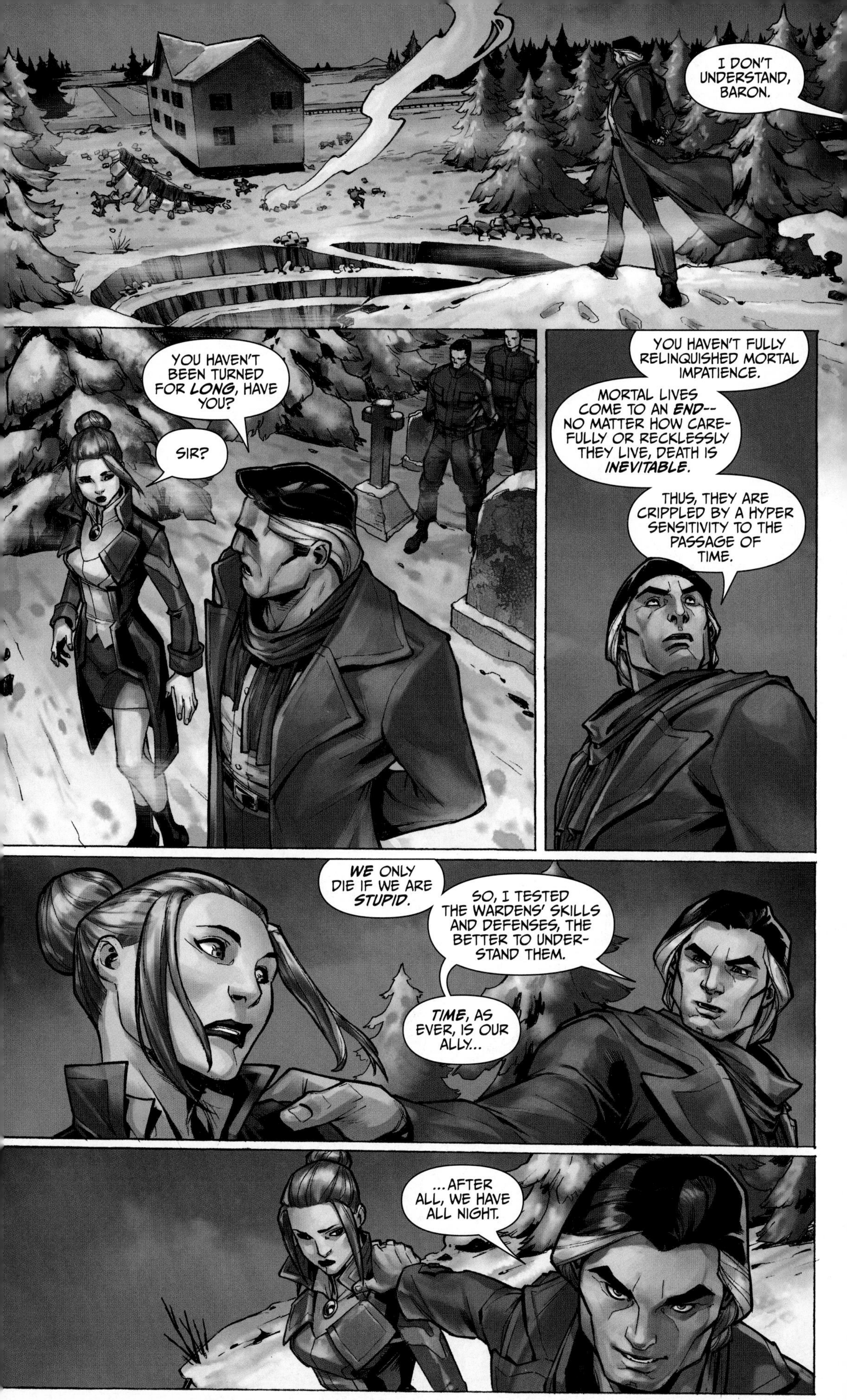

I DON'T UNDERSTAND, BARON.
YOU HAVEN'T BEEN TURNED FOR LONG, HAVE YOU?
SIR?
YOU HAVEN'T FULLY RELINQUISHED MORTAL IMPATIENCE.
MORTAL LIVES COME TO AN END-- NO MATTER HOW CAREFULLY OR RECKLESSLY THEY LIVE, DEATH IS INEVITABLE.
THUS, THEY ARE CRIPPLED BY A HYPER SENSITIVITY TO THE PASSAGE OF TIME.
WE ONLY DIE IF WE ARE STUPID.
SO, I TESTED THE WARDENS' SKILLS AND DEFENSES, THE BETTER TO UNDERSTAND THEM.
TIME, AS EVER, IS OUR ALLY...
...AFTER ALL, WE HAVE ALL NIGHT.

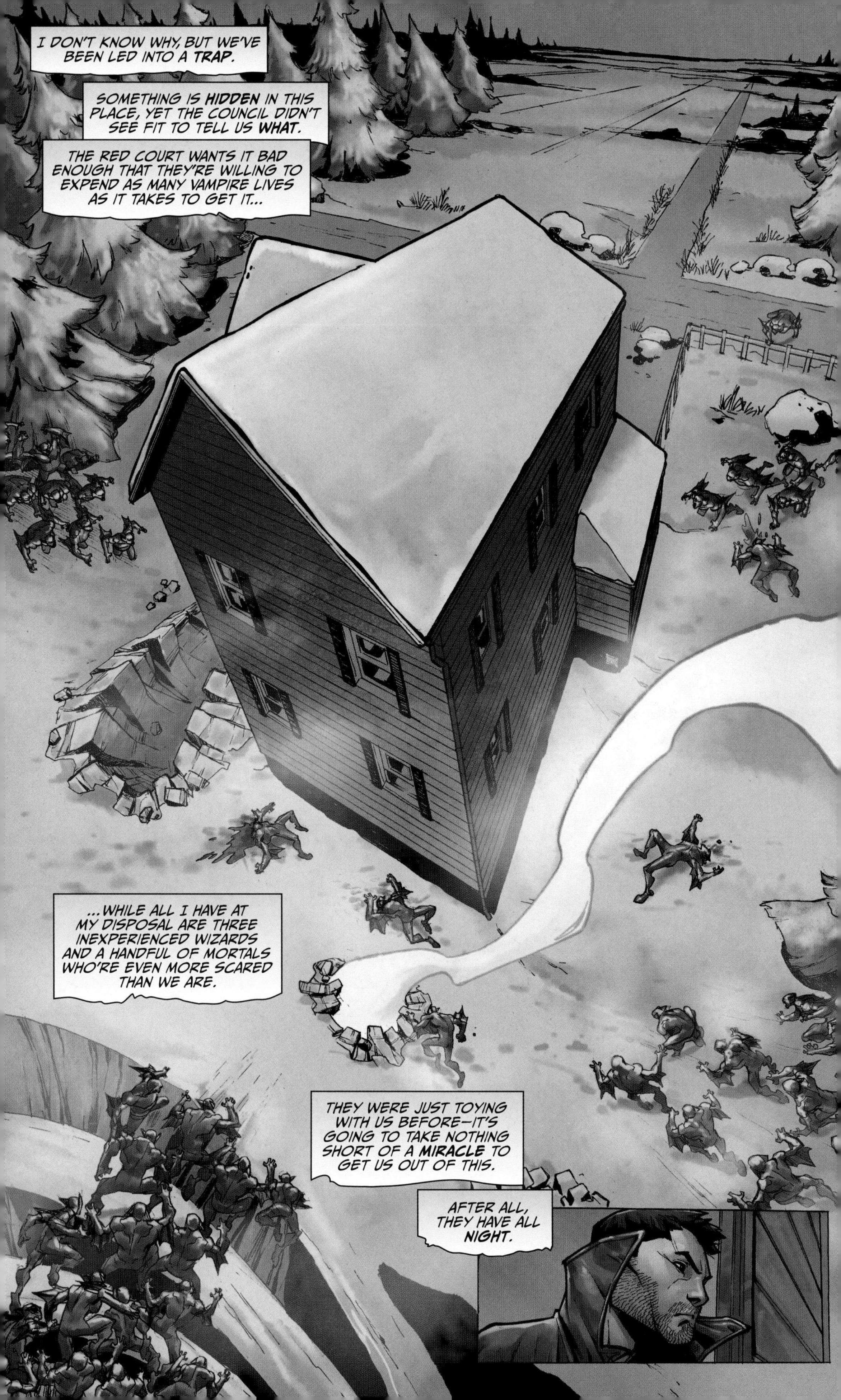

I DON'T KNOW WHY, BUT WE'VE BEEN LED INTO A TRAP.
SOMETHING IS HIDDEN IN THIS PLACE, YET THE COUNCIL DIDN'T SEE FIT TO TELL US WHAT.
THE RED COURT WANTS IT BAD ENOUGH THAT THEY'RE WILLING TO EXPEND AS MANY VAMPIRE LIVES AS IT TAKES TO GET IT...
...WHILE ALL I HAVE AT MY DISPOSAL ARE THREE INEXPERIENCED WIZARDS AND A HANDFUL OF MORTALS WHO'RE EVEN MORE SCARED THAN WE ARE.
THEY WERE JUST TOYING WITH US BEFORE—IT'S GOING TO TAKE NOTHING SHORT OF A MIRACLE TO GET US OUT OF THIS.
AFTER ALL, THEY HAVE ALL NIGHT.

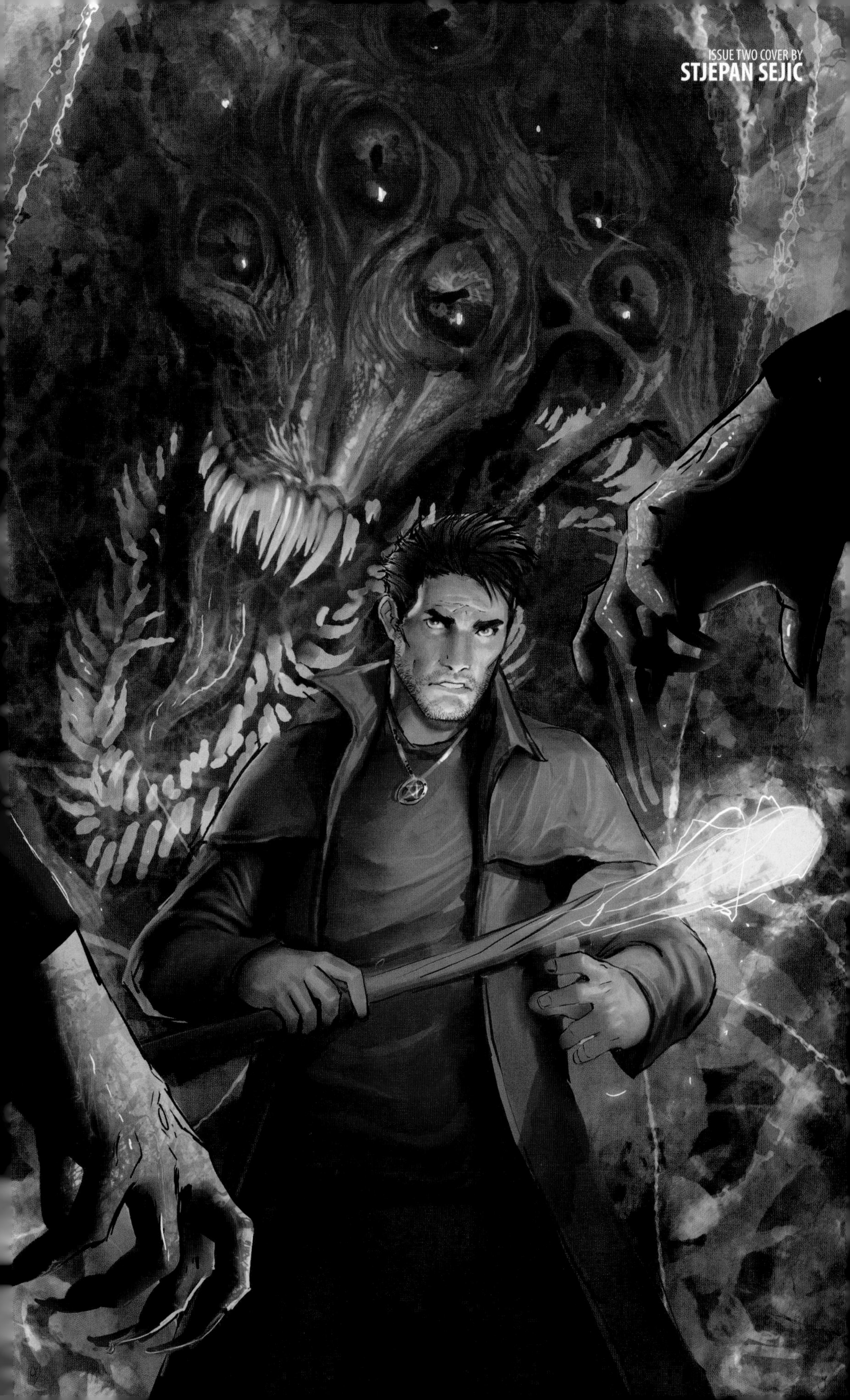
ISSUE TWO COVER BY
STJEPAN SEJIC

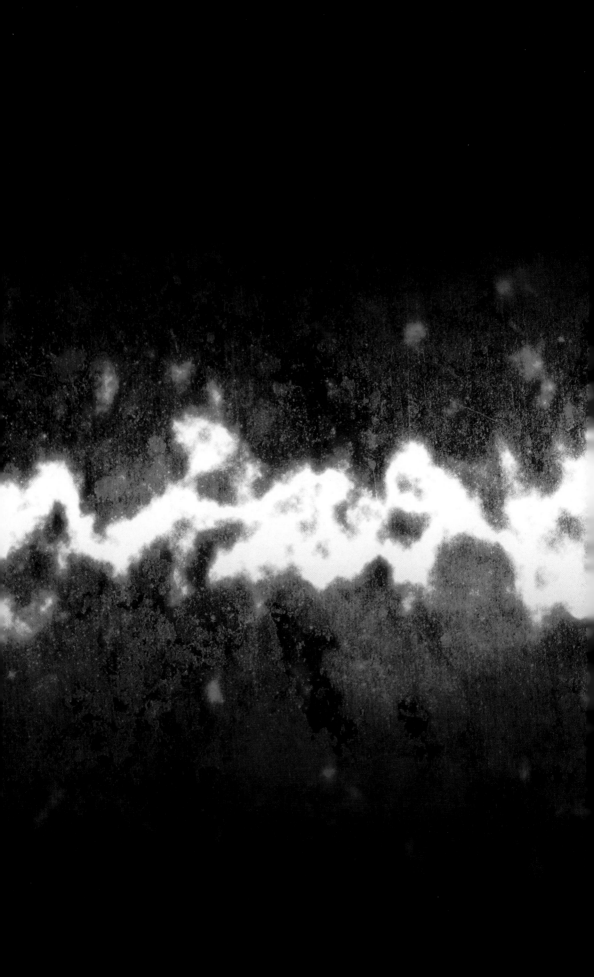

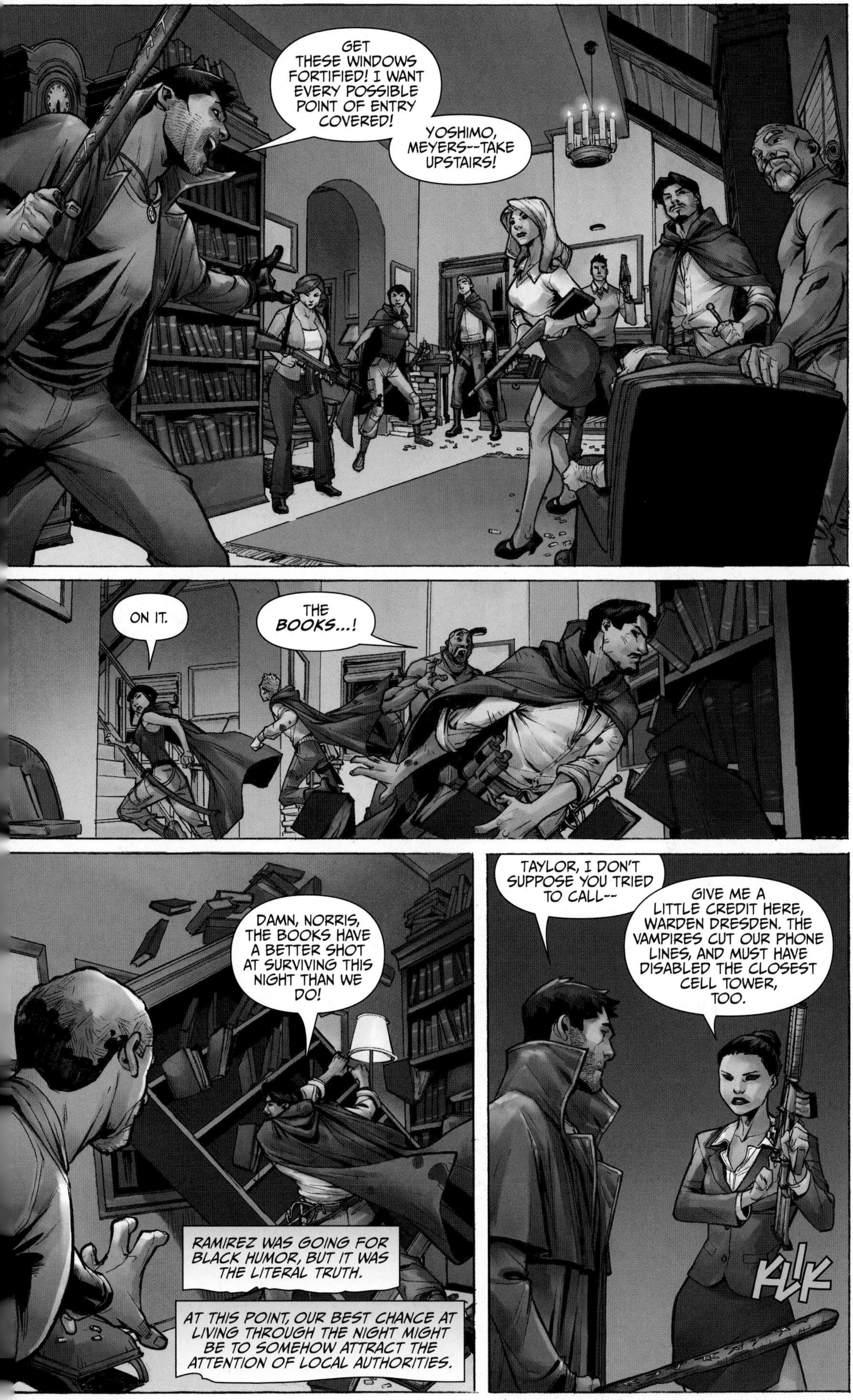
GET THESE WINDOWS FORTIFIED! I WANT EVERY POSSIBLE POINT OF ENTRY COVERED!
YOSHIMO, MEYERS--TAKE UPSTAIRS!
ON IT.
THE BOOKS...!
DAMN, NORRIS, THE BOOKS HAVE A BETTER SHOT AT SURVIVING THIS NIGHT THAN WE DO!
RAMIREZ WAS GOING FOR BLACK HUMOR, BUT IT WAS THE LITERAL TRUTH.
AT THIS POINT, OUR BEST CHANCE AT LIVING THROUGH THE NIGHT MIGHT BE TO SOMEHOW ATTRACT THE ATTENTION OF LOCAL AUTHORITIES.
TAYLOR, I DON'T SUPPOSE YOU TRIED TO CALL--
GIVE ME A LITTLE CREDIT HERE, WARDEN DRESDEN. THE VAMPIRES CUT OUR PHONE LINES, AND MUST HAVE DISABLED THE CLOSEST CELL TOWER, TOO.
KLIK

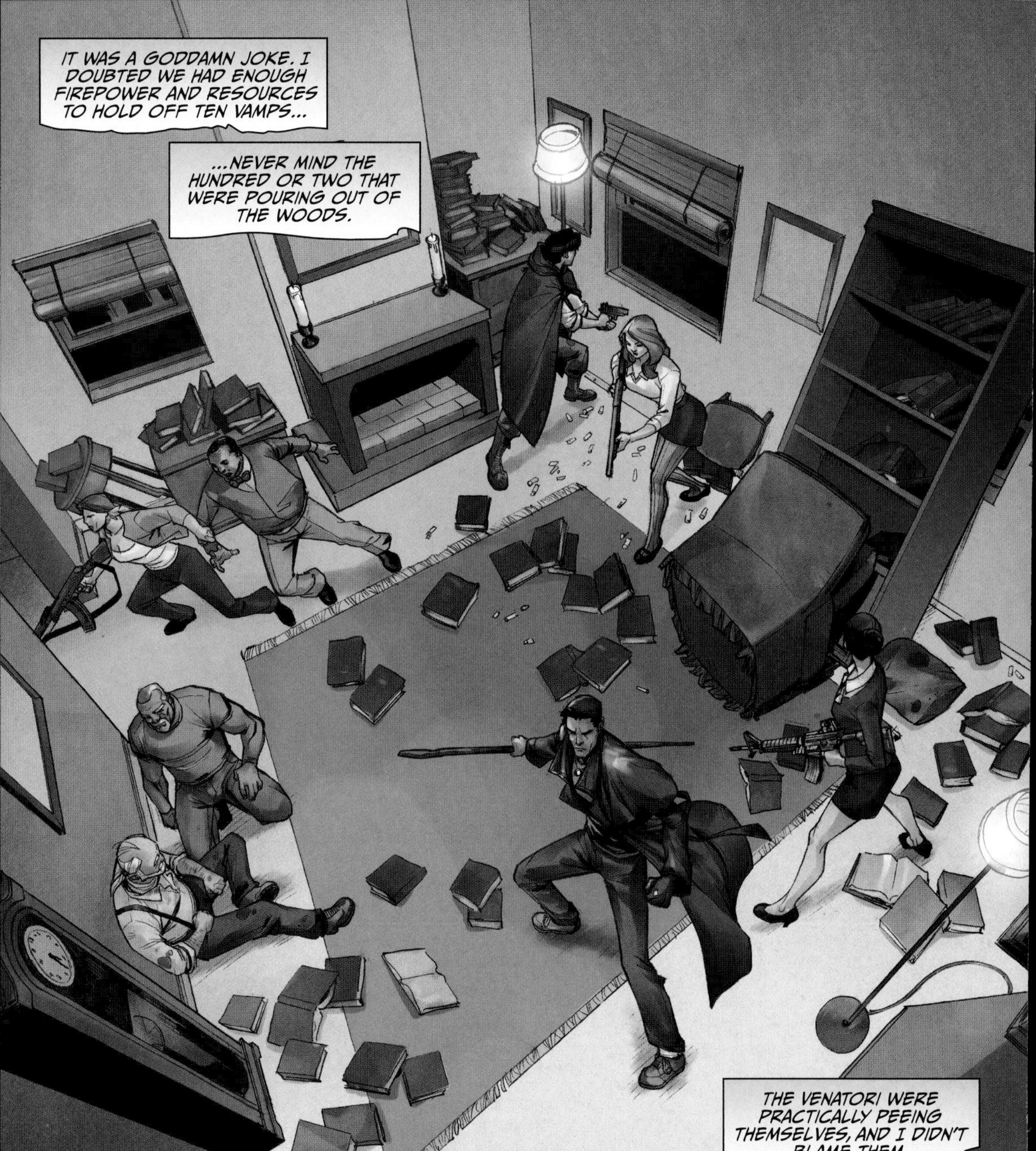
IT WAS A GODDAMN JOKE. I DOUBTED WE HAD ENOUGH FIREPOWER AND RESOURCES TO HOLD OFF TEN VAMPS...
...NEVER MIND THE HUNDRED OR TWO THAT WERE POURING OUT OF THE WOODS.
THE VENATORI WERE PRACTICALLY PEEING THEMSELVES, AND I DIDN'T BLAME THEM.

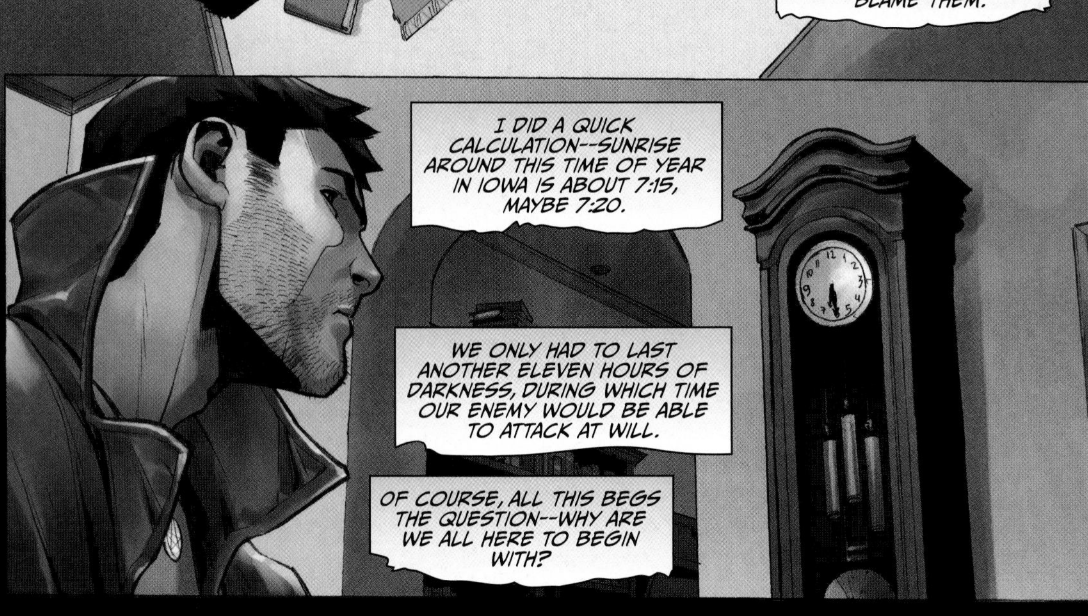
I DID A QUICK CALCULATION--SUNRISE AROUND THIS TIME OF YEAR IN IOWA IS ABOUT 7:15, MAYBE 7:20.
WE ONLY HAD TO LAST ANOTHER ELEVEN HOURS OF DARKNESS, DURING WHICH TIME OUR ENEMY WOULD BE ABLE TO ATTACK AT WILL.
OF COURSE, ALL THIS BEGS THE QUESTION--WHY ARE WE ALL HERE TO BEGIN WITH?

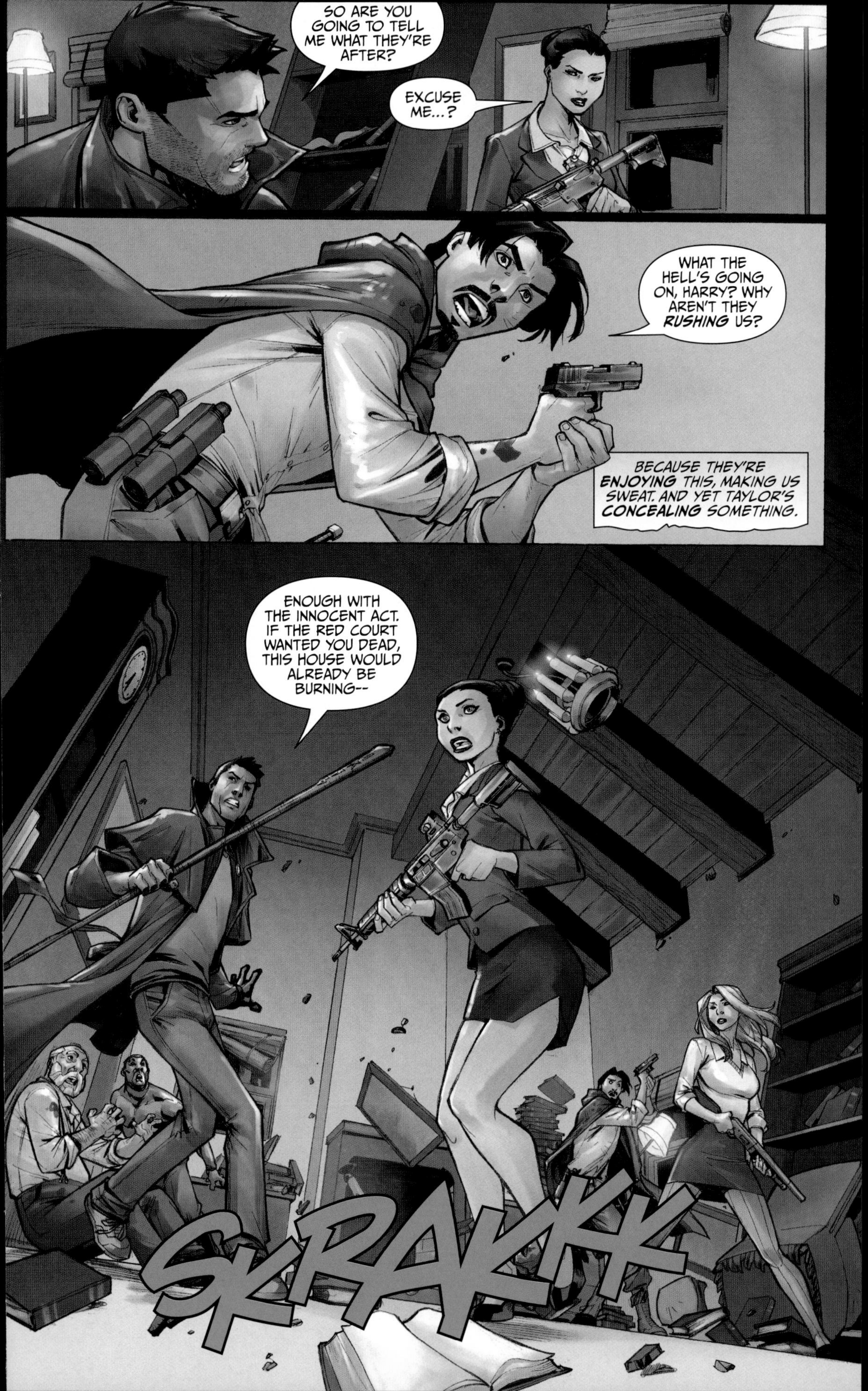
SO ARE YOU GOING TO TELL ME WHAT THEY'RE AFTER?
EXCUSE ME...?
WHAT THE HELL'S GOING ON, HARRY? WHY AREN'T THEY *RUSHING* US?
BECAUSE THEY'RE **ENJOYING** THIS, MAKING US SWEAT. AND YET TAYLOR'S **CONCEALING** SOMETHING.
ENOUGH WITH THE INNOCENT ACT. IF THE RED COURT WANTED YOU DEAD, THIS HOUSE WOULD ALREADY BE BURNING--
SKRAKK

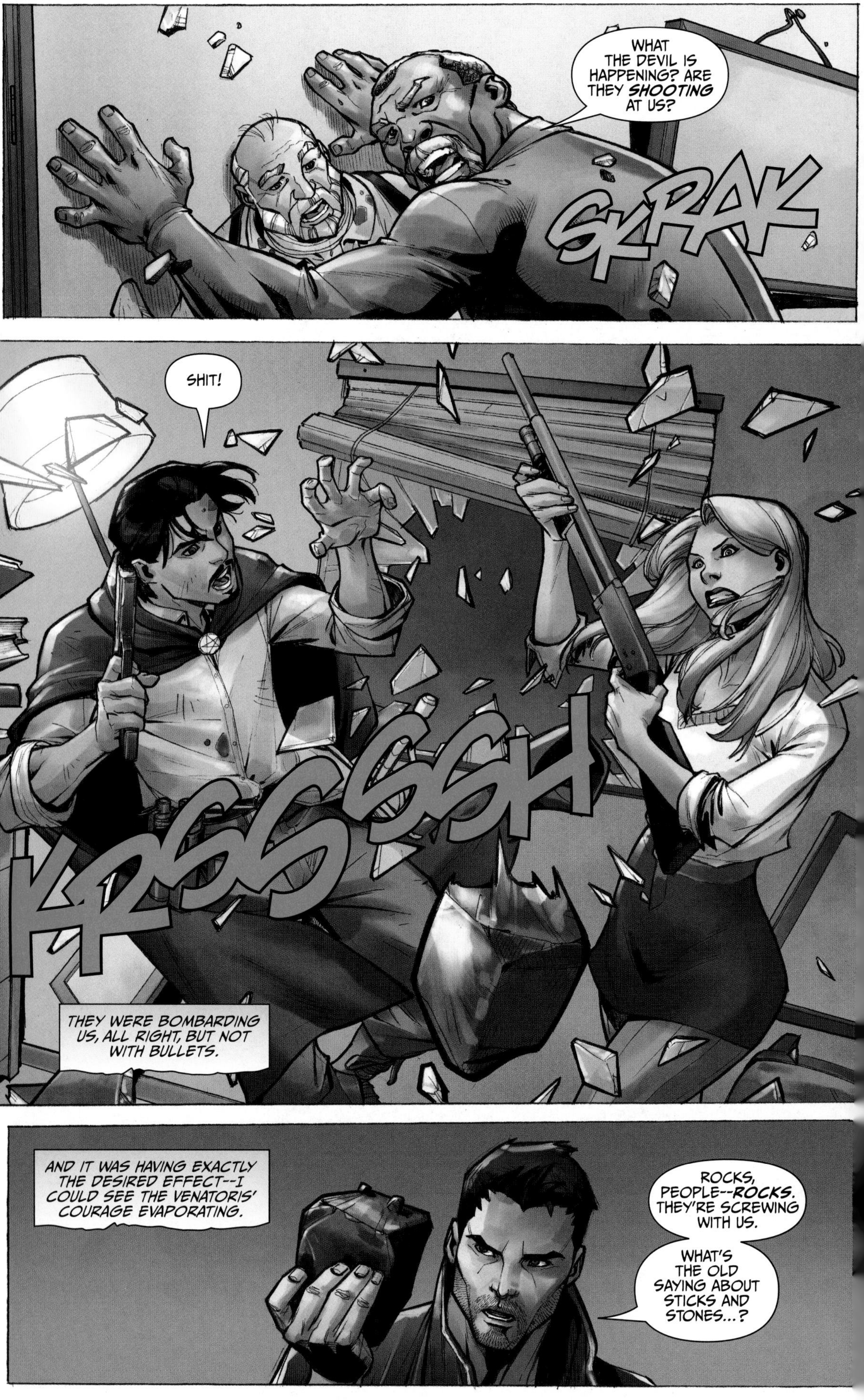
WHAT THE DEVIL IS HAPPENING? ARE THEY SHOOTING AT US?
SKRAK
SHIT!
KRSSSSSH
THEY WERE BOMBARDING US, ALL RIGHT, BUT NOT WITH BULLETS.
AND IT WAS HAVING EXACTLY THE DESIRED EFFECT--I COULD SEE THE VENATORIS' COURAGE EVAPORATING.
ROCKS, PEOPLE--ROCKS. THEY'RE SCREWING WITH US.
WHAT'S THE OLD SAYING ABOUT STICKS AND STONES...?

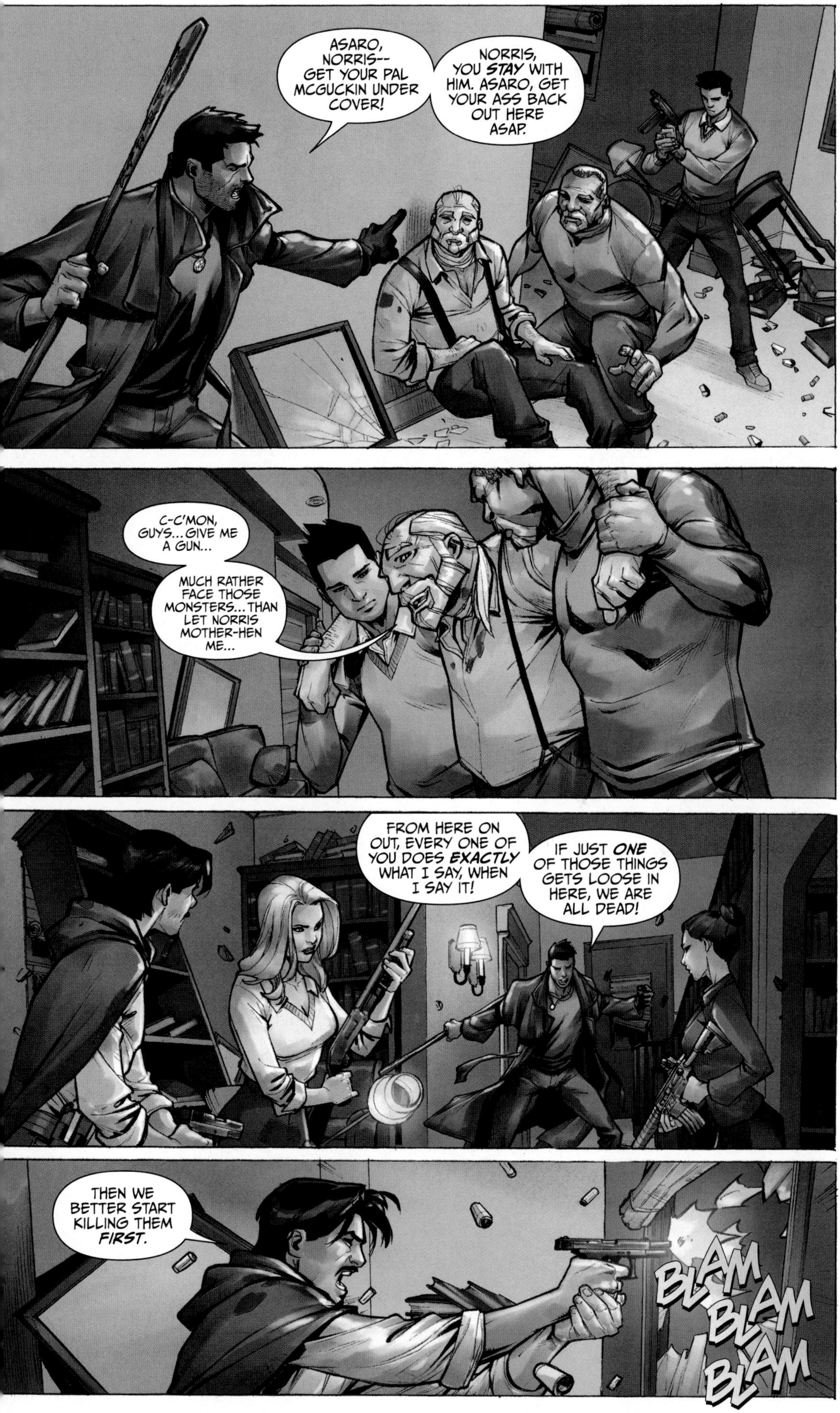
ASARO, NORRIS-- GET YOUR PAL MCGUCKIN UNDER COVER!
NORRIS, YOU STAY WITH HIM. ASARO, GET YOUR ASS BACK OUT HERE ASAP.
C-C'MON, GUYS... GIVE ME A GUN...
MUCH RATHER FACE THOSE MONSTERS... THAN LET NORRIS MOTHER-HEN ME...
FROM HERE ON OUT, EVERY ONE OF YOU DOES EXACTLY WHAT I SAY, WHEN I SAY IT!
IF JUST ONE OF THOSE THINGS GETS LOOSE IN HERE, WE ARE ALL DEAD!
THEN WE BETTER START KILLING THEM FIRST.
BLAM BLAM BLAM BLAM

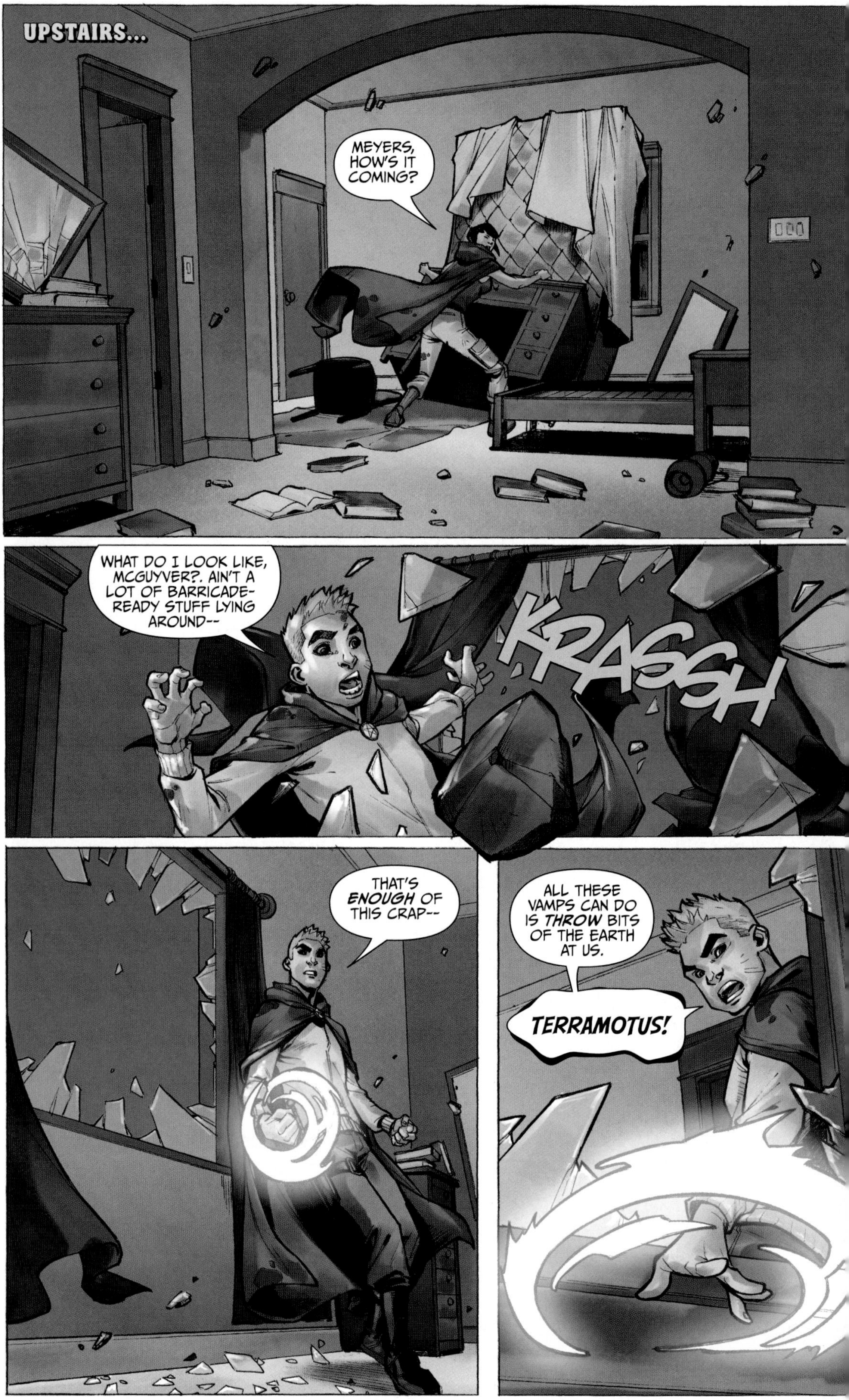
UPSTAIRS...
MEYERS, HOW'S IT COMING?
WHAT DO I LOOK LIKE, MCGUYVER?. AIN'T A LOT OF BARRICADE-READY STUFF LYING AROUND--
KRASSH
THAT'S ENOUGH OF THIS CRAP--
ALL THESE VAMPS CAN DO IS THROW BITS OF THE EARTH AT US.
TERRAMOTUS!

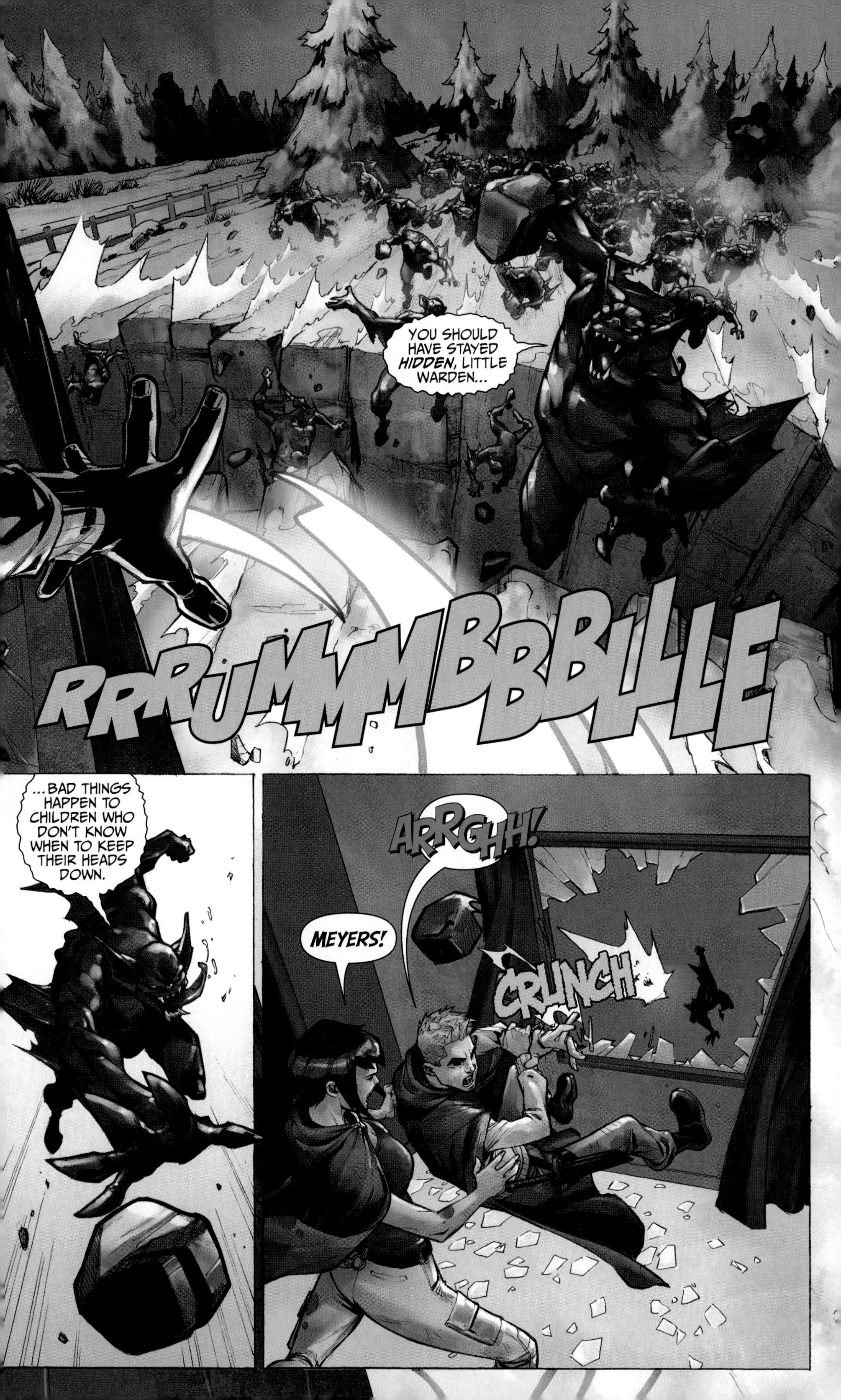
YOU SHOULD HAVE STAYED *HIDDEN*, LITTLE WARDEN...
RRRUMMMBBBLLE
...BAD THINGS HAPPEN TO CHILDREN WHO DON'T KNOW WHEN TO KEEP THEIR HEADS DOWN.
ARRGHH!
MEYERS!
CRUNCH

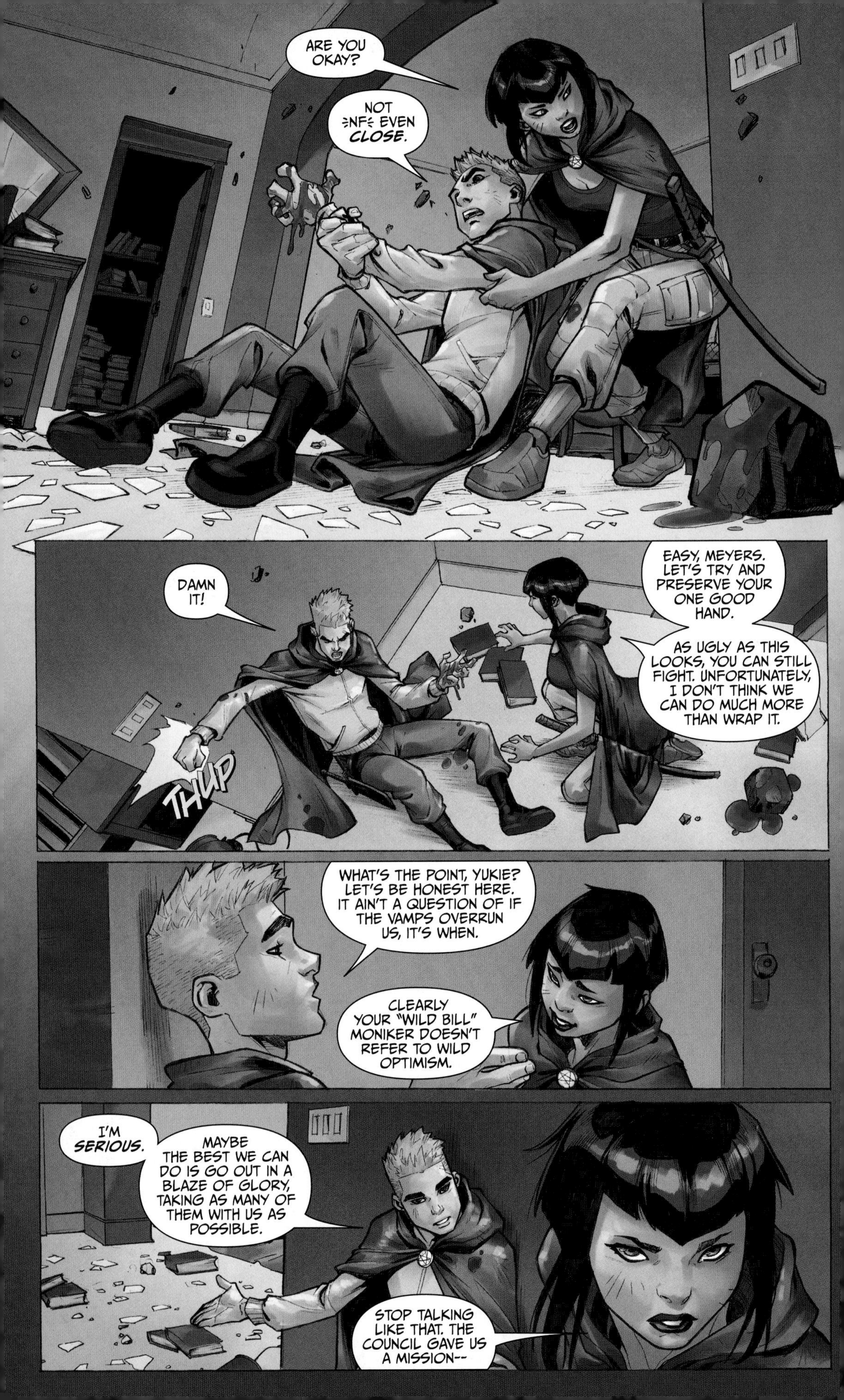
ARE YOU OKAY?
NOT NF EVEN *CLOSE*.
DAMN IT!
EASY, MEYERS. LET'S TRY AND PRESERVE YOUR ONE GOOD HAND.
AS UGLY AS THIS LOOKS, YOU CAN STILL FIGHT. UNFORTUNATELY, I DON'T THINK WE CAN DO MUCH MORE THAN WRAP IT.
THUP
WHAT'S THE POINT, YUKIE? LET'S BE HONEST HERE. IT AIN'T A QUESTION OF IF THE VAMPS OVERRUN US, IT'S WHEN.
CLEARLY YOUR "WILD BILL" MONIKER DOESN'T REFER TO WILD OPTIMISM.
I'M *SERIOUS*.
MAYBE THE BEST WE CAN DO IS GO OUT IN A BLAZE OF GLORY, TAKING AS MANY OF THEM WITH US AS POSSIBLE.
STOP TALKING LIKE THAT. THE COUNCIL GAVE US A MISSION--

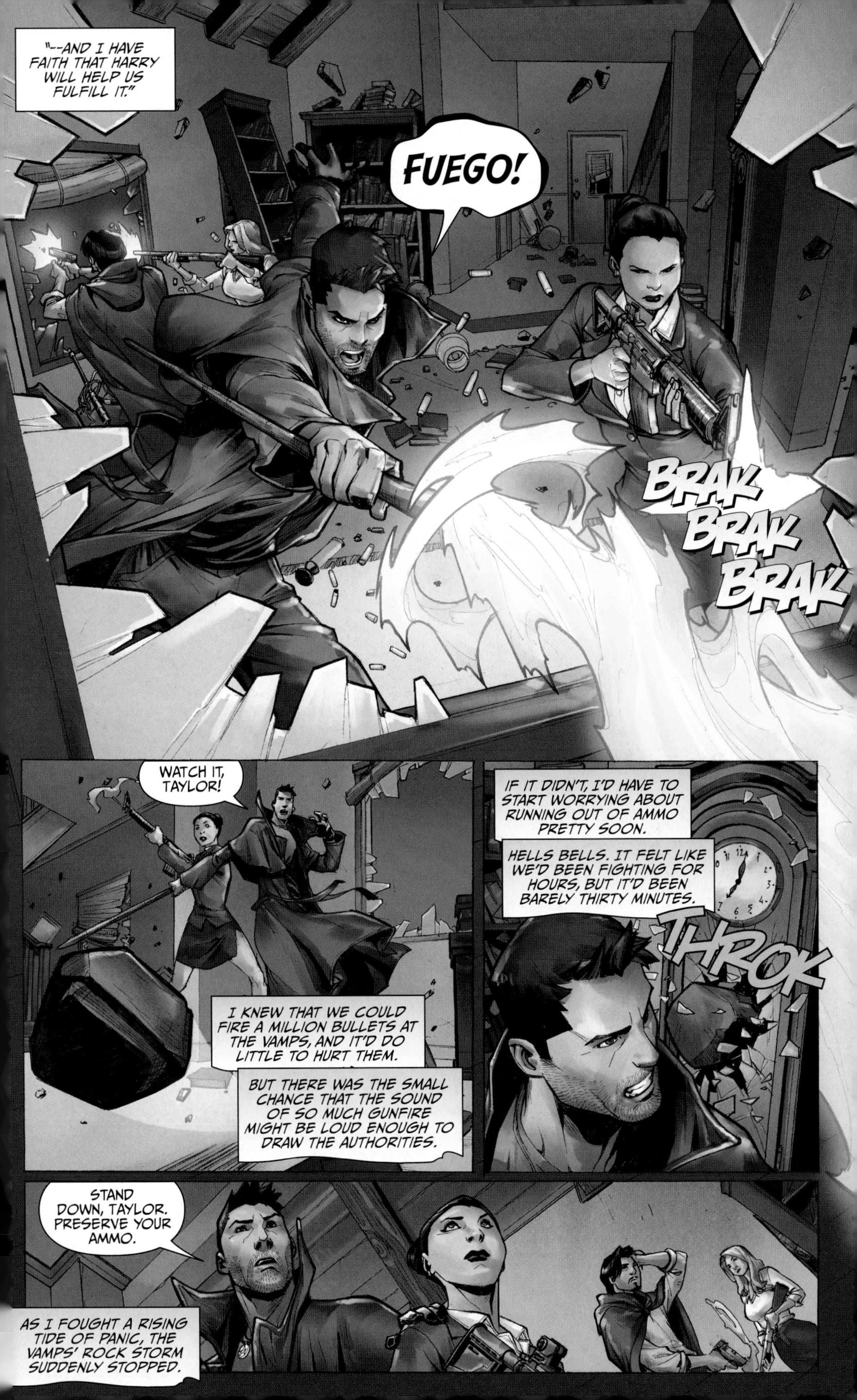

"--AND I HAVE FAITH THAT HARRY WILL HELP US FULFILL IT."
FUEGO!
BRAK BRAK BRAK
WATCH IT, TAYLOR!
I KNEW THAT WE COULD FIRE A MILLION BULLETS AT THE VAMPS, AND IT'D DO LITTLE TO HURT THEM.
BUT THERE WAS THE SMALL CHANCE THAT THE SOUND OF SO MUCH GUNFIRE MIGHT BE LOUD ENOUGH TO DRAW THE AUTHORITIES.
IF IT DIDN'T, I'D HAVE TO START WORRYING ABOUT RUNNING OUT OF AMMO PRETTY SOON.
HELLS BELLS. IT FELT LIKE WE'D BEEN FIGHTING FOR HOURS, BUT IT'D BEEN BARELY THIRTY MINUTES.
THROK
STAND DOWN, TAYLOR. PRESERVE YOUR AMMO.
AS I FOUGHT A RISING TIDE OF PANIC, THE VAMPS' ROCK STORM SUDDENLY STOPPED.

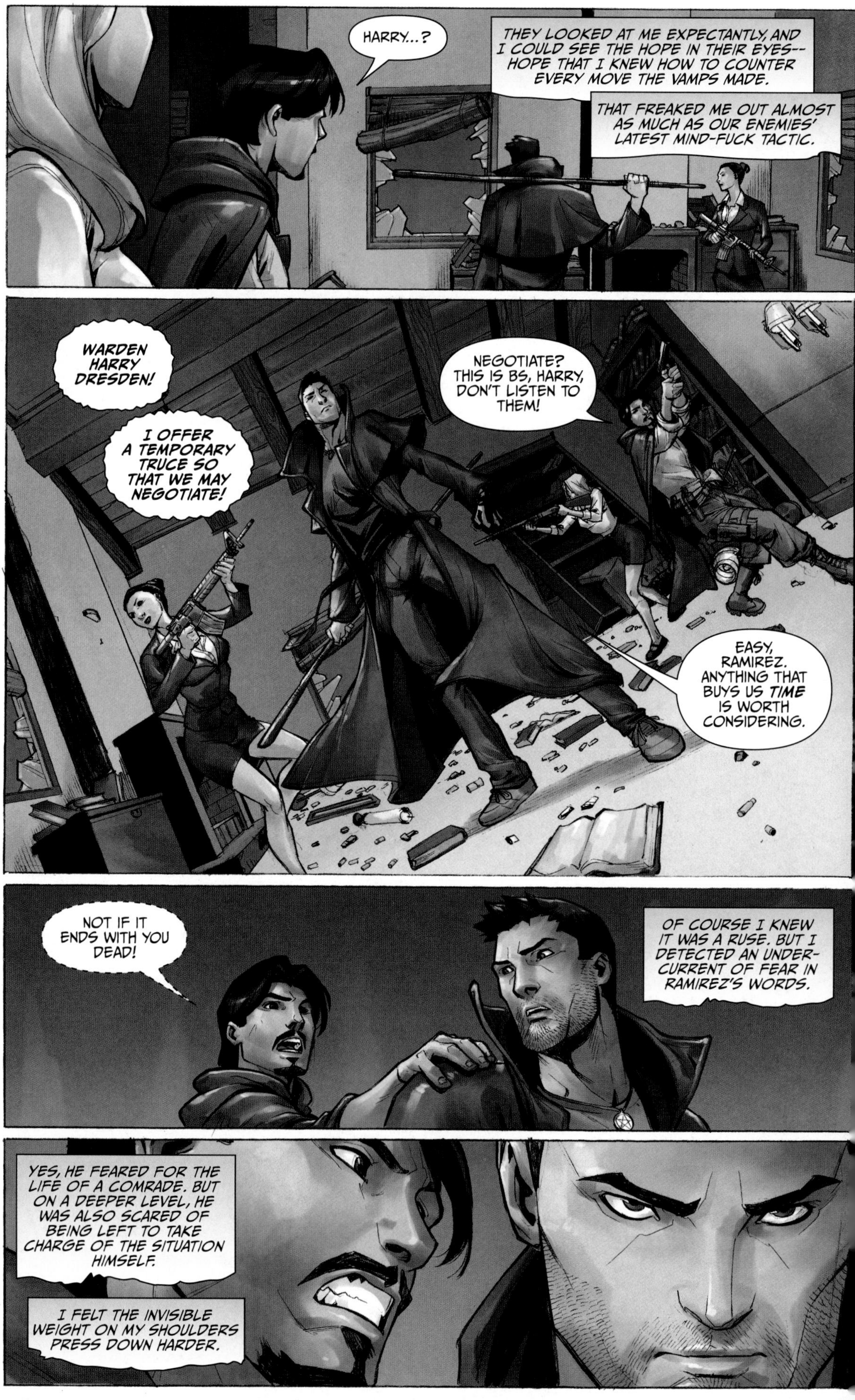
HARRY...?
THEY LOOKED AT ME EXPECTANTLY, AND I COULD SEE THE HOPE IN THEIR EYES-- HOPE THAT I KNEW HOW TO COUNTER EVERY MOVE THE VAMPS MADE.
THAT FREAKED ME OUT ALMOST AS MUCH AS OUR ENEMIES' LATEST MIND-FUCK TACTIC.
WARDEN HARRY DRESDEN!
I OFFER A TEMPORARY TRUCE SO THAT WE MAY NEGOTIATE!
NEGOTIATE? THIS IS BS, HARRY, DON'T LISTEN TO THEM!
EASY, RAMIREZ. ANYTHING THAT BUYS US TIME IS WORTH CONSIDERING.
NOT IF IT ENDS WITH YOU DEAD!
OF COURSE I KNEW IT WAS A RUSE. BUT I DETECTED AN UNDER-CURRENT OF FEAR IN RAMIREZ'S WORDS.
YES, HE FEARED FOR THE LIFE OF A COMRADE. BUT ON A DEEPER LEVEL, HE WAS ALSO SCARED OF BEING LEFT TO TAKE CHARGE OF THE SITUATION HIMSELF.
I FELT THE INVISIBLE WEIGHT ON MY SHOULDERS PRESS DOWN HARDER.

WARDEN, THIS NIGHT NEED NOT END WITH THE DEATHS OF YOU AND YOUR TEAM!

YOU HAVE THIRTY SECONDS TO COME OUT ALONE, OR WE WILL RESUME OUR BOMBARDMENT!

I--I THINK IT'S THEIR LEADER...

LISTEN TO ME, RAMIREZ, THEY CLEARLY WANT SOMETHING IN THE HOUSE.

FINDING OUT IS YOUR JOB. I'D LIKE AN ANSWER BY THE TIME I GET BACK.

BEEN THINKING THE SAME THING. BUT WHAT?

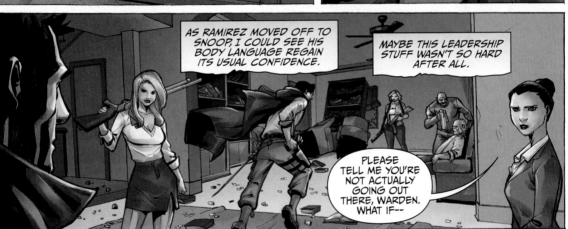

AS RAMIREZ MOVED OFF TO SNOOP, I COULD SEE HIS BODY LANGUAGE REGAIN ITS USUAL CONFIDENCE.

MAYBE THIS LEADERSHIP STUFF WASN'T SO HARD AFTER ALL.

PLEASE TELL ME YOU'RE NOT ACTUALLY GOING OUT THERE, WARDEN. WHAT IF--

IF THEY KILL ME, THEN YOU GIVE RAMIREZ YOUR UNQUESTIONING OBEDIENCE.

BUT DON'T WORRY--THEY'RE NOT KILLING ME.

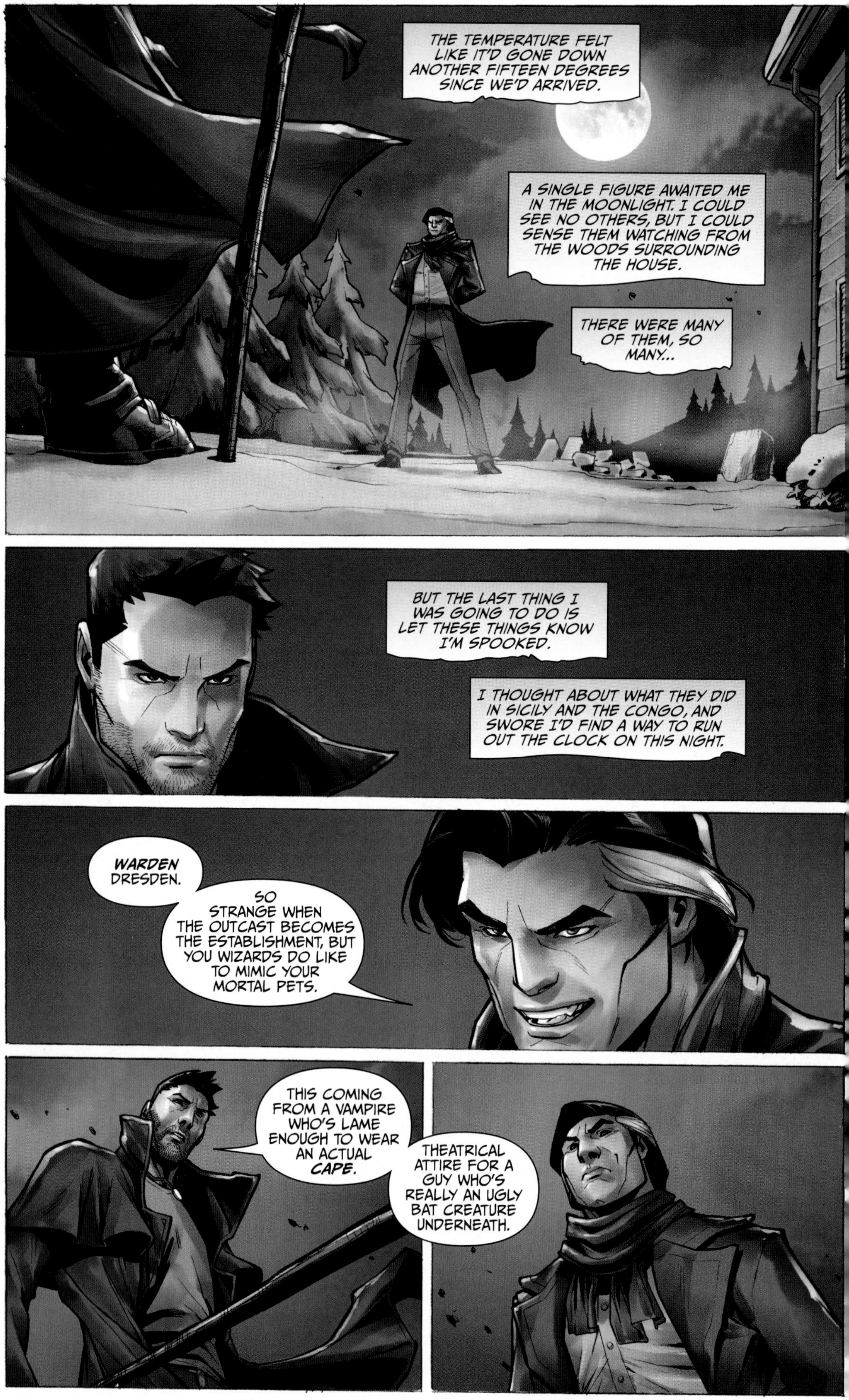
THE TEMPERATURE FELT LIKE IT'D GONE DOWN ANOTHER FIFTEEN DEGREES SINCE WE'D ARRIVED.
A SINGLE FIGURE AWAITED ME IN THE MOONLIGHT. I COULD SEE NO OTHERS, BUT I COULD SENSE THEM WATCHING FROM THE WOODS SURROUNDING THE HOUSE.
THERE WERE MANY OF THEM, SO MANY...
BUT THE LAST THING I WAS GOING TO DO IS LET THESE THINGS KNOW I'M SPOOKED.
I THOUGHT ABOUT WHAT THEY DID IN SICILY AND THE CONGO, AND SWORE I'D FIND A WAY TO RUN OUT THE CLOCK ON THIS NIGHT.
WARDEN DRESDEN.
SO STRANGE WHEN THE OUTCAST BECOMES THE ESTABLISHMENT, BUT YOU WIZARDS DO LIKE TO MIMIC YOUR MORTAL PETS.
THIS COMING FROM A VAMPIRE WHO'S LAME ENOUGH TO WEAR AN ACTUAL CAPE.
THEATRICAL ATTIRE FOR A GUY WHO'S REALLY AN UGLY BAT CREATURE UNDERNEATH.

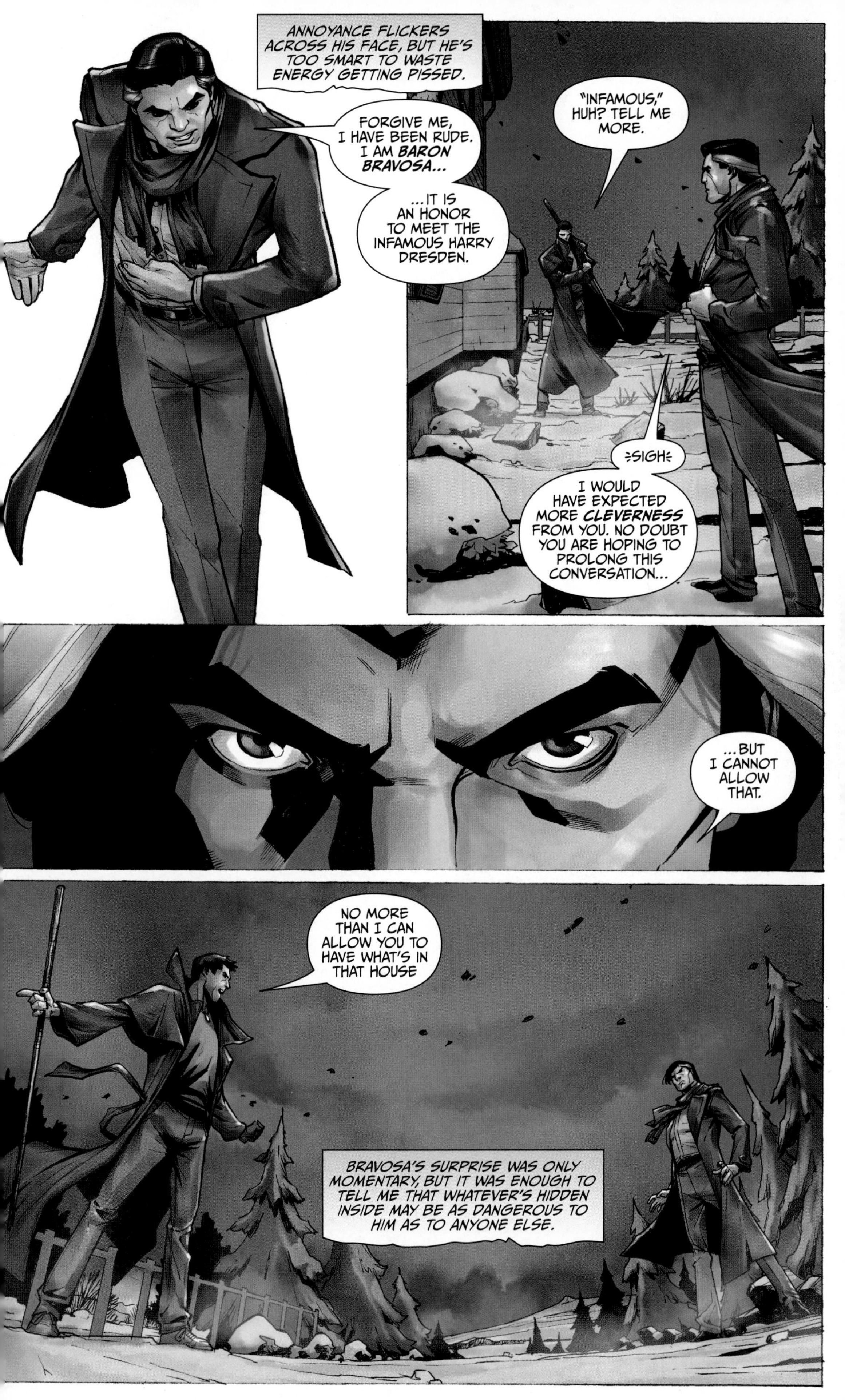
ANNOYANCE FLICKERS ACROSS HIS FACE, BUT HE'S TOO SMART TO WASTE ENERGY GETTING PISSED.
FORGIVE ME, I HAVE BEEN RUDE. I AM BARON BRAVOSA...
...IT IS AN HONOR TO MEET THE INFAMOUS HARRY DRESDEN.
"INFAMOUS," HUH? TELL ME MORE.
SIGH
I WOULD HAVE EXPECTED MORE CLEVERNESS FROM YOU. NO DOUBT YOU ARE HOPING TO PROLONG THIS CONVERSATION...
...BUT I CANNOT ALLOW THAT.
NO MORE THAN I CAN ALLOW YOU TO HAVE WHAT'S IN THAT HOUSE
BRAVOSA'S SURPRISE WAS ONLY MOMENTARY, BUT IT WAS ENOUGH TO TELL ME THAT WHATEVER'S HIDDEN INSIDE MAY BE AS DANGEROUS TO HIM AS TO ANYONE ELSE.

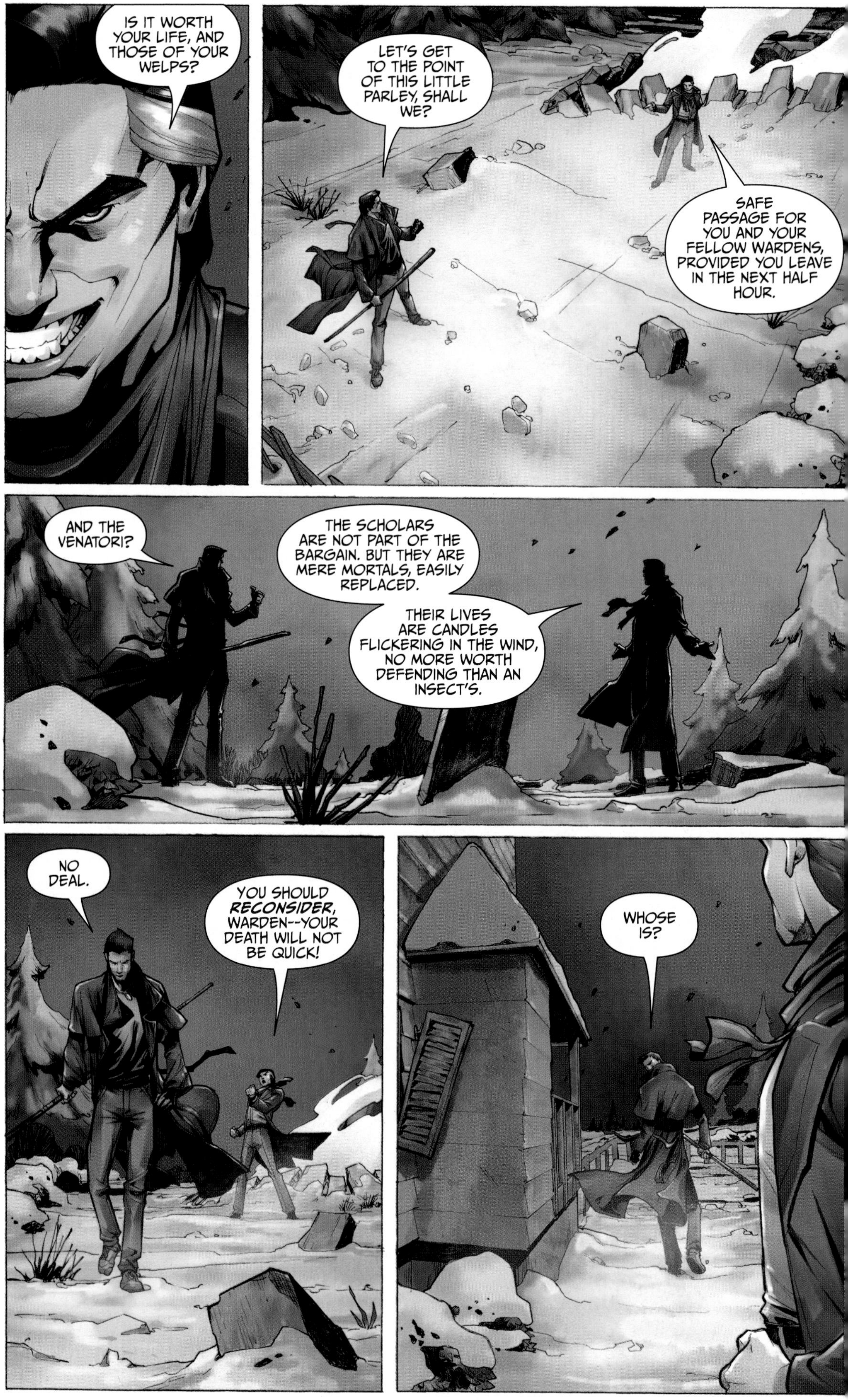

IS IT WORTH YOUR LIFE, AND THOSE OF YOUR WELPS?
LET'S GET TO THE POINT OF THIS LITTLE PARLEY, SHALL WE?
SAFE PASSAGE FOR YOU AND YOUR FELLOW WARDENS, PROVIDED YOU LEAVE IN THE NEXT HALF HOUR.
AND THE VENATORI?
THE SCHOLARS ARE NOT PART OF THE BARGAIN. BUT THEY ARE MERE MORTALS, EASILY REPLACED.
THEIR LIVES ARE CANDLES FLICKERING IN THE WIND, NO MORE WORTH DEFENDING THAN AN INSECT'S.
NO DEAL.
YOU SHOULD *RECONSIDER*, WARDEN--YOUR DEATH WILL NOT BE QUICK!
WHOSE IS?

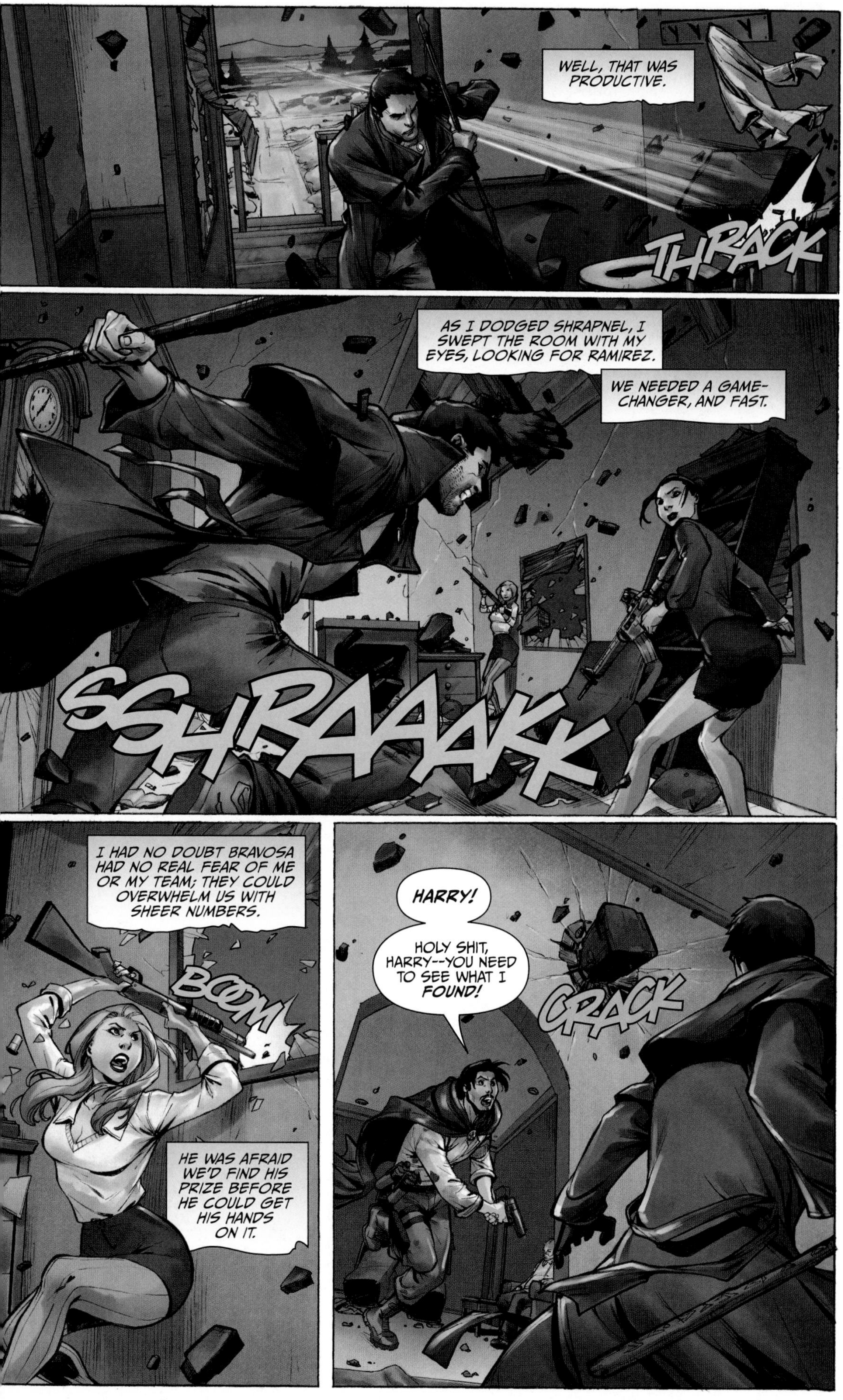
WELL, THAT WAS PRODUCTIVE.
THRACK
AS I DODGED SHRAPNEL, I SWEPT THE ROOM WITH MY EYES, LOOKING FOR RAMIREZ.
WE NEEDED A GAME-CHANGER, AND FAST.
SSHRAAAKK
I HAD NO DOUBT BRAVOSA HAD NO REAL FEAR OF ME OR MY TEAM; THEY COULD OVERWHELM US WITH SHEER NUMBERS.
BOOM
HE WAS AFRAID WE'D FIND HIS PRIZE BEFORE HE COULD GET HIS HANDS ON IT.
HARRY!
HOLY SHIT, HARRY--YOU NEED TO SEE WHAT I FOUND!
CRACK

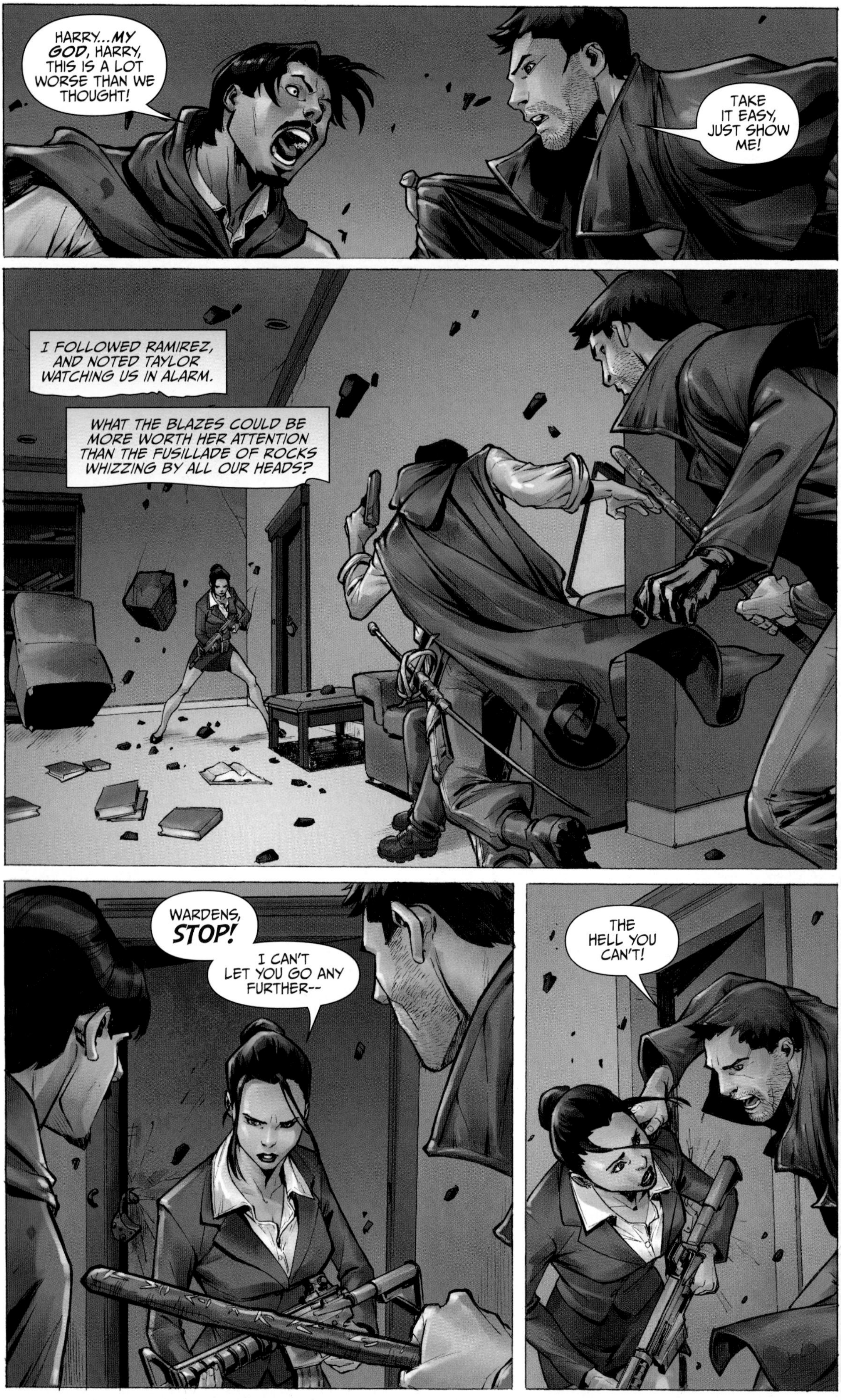
HARRY...MY GOD, HARRY, THIS IS A LOT WORSE THAN WE THOUGHT!
TAKE IT EASY, JUST SHOW ME!
I FOLLOWED RAMIREZ, AND NOTED TAYLOR WATCHING US IN ALARM.
WHAT THE BLAZES COULD BE MORE WORTH HER ATTENTION THAN THE FUSILLADE OF ROCKS WHIZZING BY ALL OUR HEADS?
WARDENS, STOP!
I CAN'T LET YOU GO ANY FURTHER--
THE HELL YOU CAN'T!

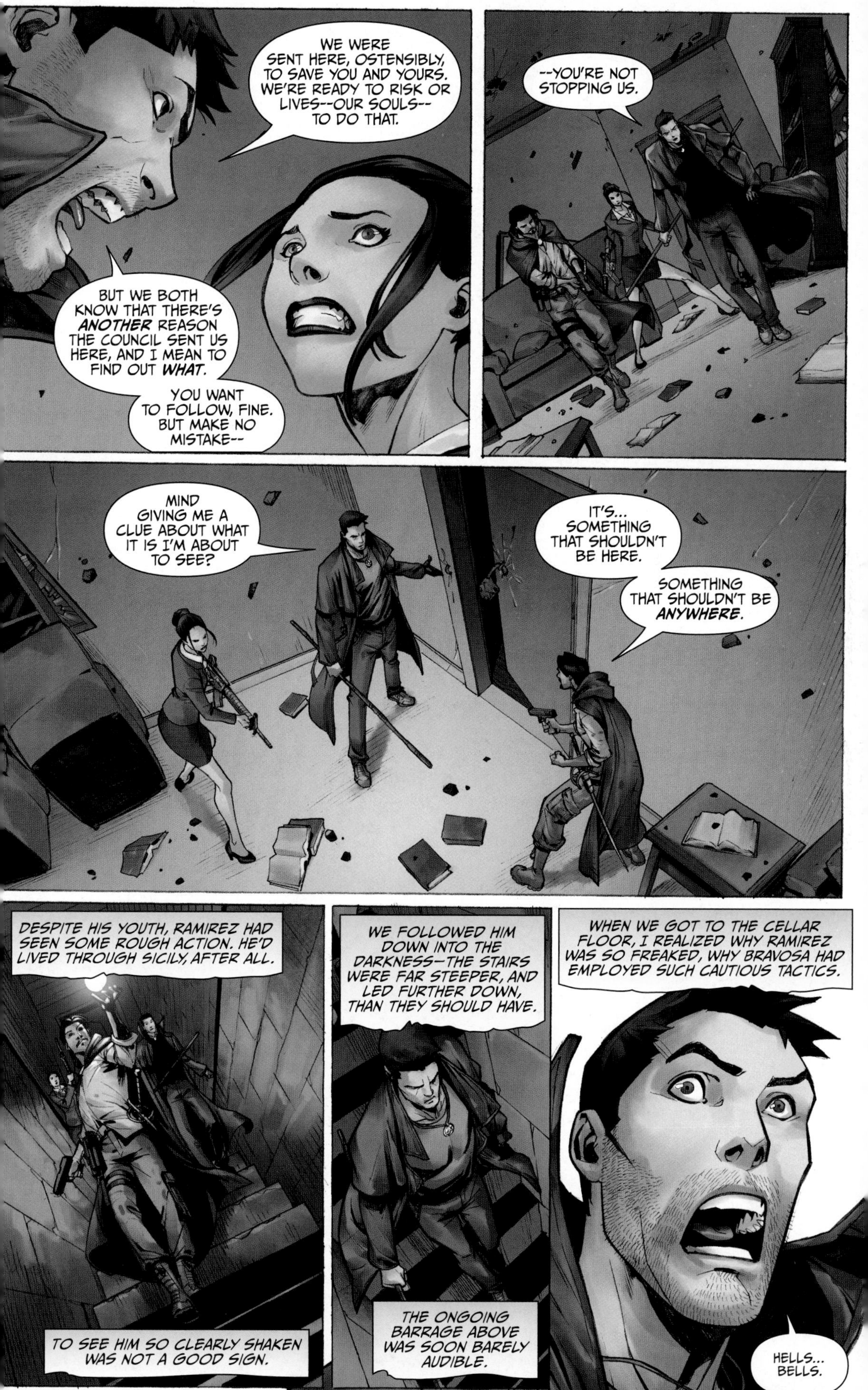
WE WERE SENT HERE, OSTENSIBLY, TO SAVE YOU AND YOURS. WE'RE READY TO RISK OR LIVES--OUR SOULS-- TO DO THAT.
BUT WE BOTH KNOW THAT THERE'S ANOTHER REASON THE COUNCIL SENT US HERE, AND I MEAN TO FIND OUT WHAT.
YOU WANT TO FOLLOW, FINE. BUT MAKE NO MISTAKE--
--YOU'RE NOT STOPPING US.
MIND GIVING ME A CLUE ABOUT WHAT IT IS I'M ABOUT TO SEE?
IT'S... SOMETHING THAT SHOULDN'T BE HERE.
SOMETHING THAT SHOULDN'T BE ANYWHERE.
DESPITE HIS YOUTH, RAMIREZ HAD SEEN SOME ROUGH ACTION. HE'D LIVED THROUGH SICILY, AFTER ALL.
TO SEE HIM SO CLEARLY SHAKEN WAS NOT A GOOD SIGN.
WE FOLLOWED HIM DOWN INTO THE DARKNESS—THE STAIRS WERE FAR STEEPER, AND LED FURTHER DOWN, THAN THEY SHOULD HAVE.
THE ONGOING BARRAGE ABOVE WAS SOON BARELY AUDIBLE.
WHEN WE GOT TO THE CELLAR FLOOR, I REALIZED WHY RAMIREZ WAS SO FREAKED, WHY BRAVOSA HAD EMPLOYED SUCH CAUTIOUS TACTICS.
HELLS... BELLS.

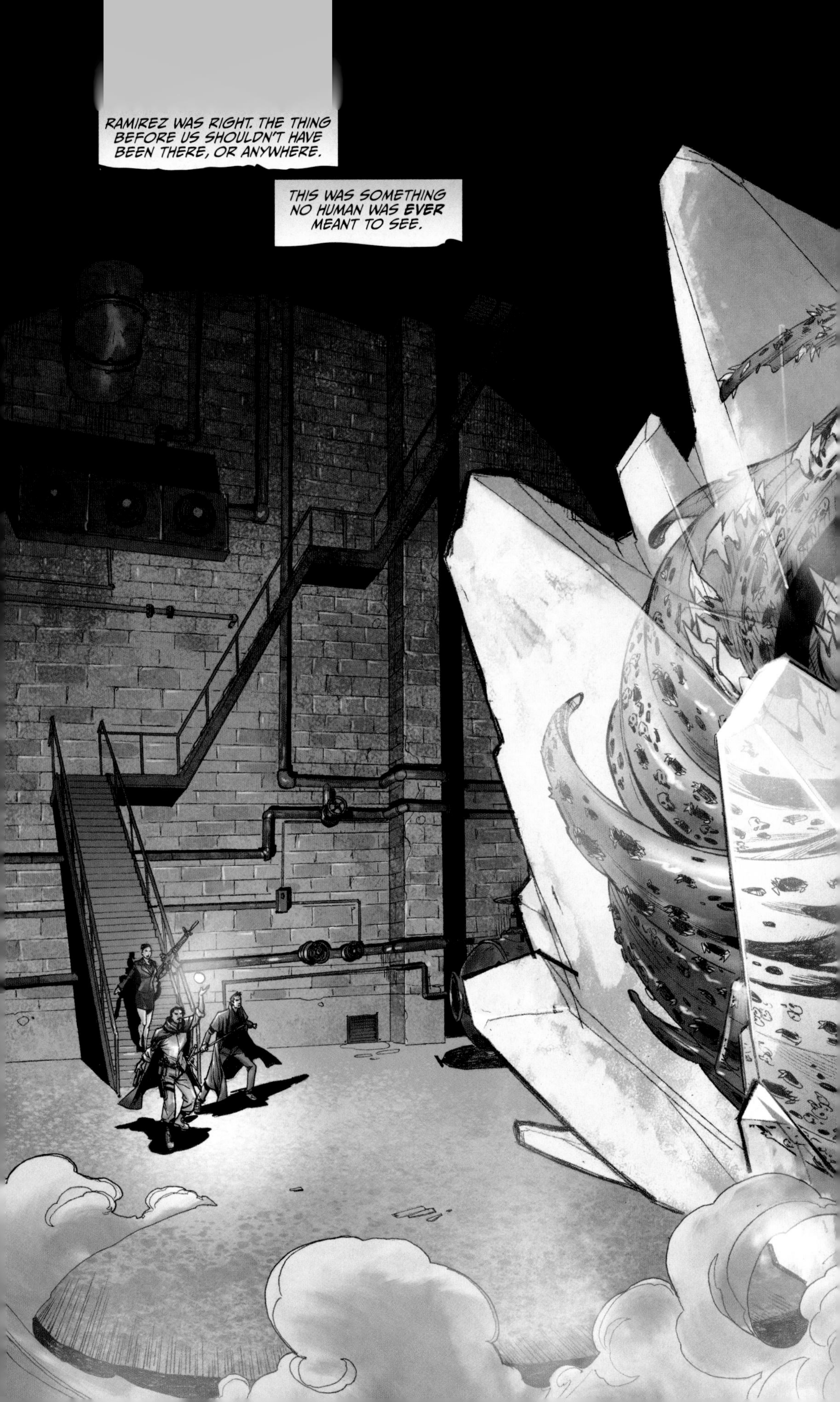
RAMIREZ WAS RIGHT. THE THING BEFORE US SHOULDN'T HAVE BEEN THERE, OR ANYWHERE.
THIS WAS SOMETHING NO HUMAN WAS **EVER** MEANT TO SEE.

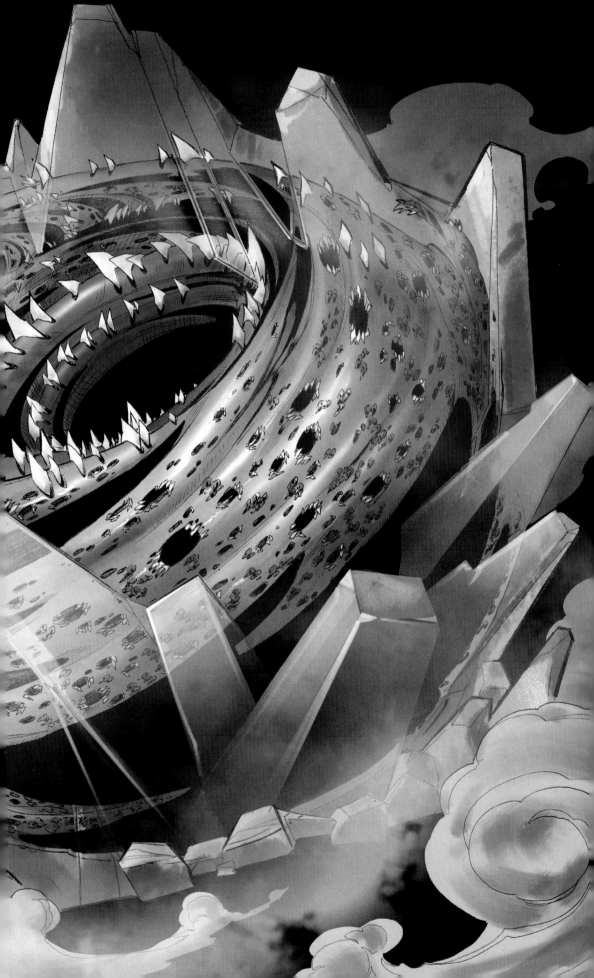

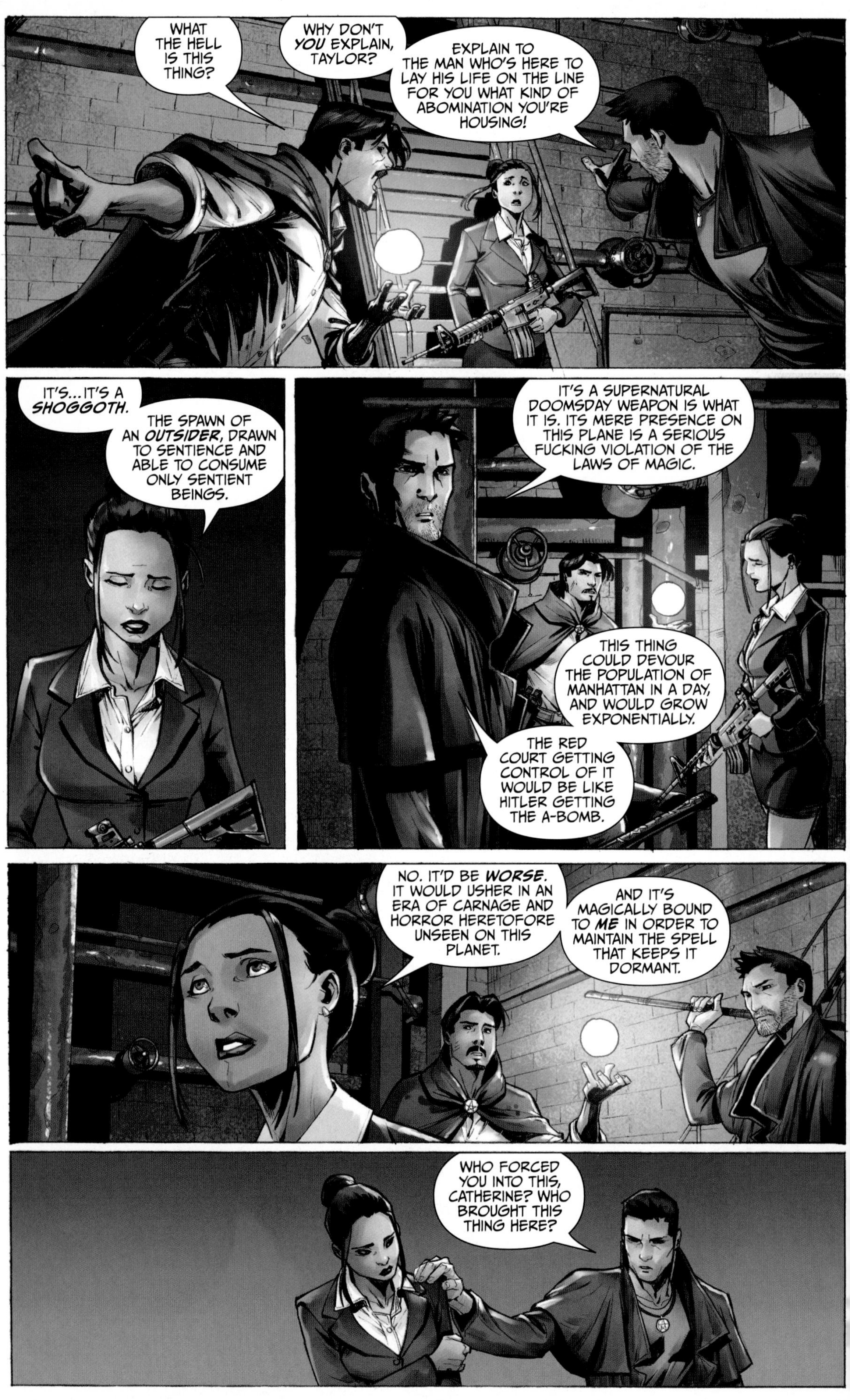
WHAT THE HELL IS THIS THING?
WHY DON'T *YOU* EXPLAIN, TAYLOR?
EXPLAIN TO THE MAN WHO'S HERE TO LAY HIS LIFE ON THE LINE FOR YOU WHAT KIND OF ABOMINATION YOU'RE HOUSING!
IT'S...IT'S A *SHOGGOTH*.
THE SPAWN OF AN *OUTSIDER*, DRAWN TO SENTIENCE AND ABLE TO CONSUME ONLY SENTIENT BEINGS.
IT'S A SUPERNATURAL DOOMSDAY WEAPON IS WHAT IT IS. ITS MERE PRESENCE ON THIS PLANE IS A SERIOUS FUCKING VIOLATION OF THE LAWS OF MAGIC.
THIS THING COULD DEVOUR THE POPULATION OF MANHATTAN IN A DAY, AND WOULD GROW EXPONENTIALLY.
THE RED COURT GETTING CONTROL OF IT WOULD BE LIKE HITLER GETTING THE A-BOMB.
NO. IT'D BE *WORSE*. IT WOULD USHER IN AN ERA OF CARNAGE AND HORROR HERETOFORE UNSEEN ON THIS PLANET.
AND IT'S MAGICALLY BOUND TO *ME* IN ORDER TO MAINTAIN THE SPELL THAT KEEPS IT DORMANT.
WHO FORCED YOU INTO THIS, CATHERINE? WHO BROUGHT THIS THING HERE?

"IT WAS DELIVERED THROUGH ULTRA-BLACK SECURITY PROTOCOLS..."

PLEASE, DO NOT ASK THIS OF ME!

I--WE-- HAVE ALWAYS BEEN THE COUNCIL'S STALWART ALLIES!

THAT IS WHY WE KNOW WE CAN TRUST YOU WITH SO *IMPORTANT* A TASK.

TASK? IS THAT WHAT YOU CALL THIS? YOU'RE MAKING ME AN ACCOMPLICE TO--

TO *WHAT?* I SUGGEST YOU HAVE A CARE WHAT TONE YOU TAKE WITH ME.

AND HAVE *FAITH* THAT THE WHITE COUNCIL ACTS WITH THE GREATER GOOD IN MIND.

THE CREATURE HAS BEEN BOUND TO YOU. STAY CLOSE TO IT...

...AND BE READY TO DO ANYTHING IT TAKES TO KEEP IT HIDDEN.

I NEVER SAW HIS FACE...I HAVE NO IDEA WHO HE WAS...

ANY MORE THAN I KNEW WHO GAVE US *OUR* ORDERS. BUT I BET THEY WERE ONE AND THE SAME.

TRAPPING THE SHOGGOTH HAD TO BE THE WORK OF AN INCREDIBLY POWERFUL WIZARD.

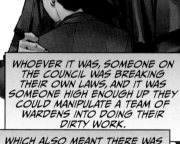

COULD IT BE EBENEZAR?

WHOEVER IT WAS, SOMEONE ON THE COUNCIL WAS BREAKING THEIR OWN LAWS, AND IT WAS SOMEONE HIGH ENOUGH UP THEY COULD MANIPULATE A TEAM OF WARDENS INTO DOING THEIR DIRTY WORK.

WHICH ALSO MEANT THERE WAS NO *CAVALRY* FORTHCOMING. WE'D BEEN SCREWED...

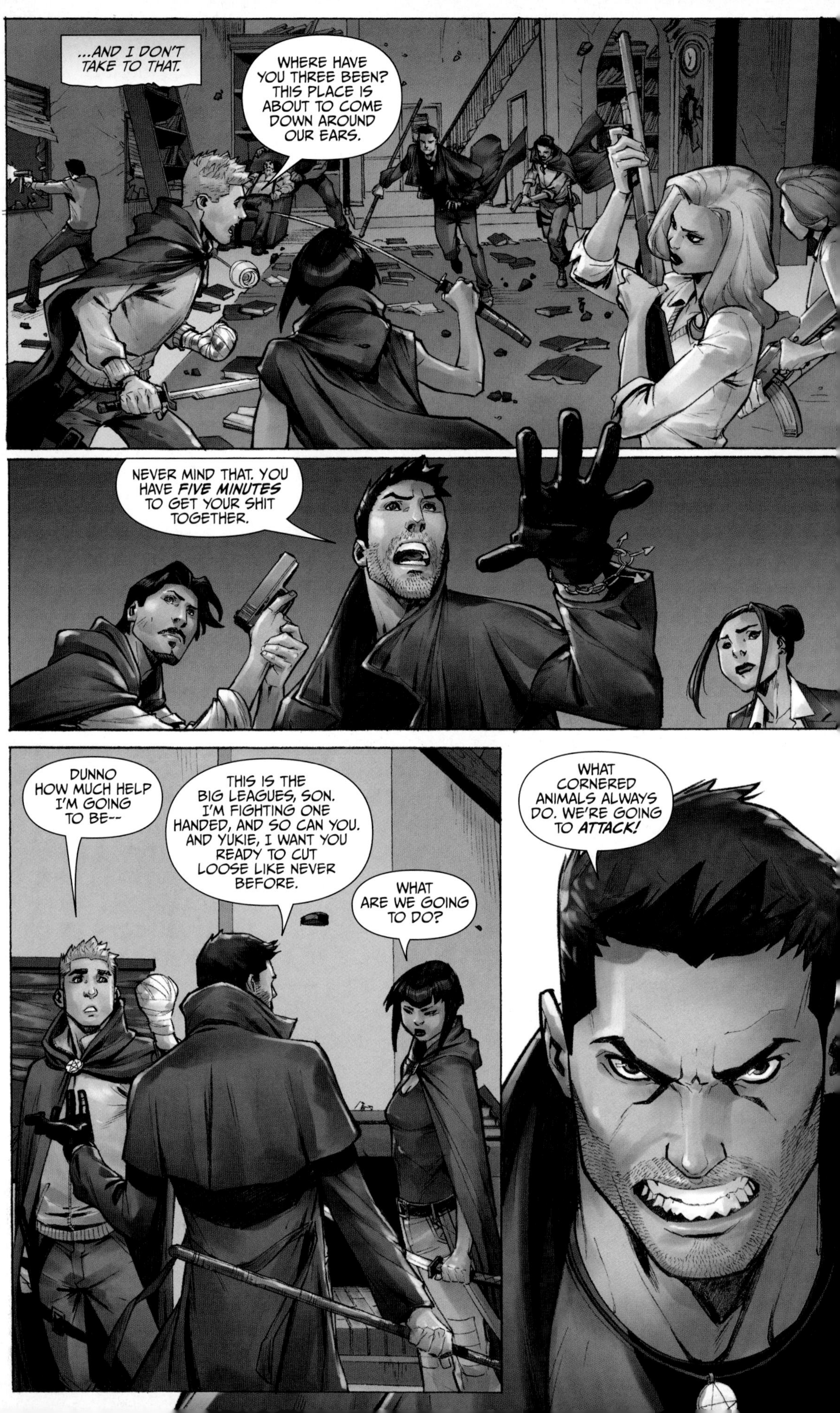
...AND I DON'T TAKE TO THAT.
WHERE HAVE YOU THREE BEEN? THIS PLACE IS ABOUT TO COME DOWN AROUND OUR EARS.
NEVER MIND THAT. YOU HAVE FIVE MINUTES TO GET YOUR SHIT TOGETHER.
DUNNO HOW MUCH HELP I'M GOING TO BE--
THIS IS THE BIG LEAGUES, SON. I'M FIGHTING ONE HANDED, AND SO CAN YOU. AND YUKIE, I WANT YOU READY TO CUT LOOSE LIKE NEVER BEFORE.
WHAT ARE WE GOING TO DO?
WHAT CORNERED ANIMALS ALWAYS DO. WE'RE GOING TO ATTACK!

ISSUE THREE COVER BY
STJEPAN SEJIC

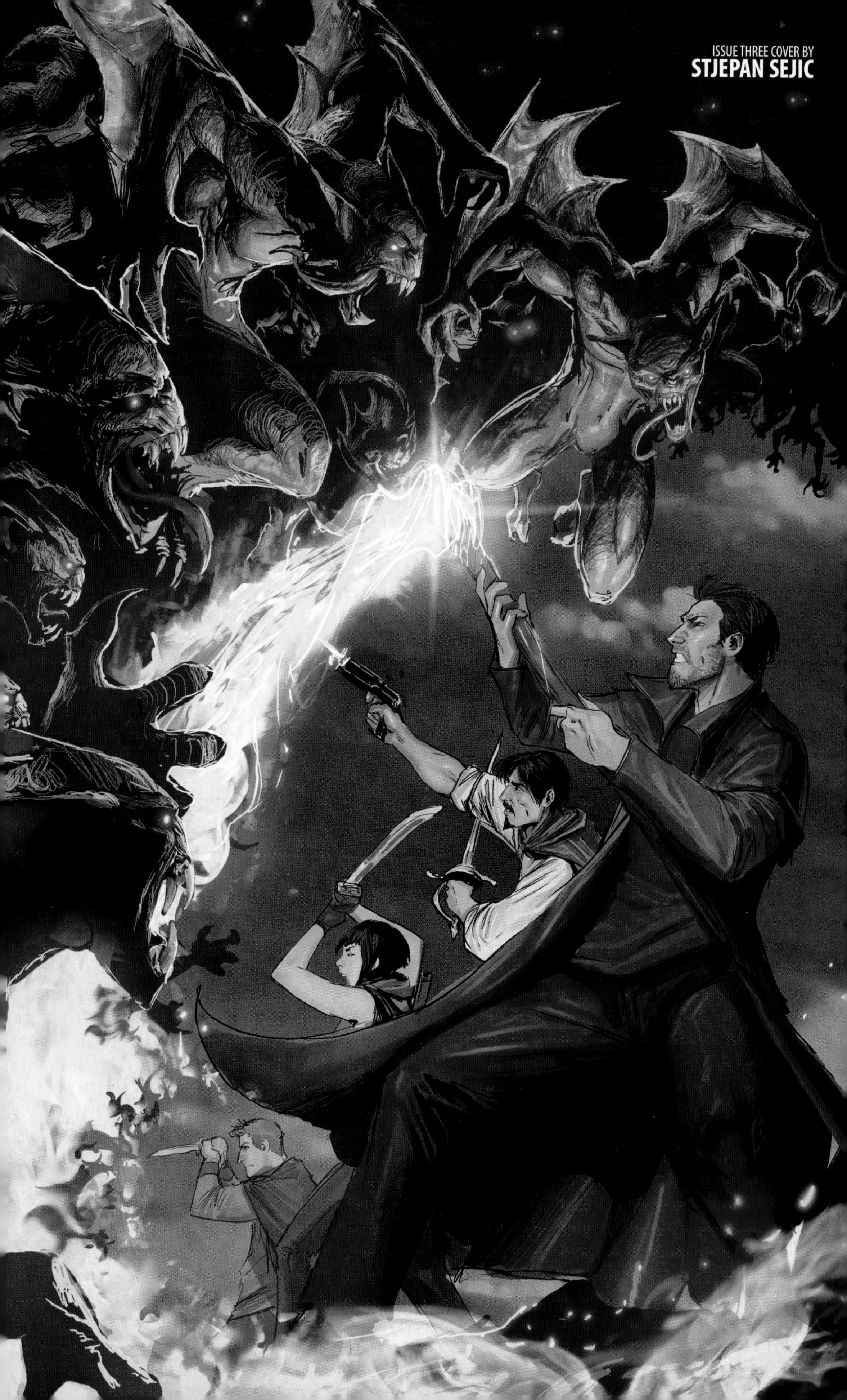

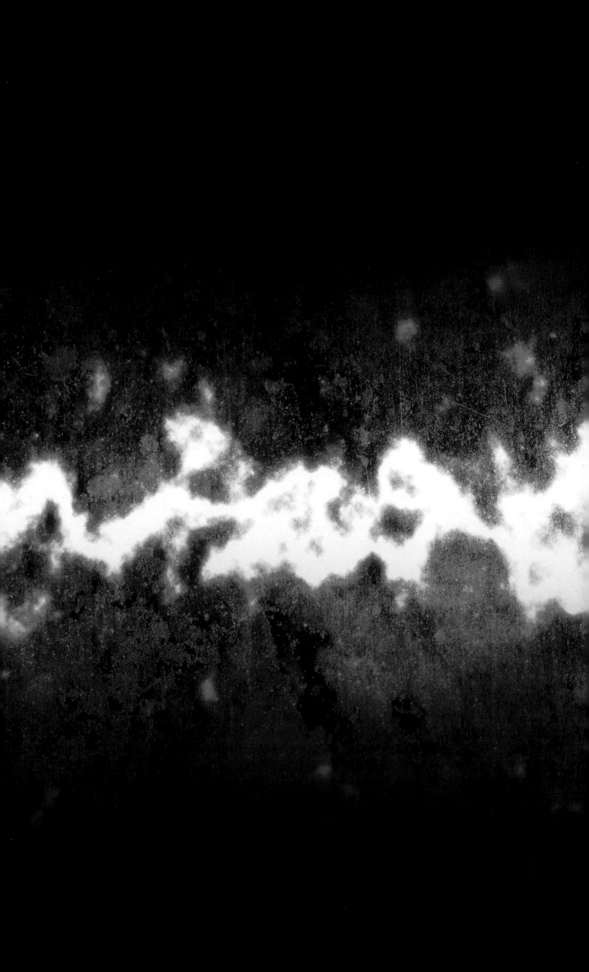

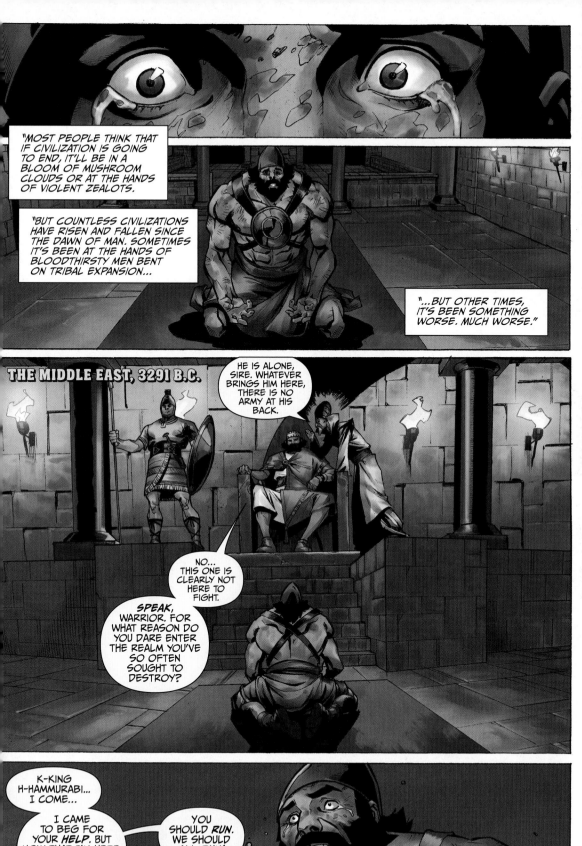

"MOST PEOPLE THINK THAT IF CIVILIZATION IS GOING TO END, IT'LL BE IN A BLOOM OF MUSHROOM CLOUDS OR AT THE HANDS OF VIOLENT ZEALOTS.

"BUT COUNTLESS CIVILIZATIONS HAVE RISEN AND FALLEN SINCE THE DAWN OF MAN. SOMETIMES IT'S BEEN AT THE HANDS OF BLOODTHIRSTY MEN BENT ON TRIBAL EXPANSION...

"...BUT OTHER TIMES, IT'S BEEN SOMETHING WORSE. MUCH WORSE."

THE MIDDLE EAST, 3291 B.C.

HE IS ALONE, SIRE. WHATEVER BRINGS HIM HERE, THERE IS NO ARMY AT HIS BACK.

NO... THIS ONE IS CLEARLY NOT HERE TO FIGHT.

SPEAK, WARRIOR. FOR WHAT REASON DO YOU DARE ENTER THE REALM YOU'VE SO OFTEN SOUGHT TO DESTROY?

K-KING H-HAMMURABI... I COME...

I CAME TO BEG FOR YOUR HELP. BUT NOW THAT I'M HERE, I KNOW THAT...THAT WOULD BE FOLLY.

YOU SHOULD RUN. WE SHOULD ALL RUN!

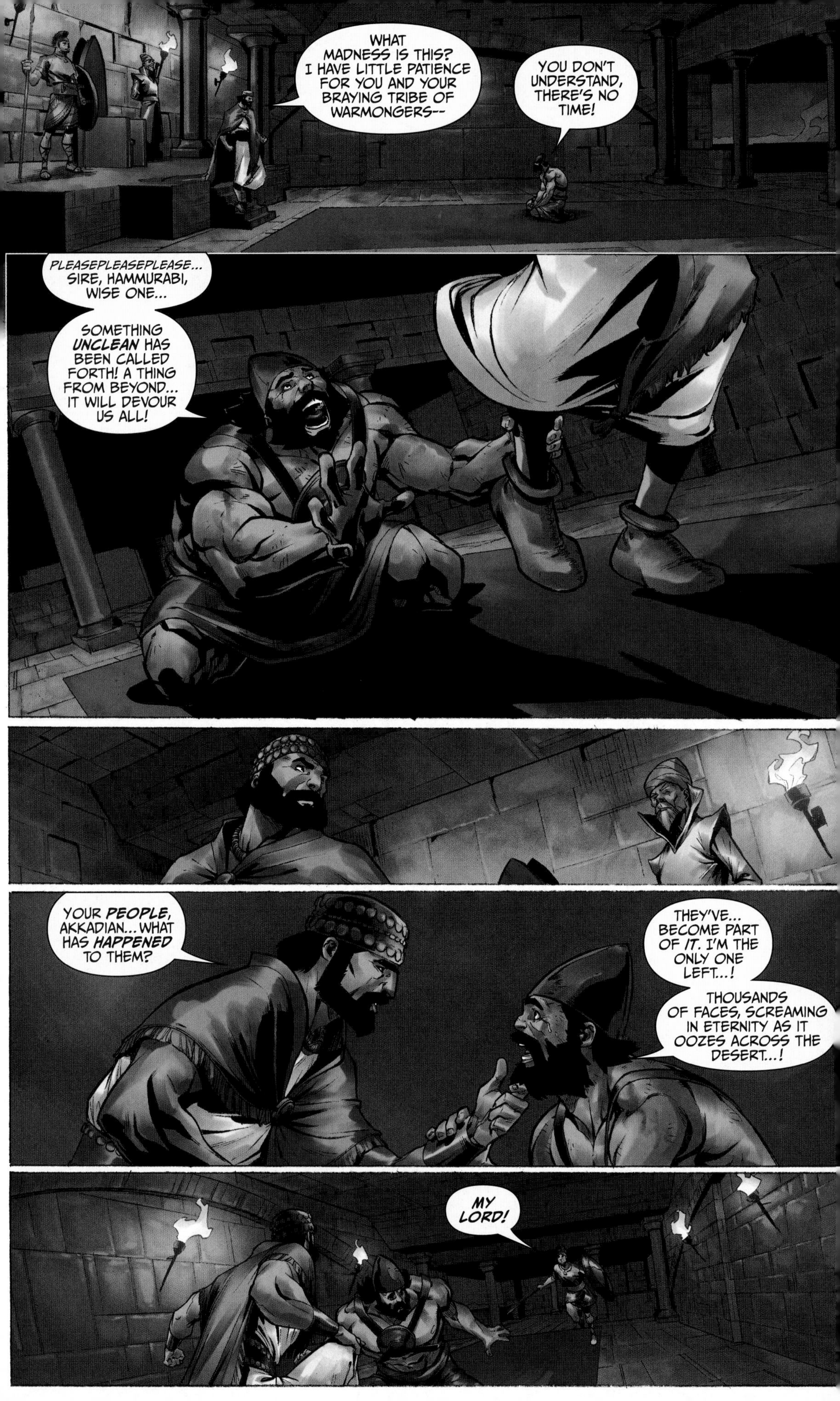
WHAT MADNESS IS THIS? I HAVE LITTLE PATIENCE FOR YOU AND YOUR BRAYING TRIBE OF WARMONGERS--
YOU DON'T UNDERSTAND, THERE'S NO TIME!
PLEASEPLEASEPLEASE... SIRE, HAMMURABI, WISE ONE...
SOMETHING UNCLEAN HAS BEEN CALLED FORTH! A THING FROM BEYOND... IT WILL DEVOUR US ALL!
YOUR PEOPLE, AKKADIAN... WHAT HAS HAPPENED TO THEM?
THEY'VE... BECOME PART OF IT. I'M THE ONLY ONE LEFT...!
THOUSANDS OF FACES, SCREAMING IN ETERNITY AS IT OOZES ACROSS THE DESERT...!
MY LORD!

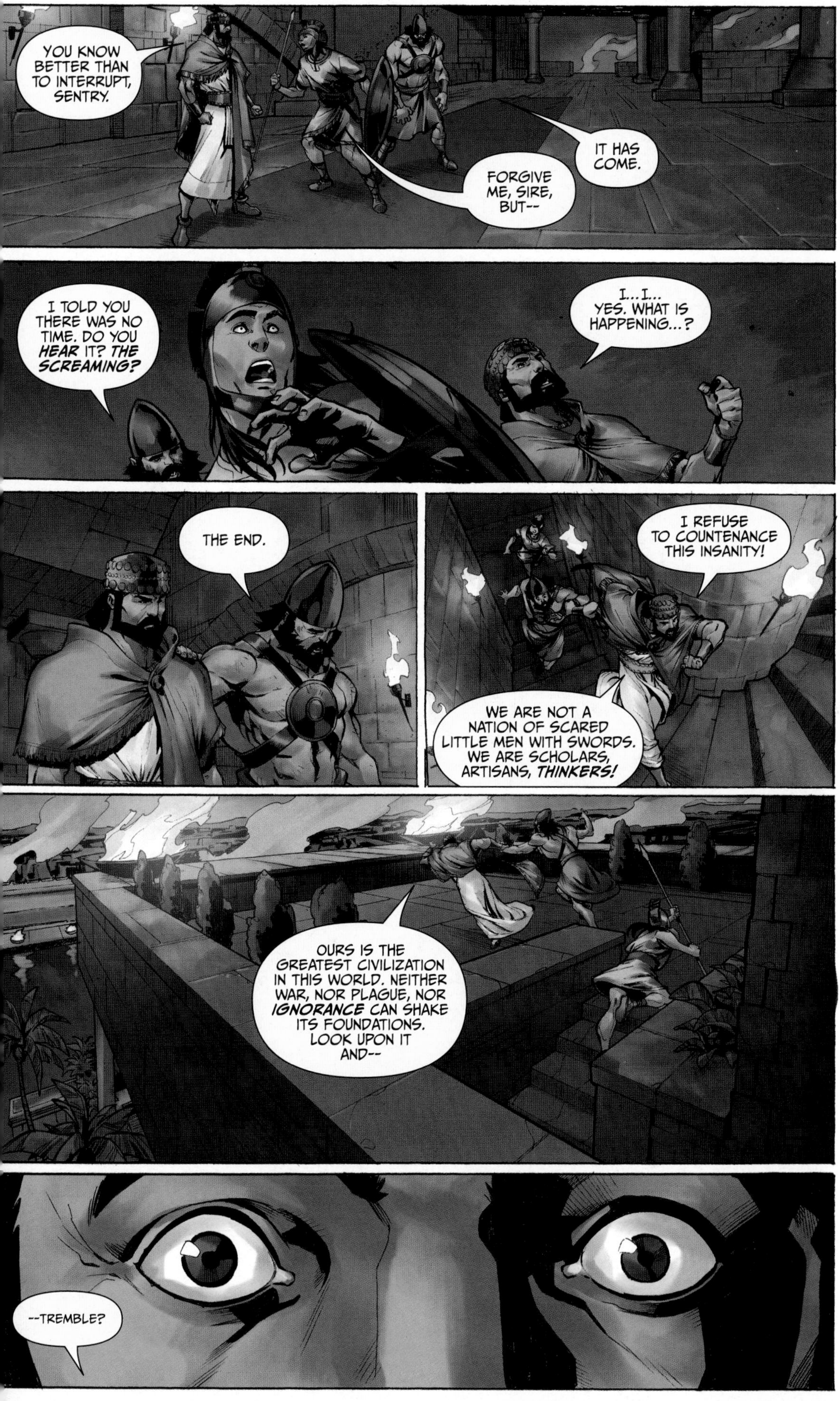

YOU KNOW BETTER THAN TO INTERRUPT, SENTRY.
FORGIVE ME, SIRE, BUT--
IT HAS COME.
I TOLD YOU THERE WAS NO TIME. DO YOU HEAR IT? THE SCREAMING?
I... I... YES. WHAT IS HAPPENING...?
THE END.
I REFUSE TO COUNTENANCE THIS INSANITY!
WE ARE NOT A NATION OF SCARED LITTLE MEN WITH SWORDS. WE ARE SCHOLARS, ARTISANS, THINKERS!
OURS IS THE GREATEST CIVILIZATION IN THIS WORLD. NEITHER WAR, NOR PLAGUE, NOR IGNORANCE CAN SHAKE ITS FOUNDATIONS. LOOK UPON IT AND--
--TREMBLE?

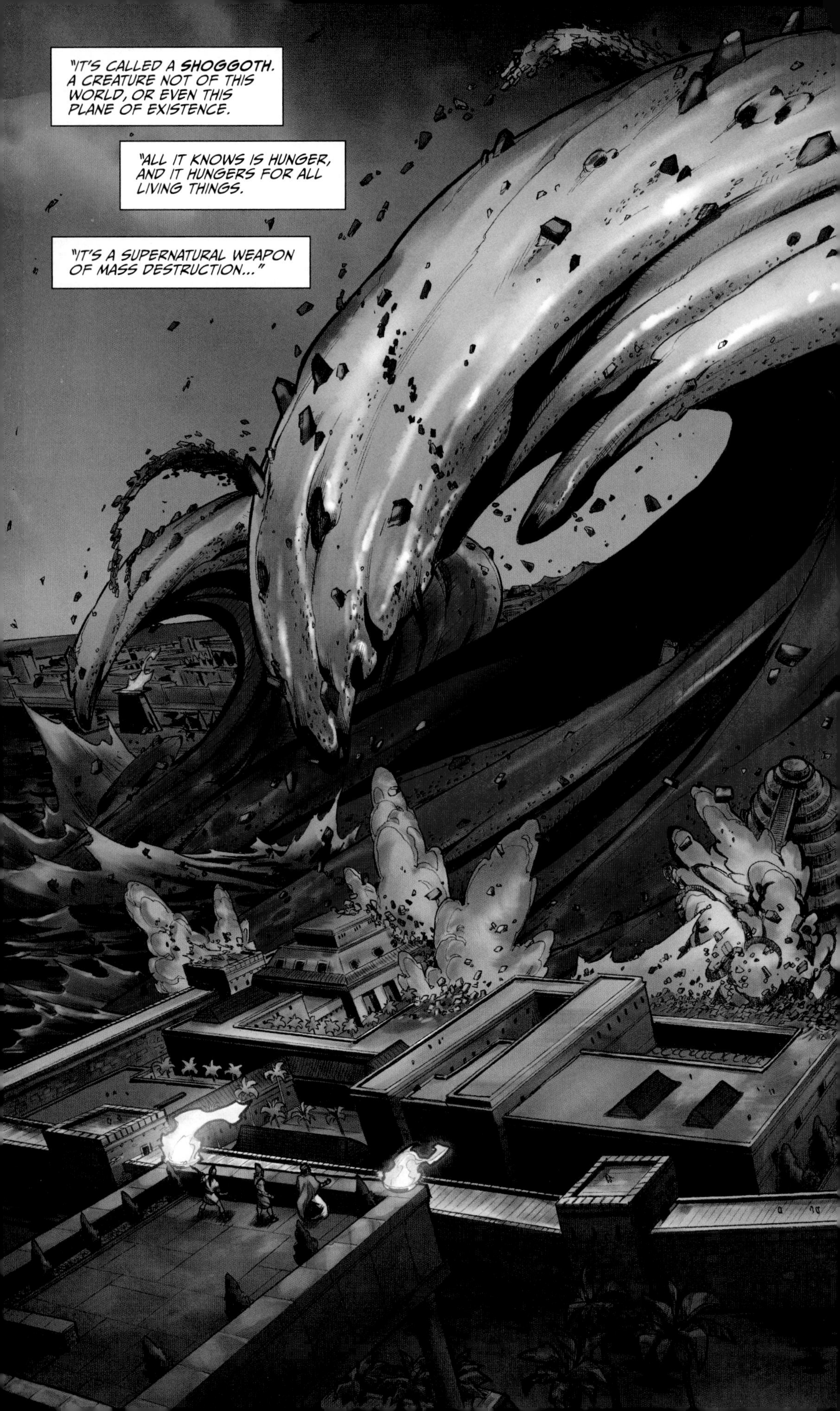
"IT'S CALLED A SHOGGOTH. A CREATURE NOT OF THIS WORLD, OR EVEN THIS PLANE OF EXISTENCE.
"ALL IT KNOWS IS HUNGER, AND IT HUNGERS FOR ALL LIVING THINGS.
"IT'S A SUPERNATURAL WEAPON OF MASS DESTRUCTION..."

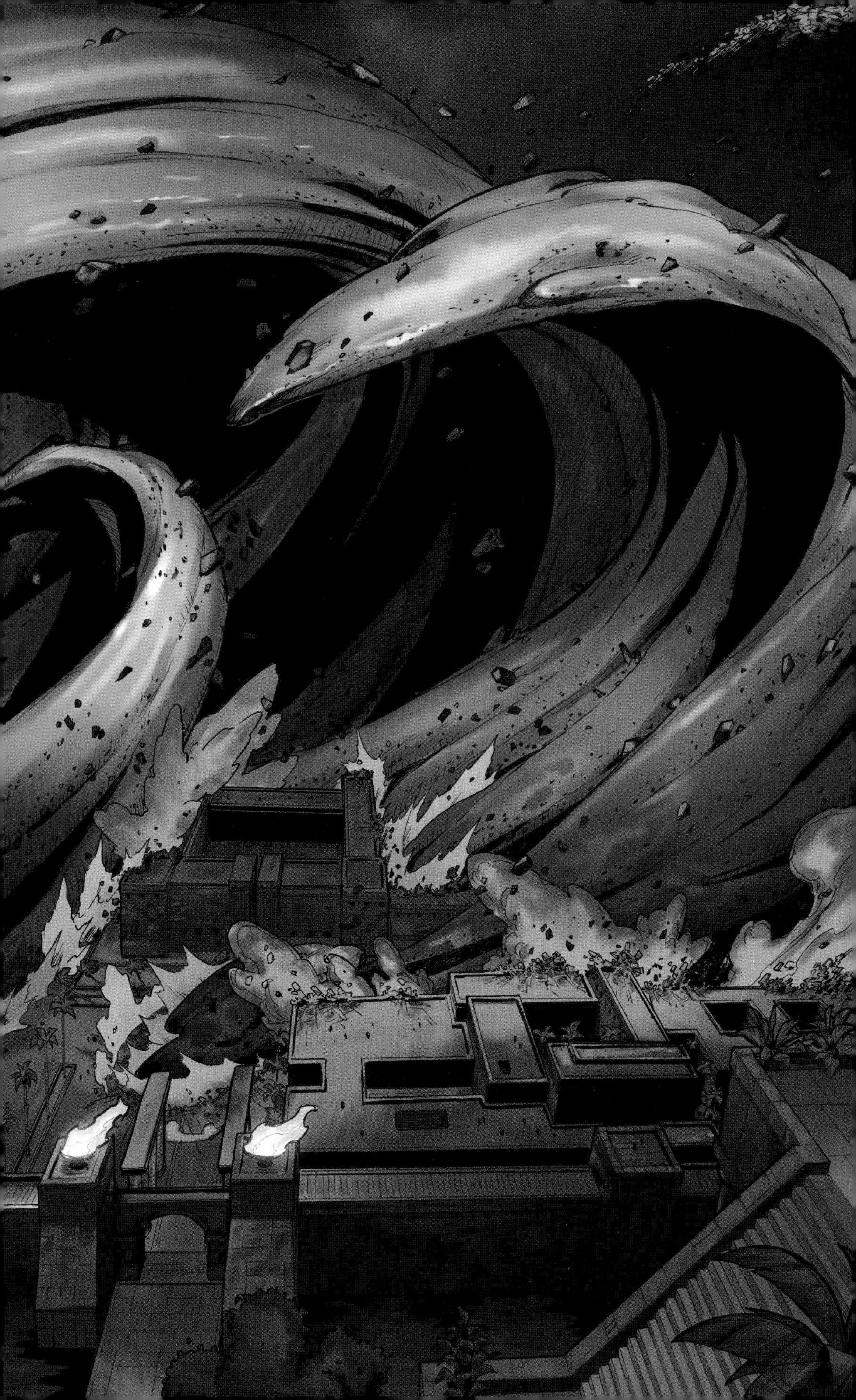

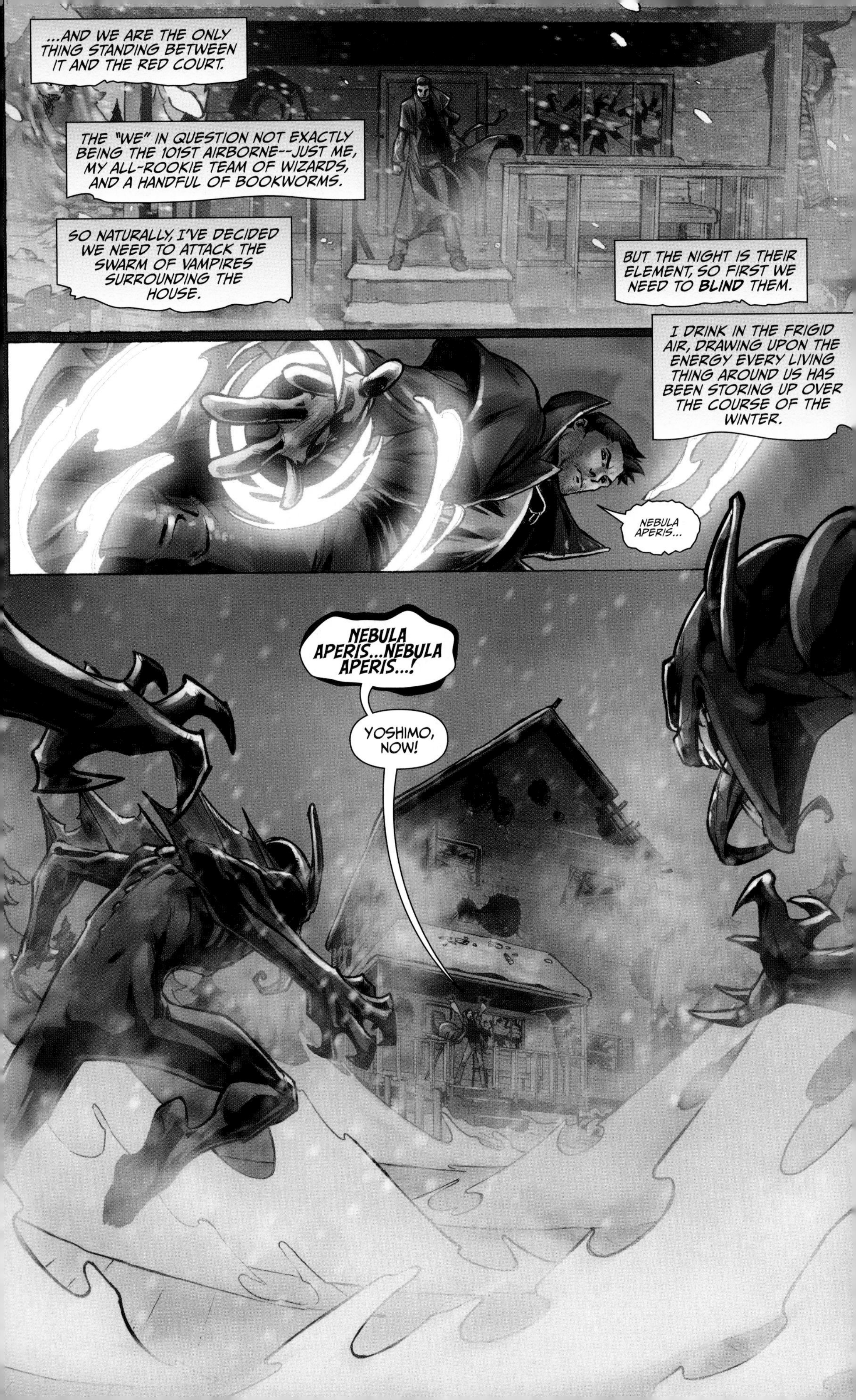
...AND WE ARE THE ONLY THING STANDING BETWEEN IT AND THE RED COURT.
THE "WE" IN QUESTION NOT EXACTLY BEING THE 101ST AIRBORNE--JUST ME, MY ALL-ROOKIE TEAM OF WIZARDS, AND A HANDFUL OF BOOKWORMS.
SO NATURALLY, I'VE DECIDED WE NEED TO ATTACK THE SWARM OF VAMPIRES SURROUNDING THE HOUSE.
BUT THE NIGHT IS THEIR ELEMENT, SO FIRST WE NEED TO **BLIND** THEM.
I DRINK IN THE FRIGID AIR, DRAWING UPON THE ENERGY EVERY LIVING THING AROUND US HAS BEEN STORING UP OVER THE COURSE OF THE WINTER.
NEBULA APERIS...
NEBULA APERIS...NEBULA APERIS...!
YOSHIMO, NOW!

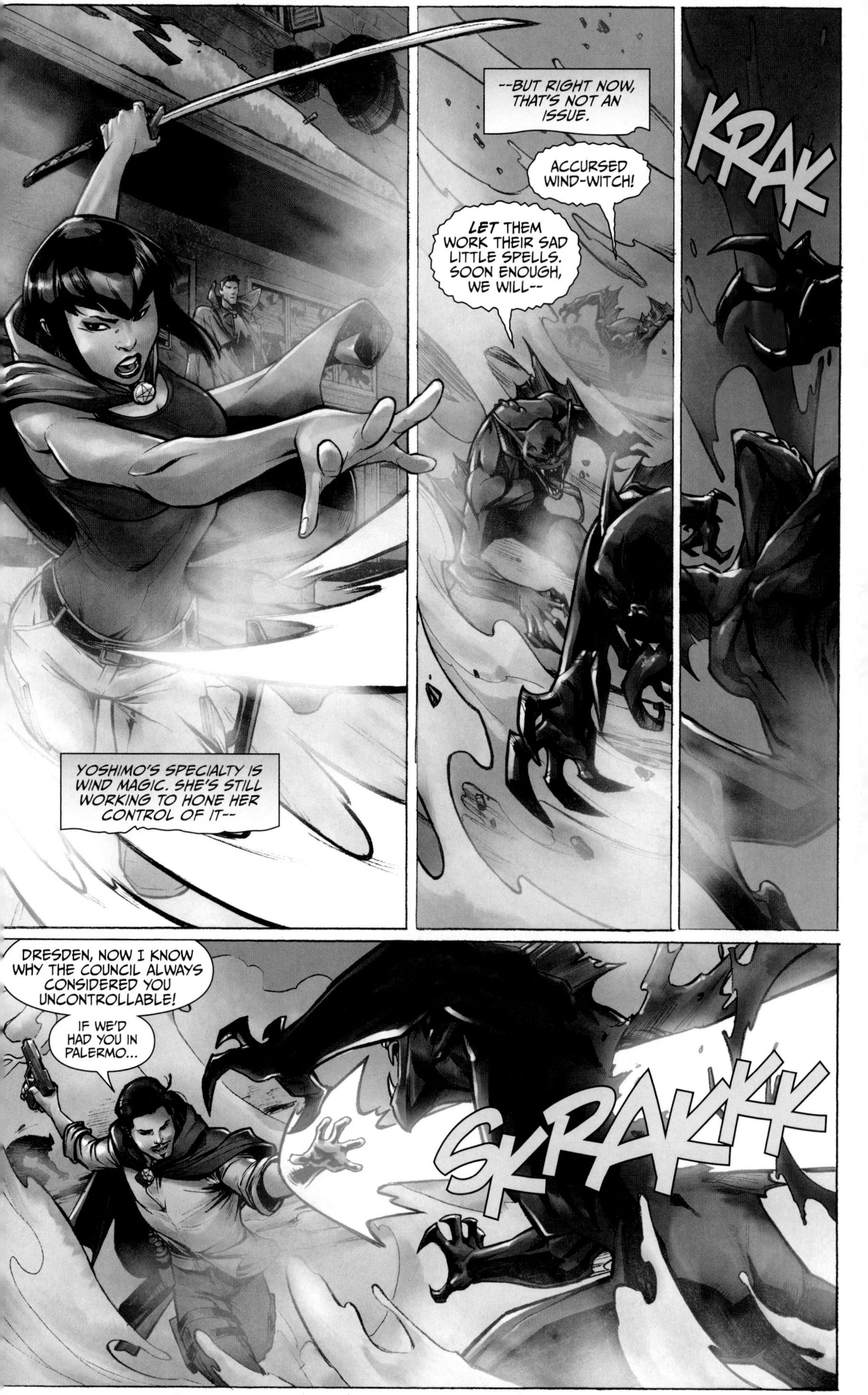
YOSHIMO'S SPECIALTY IS WIND MAGIC. SHE'S STILL WORKING TO HONE HER CONTROL OF IT--
--BUT RIGHT NOW, THAT'S NOT AN ISSUE.
ACCURSED WIND-WITCH!
LET THEM WORK THEIR SAD LITTLE SPELLS. SOON ENOUGH, WE WILL--
KRAK
DRESDEN, NOW I KNOW WHY THE COUNCIL ALWAYS CONSIDERED YOU UNCONTROLLABLE!
IF WE'D HAD YOU IN PALERMO...
SKRAKKK

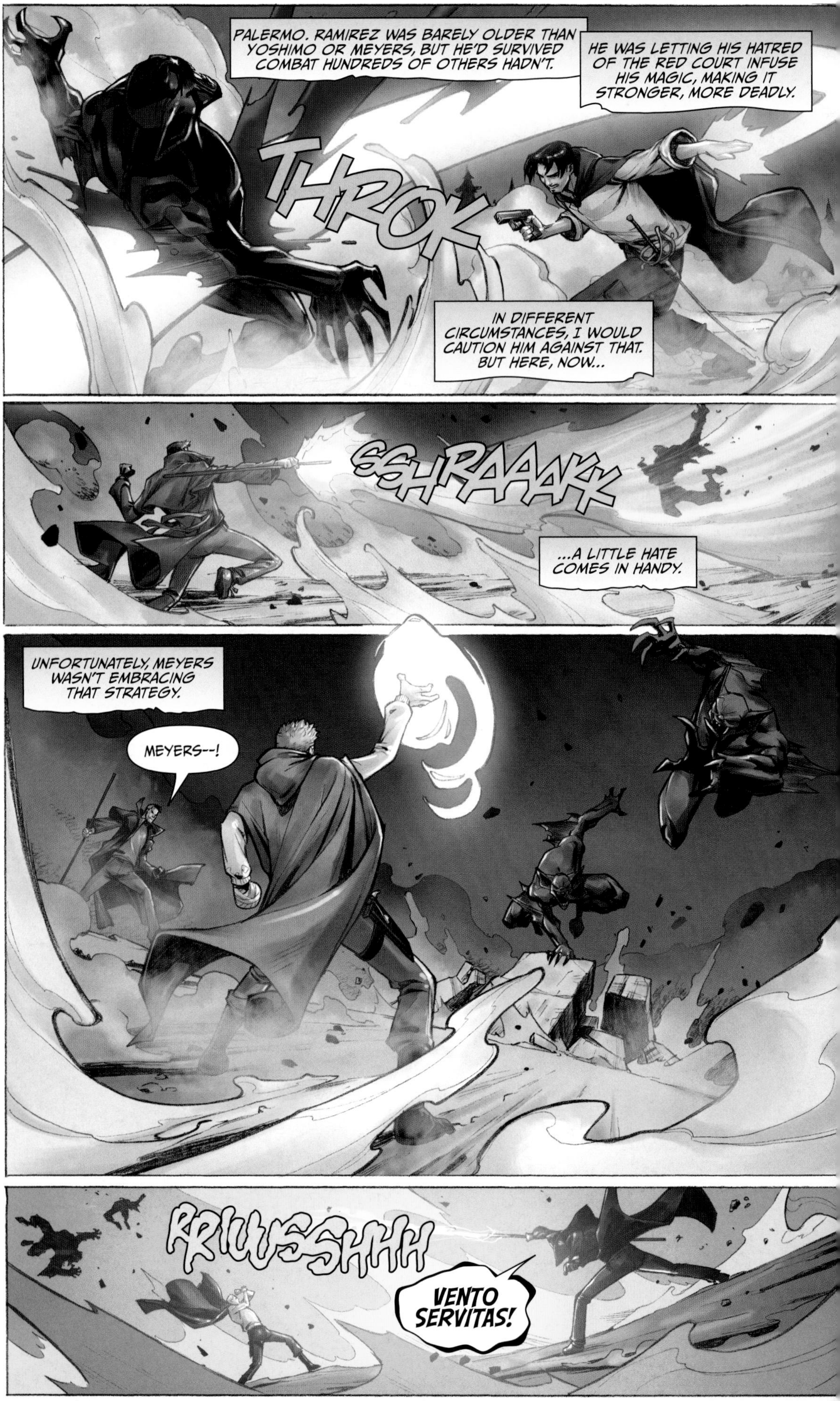
PALERMO. RAMIREZ WAS BARELY OLDER THAN YOSHIMO OR MEYERS, BUT HE'D SURVIVED COMBAT HUNDREDS OF OTHERS HADN'T.
HE WAS LETTING HIS HATRED OF THE RED COURT INFUSE HIS MAGIC, MAKING IT STRONGER, MORE DEADLY.
THROK
IN DIFFERENT CIRCUMSTANCES, I WOULD CAUTION HIM AGAINST THAT. BUT HERE, NOW...
SSHRAAAKK
...A LITTLE HATE COMES IN HANDY.
UNFORTUNATELY, MEYERS WASN'T EMBRACING THAT STRATEGY.
MEYERS--!
RRUUSSHHH
VENTO SERVITAS!

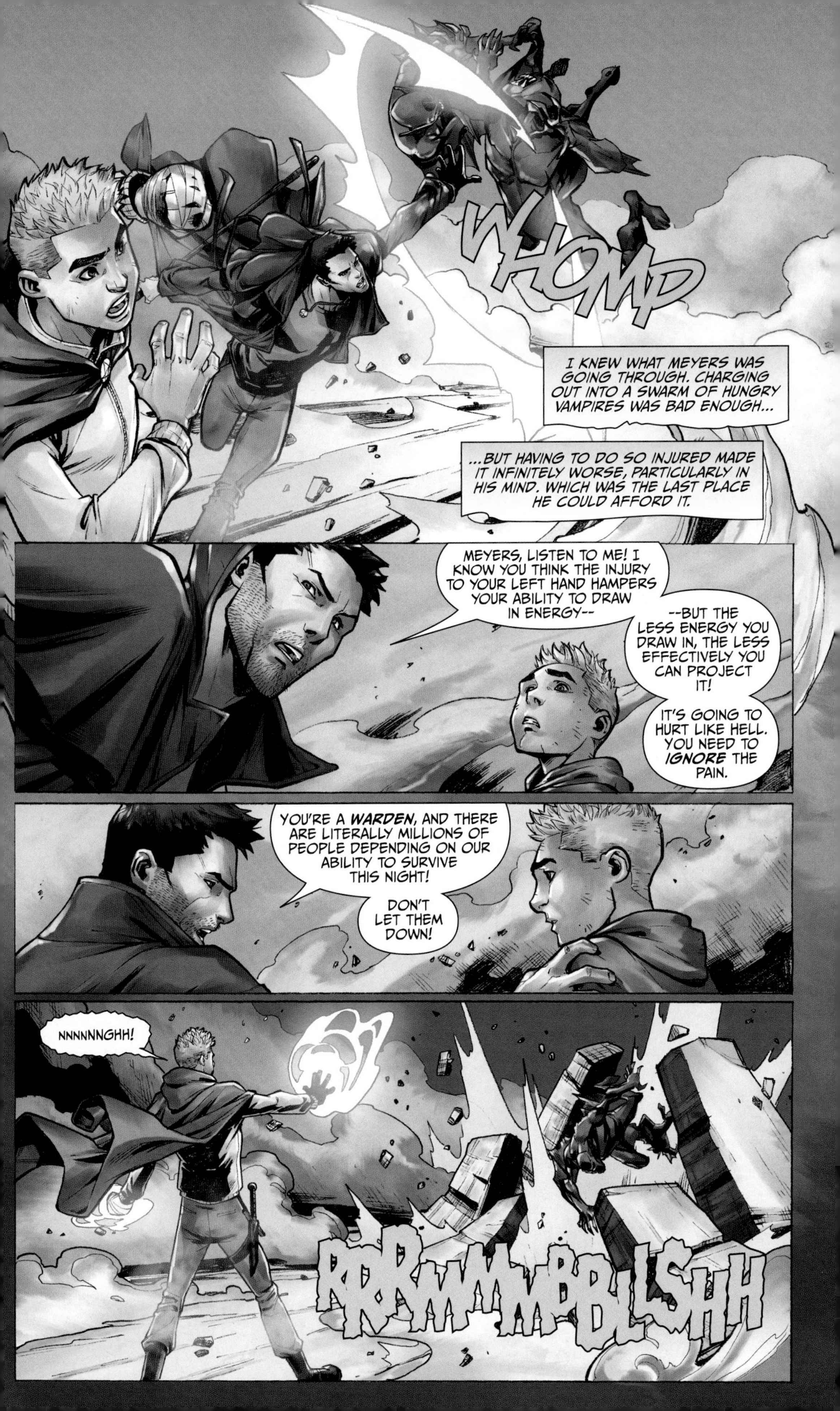
WHOMP
I KNEW WHAT MEYERS WAS GOING THROUGH. CHARGING OUT INTO A SWARM OF HUNGRY VAMPIRES WAS BAD ENOUGH...
...BUT HAVING TO DO SO INJURED MADE IT INFINITELY WORSE, PARTICULARLY IN HIS MIND. WHICH WAS THE LAST PLACE HE COULD AFFORD IT.
MEYERS, LISTEN TO ME! I KNOW YOU THINK THE INJURY TO YOUR LEFT HAND HAMPERS YOUR ABILITY TO DRAW IN ENERGY--
--BUT THE LESS ENERGY YOU DRAW IN, THE LESS EFFECTIVELY YOU CAN PROJECT IT!
IT'S GOING TO HURT LIKE HELL. YOU NEED TO *IGNORE* THE PAIN.
YOU'RE A *WARDEN*, AND THERE ARE LITERALLY MILLIONS OF PEOPLE DEPENDING ON OUR ABILITY TO SURVIVE THIS NIGHT!
DON'T LET THEM DOWN!
NNNNNNGHH!
RRRWWWMBBLSHH

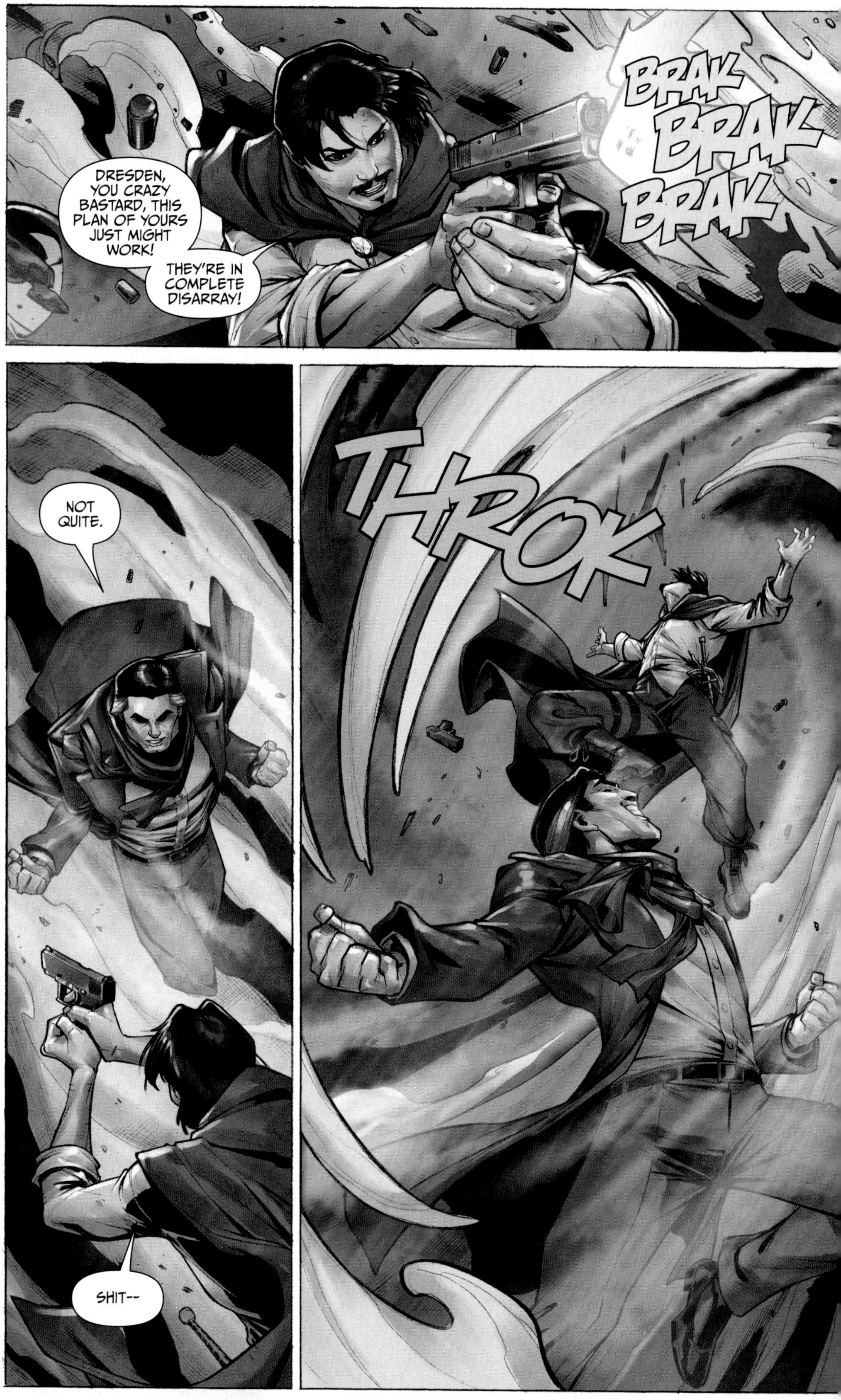
BRAK BRAK BRAK
DRESDEN, YOU CRAZY BASTARD, THIS PLAN OF YOURS JUST MIGHT WORK!
THEY'RE IN COMPLETE DISARRAY!
NOT QUITE.
SHIT--
THROK

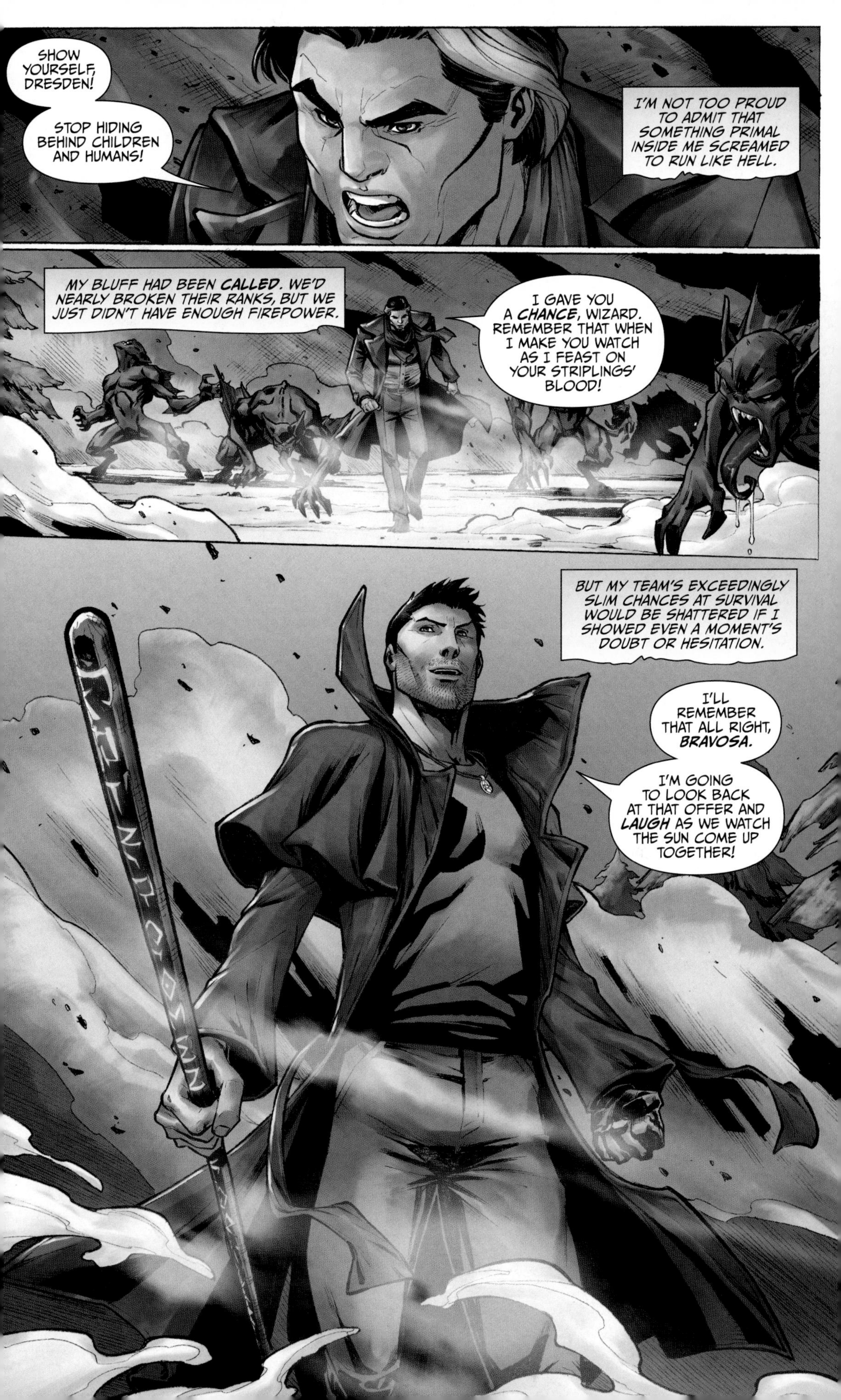
SHOW YOURSELF, DRESDEN!
STOP HIDING BEHIND CHILDREN AND HUMANS!
I'M NOT TOO PROUD TO ADMIT THAT SOMETHING PRIMAL INSIDE ME SCREAMED TO RUN LIKE HELL.
MY BLUFF HAD BEEN CALLED. WE'D NEARLY BROKEN THEIR RANKS, BUT WE JUST DIDN'T HAVE ENOUGH FIREPOWER.
I GAVE YOU A CHANCE, WIZARD. REMEMBER THAT WHEN I MAKE YOU WATCH AS I FEAST ON YOUR STRIPLINGS' BLOOD!
BUT MY TEAM'S EXCEEDINGLY SLIM CHANCES AT SURVIVAL WOULD BE SHATTERED IF I SHOWED EVEN A MOMENT'S DOUBT OR HESITATION.
I'LL REMEMBER THAT ALL RIGHT, BRAVOSA.
I'M GOING TO LOOK BACK AT THAT OFFER AND LAUGH AS WE WATCH THE SUN COME UP TOGETHER!

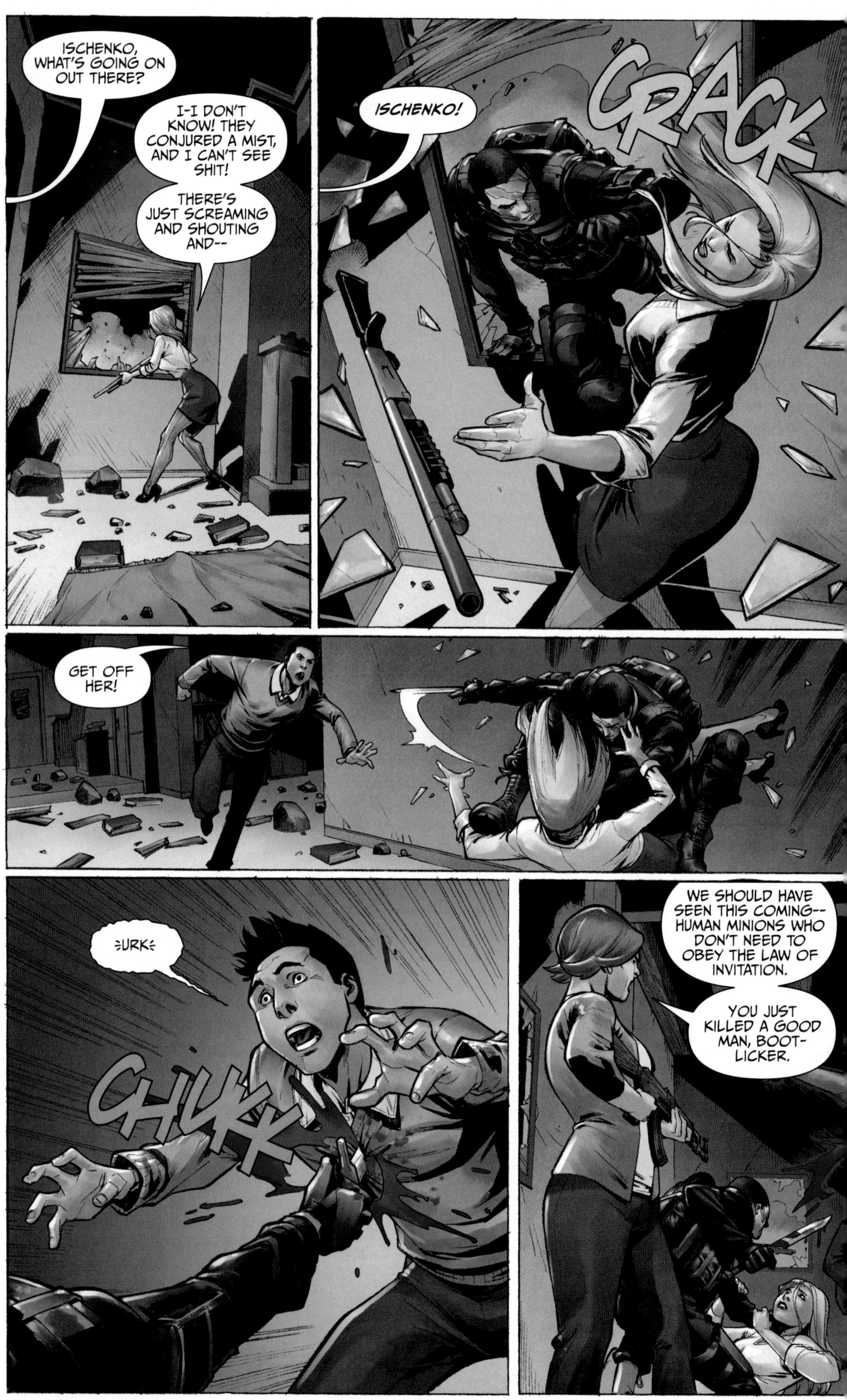
ISCHENKO, WHAT'S GOING ON OUT THERE?
I-I DON'T KNOW! THEY CONJURED A MIST, AND I CAN'T SEE SHIT!
THERE'S JUST SCREAMING AND SHOUTING AND--
ISCHENKO!
CRACK
GET OFF HER!
=URK=
CHUKK
WE SHOULD HAVE SEEN THIS COMING--HUMAN MINIONS WHO DON'T NEED TO OBEY THE LAW OF INVITATION.
YOU JUST KILLED A GOOD MAN, BOOT-LICKER.

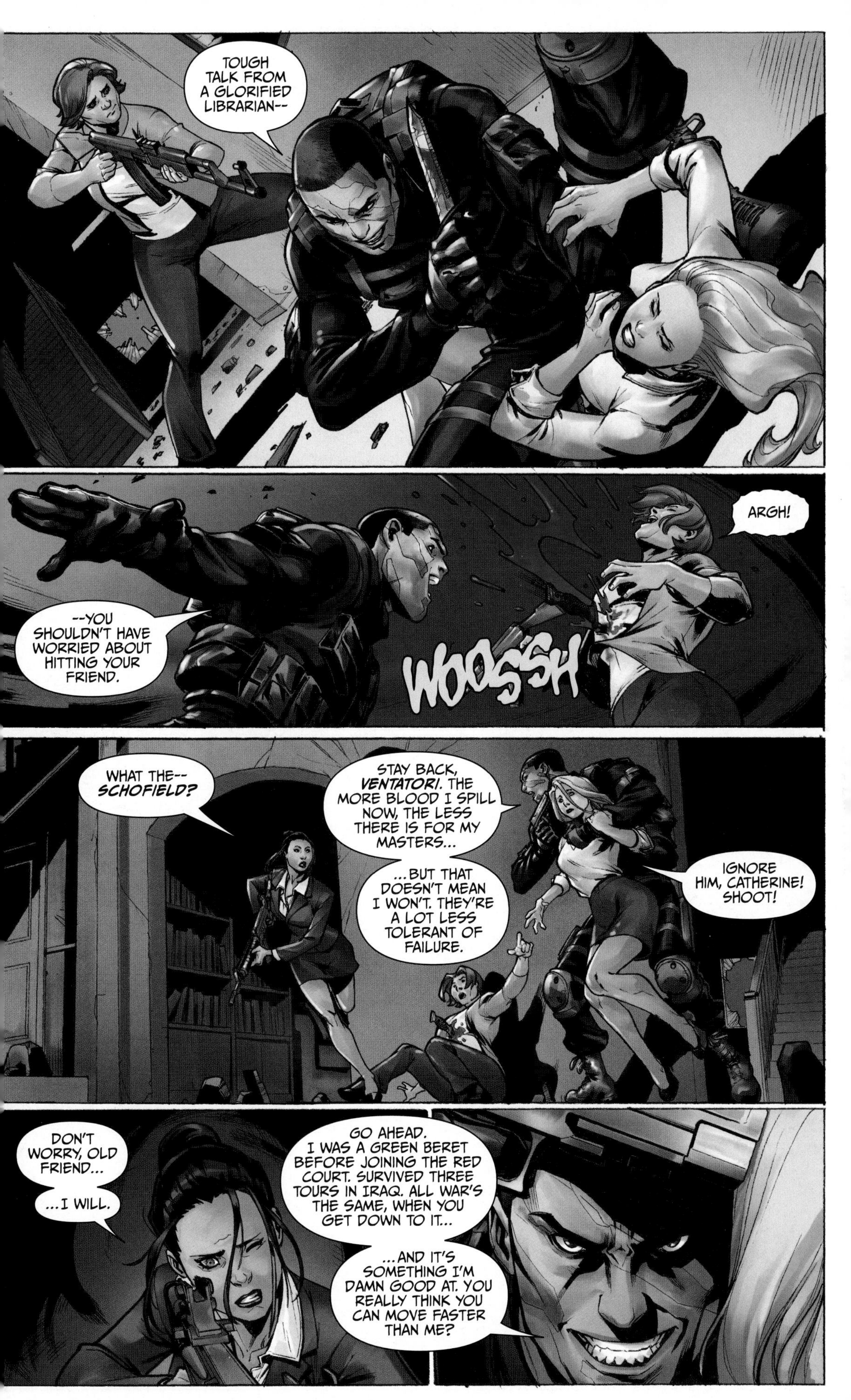
TOUGH TALK FROM A GLORIFIED LIBRARIAN--
ARGH!
--YOU SHOULDN'T HAVE WORRIED ABOUT HITTING YOUR FRIEND.
WOOSSH
WHAT THE-- *SCHOFIELD?*
STAY BACK, *VENTATORI*. THE MORE BLOOD I SPILL NOW, THE LESS THERE IS FOR MY MASTERS...
...BUT THAT DOESN'T MEAN I WON'T. THEY'RE A LOT LESS TOLERANT OF FAILURE.
IGNORE HIM, CATHERINE! SHOOT!
DON'T WORRY, OLD FRIEND...
...I WILL.
GO AHEAD. I WAS A GREEN BERET BEFORE JOINING THE RED COURT. SURVIVED THREE TOURS IN IRAQ. ALL WAR'S THE SAME, WHEN YOU GET DOWN TO IT...
...AND IT'S SOMETHING I'M DAMN GOOD AT. YOU REALLY THINK YOU CAN MOVE FASTER THAN ME?

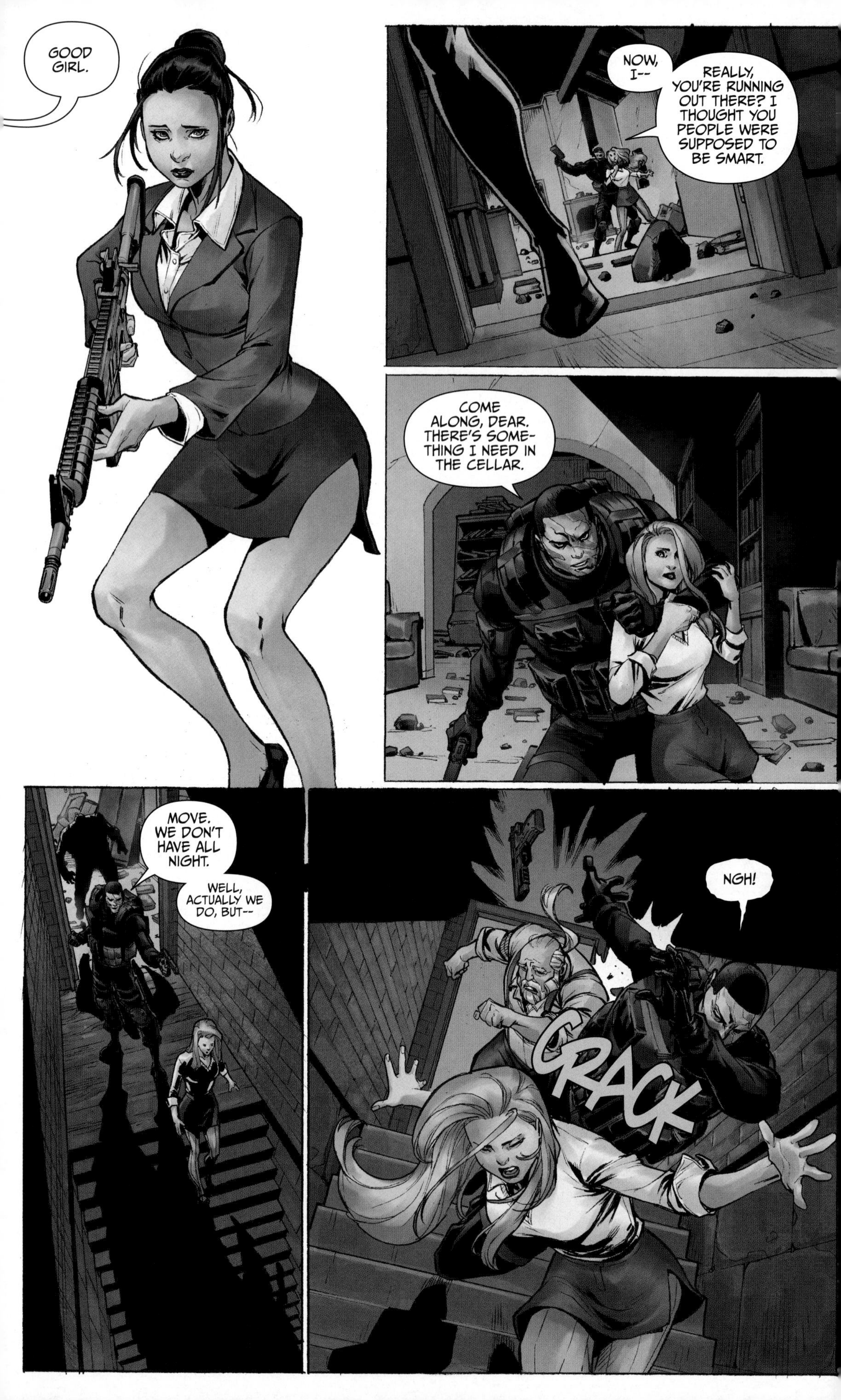
GOOD GIRL.
NOW, I--
REALLY, YOU'RE RUNNING OUT THERE? I THOUGHT YOU PEOPLE WERE SUPPOSED TO BE SMART.
COME ALONG, DEAR. THERE'S SOME-THING I NEED IN THE CELLAR.
MOVE. WE DON'T HAVE ALL NIGHT.
WELL, ACTUALLY WE DO, BUT--
NGH!
CRACK

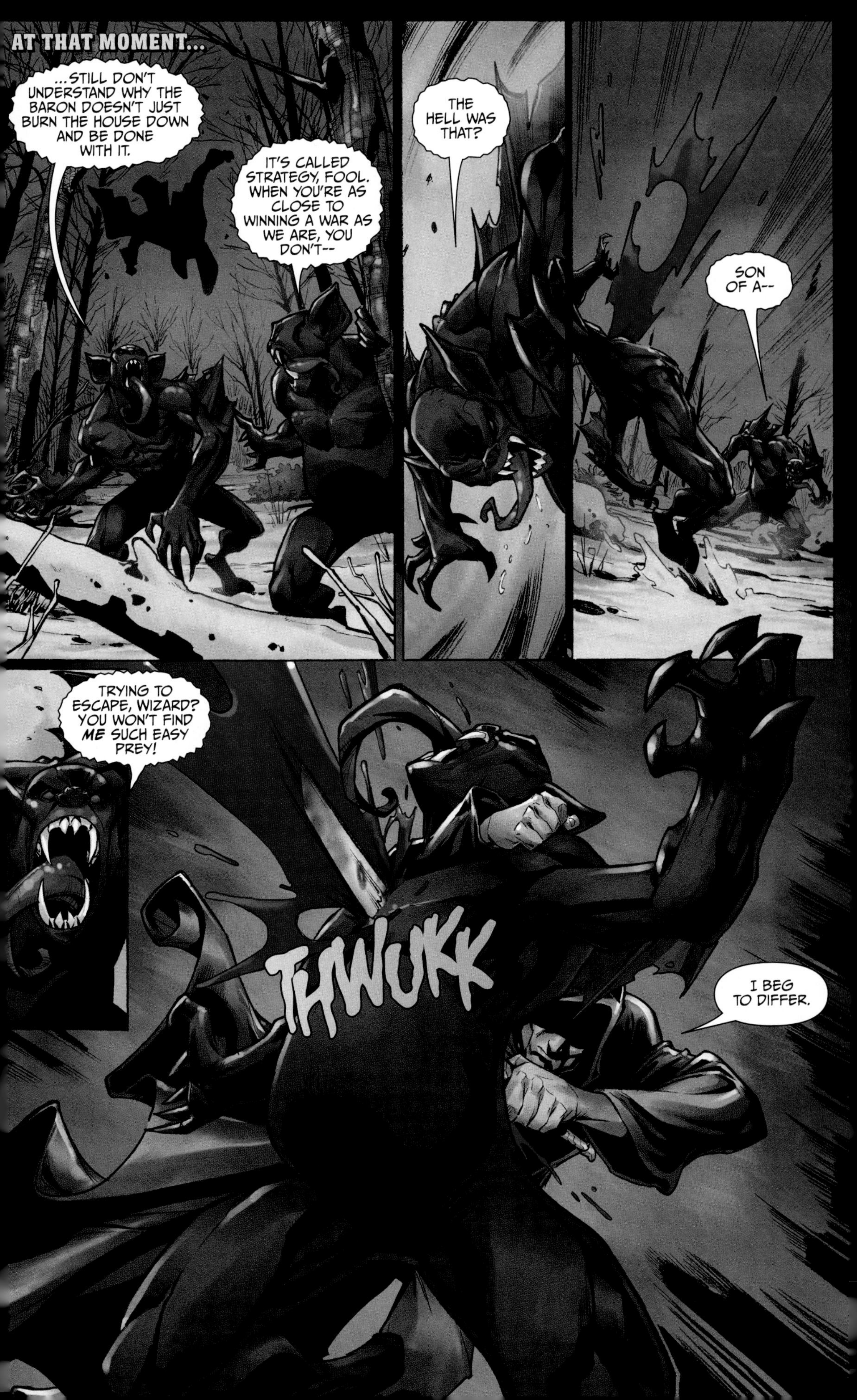
AT THAT MOMENT...
...STILL DON'T UNDERSTAND WHY THE BARON DOESN'T JUST BURN THE HOUSE DOWN AND BE DONE WITH IT.
IT'S CALLED STRATEGY, FOOL. WHEN YOU'RE AS CLOSE TO WINNING A WAR AS WE ARE, YOU DON'T--
THE HELL WAS THAT?
SON OF A--
TRYING TO ESCAPE, WIZARD? YOU WON'T FIND ME SUCH EASY PREY!
THWUKK
I BEG TO DIFFER.

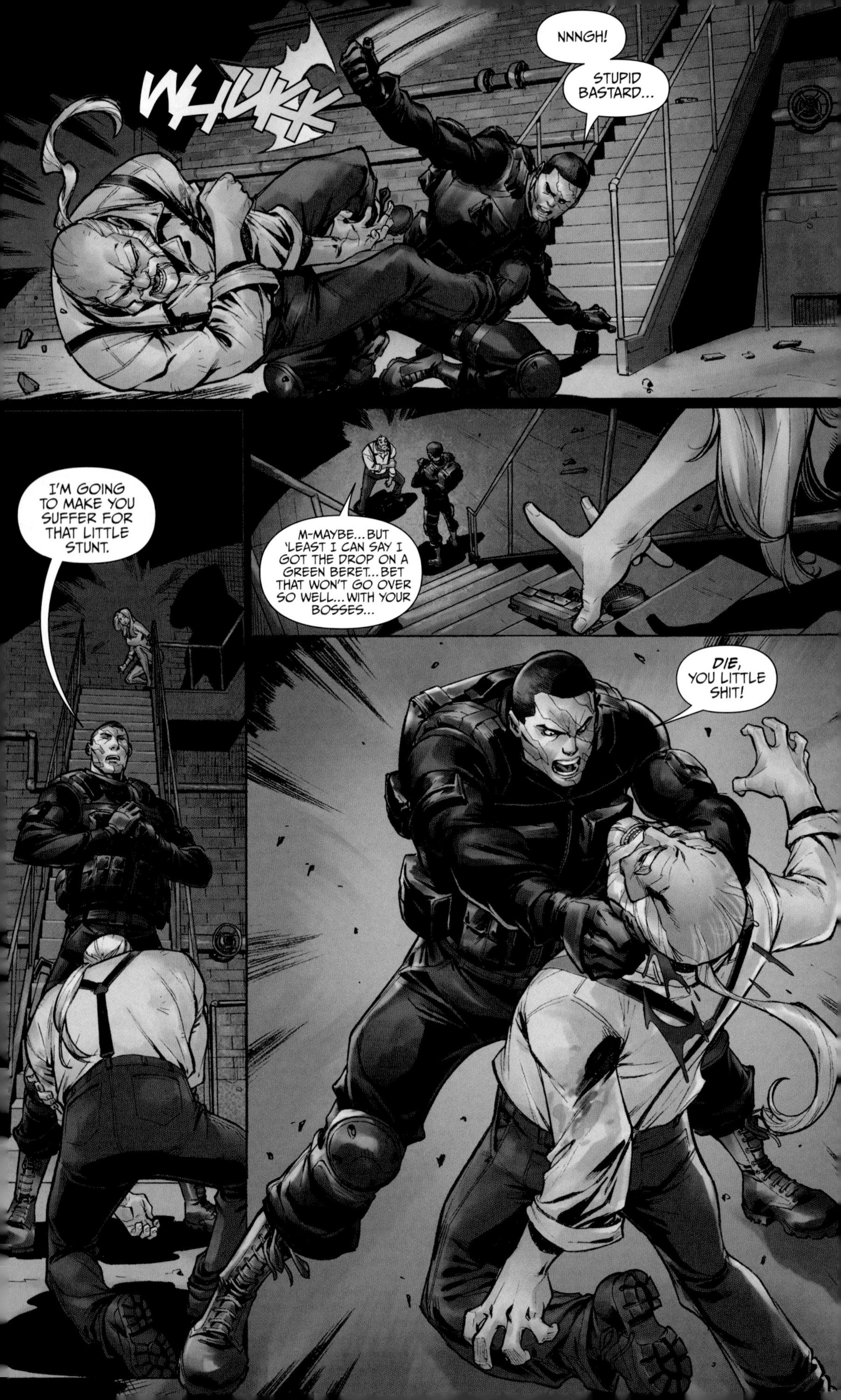
WHUKK
NNNGH!
STUPID BASTARD...
I'M GOING TO MAKE YOU SUFFER FOR THAT LITTLE STUNT.
M-MAYBE...BUT 'LEAST I CAN SAY I GOT THE DROP ON A GREEN BERET...BET THAT WON'T GO OVER SO WELL...WITH YOUR BOSSES...
DIE, YOU LITTLE SHIT!

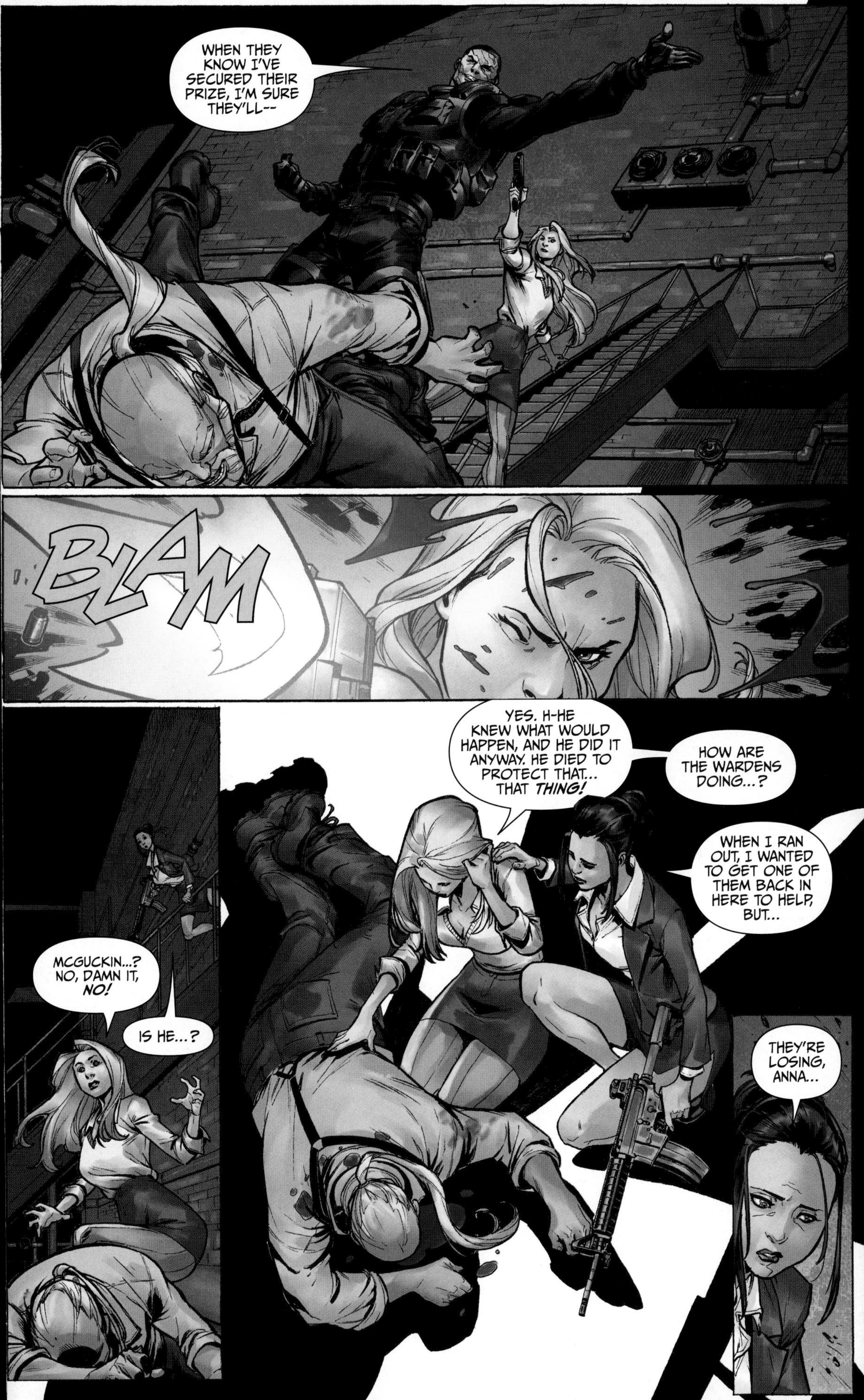
WHEN THEY KNOW I'VE SECURED THEIR PRIZE, I'M SURE THEY'LL--
BLAM
MCGUCKIN...? NO, DAMN IT, *NO!*
IS HE...?
YES. H-HE KNEW WHAT WOULD HAPPEN, AND HE DID IT ANYWAY. HE DIED TO PROTECT THAT... THAT *THING!*
HOW ARE THE WARDENS DOING...?
WHEN I RAN OUT, I WANTED TO GET ONE OF THEM BACK IN HERE TO HELP, BUT...
THEY'RE LOSING, ANNA...

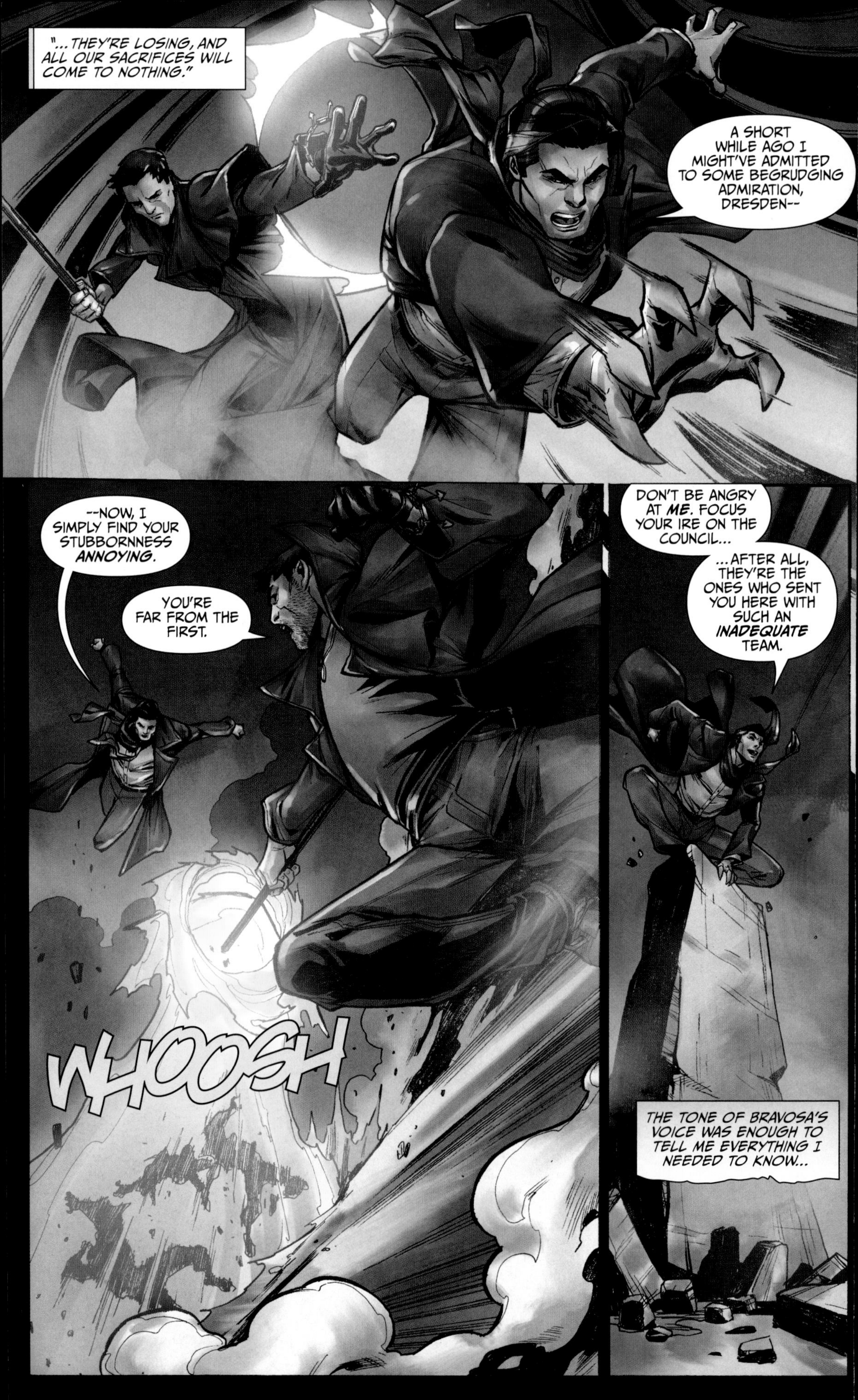
"...THEY'RE LOSING, AND ALL OUR SACRIFICES WILL COME TO NOTHING."
A SHORT WHILE AGO I MIGHT'VE ADMITTED TO SOME BEGRUDGING ADMIRATION, DRESDEN--
--NOW, I SIMPLY FIND YOUR STUBBORNNESS ANNOYING.
YOU'RE FAR FROM THE FIRST.
WHOOSH
DON'T BE ANGRY AT ME. FOCUS YOUR IRE ON THE COUNCIL...
...AFTER ALL, THEY'RE THE ONES WHO SENT YOU HERE WITH SUCH AN INADEQUATE TEAM.
THE TONE OF BRAVOSA'S VOICE WAS ENOUGH TO TELL ME EVERYTHING I NEEDED TO KNOW...

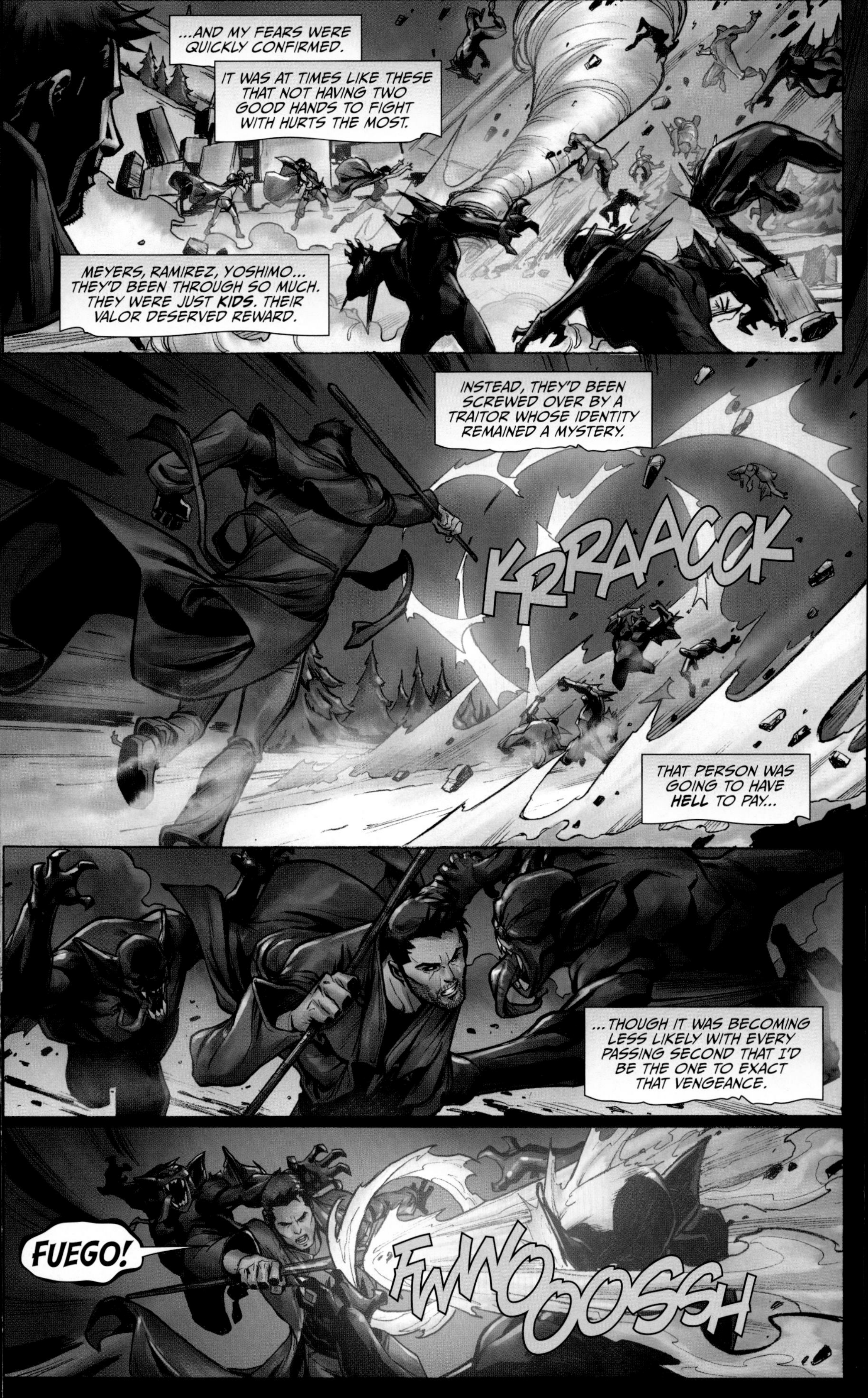
...AND MY FEARS WERE QUICKLY CONFIRMED.
IT WAS AT TIMES LIKE THESE THAT NOT HAVING TWO GOOD HANDS TO FIGHT WITH HURTS THE MOST.
MEYERS, RAMIREZ, YOSHIMO... THEY'D BEEN THROUGH SO MUCH. THEY WERE JUST KIDS. THEIR VALOR DESERVED REWARD.
INSTEAD, THEY'D BEEN SCREWED OVER BY A TRAITOR WHOSE IDENTITY REMAINED A MYSTERY.
KRRAACCK
THAT PERSON WAS GOING TO HAVE HELL TO PAY...
...THOUGH IT WAS BECOMING LESS LIKELY WITH EVERY PASSING SECOND THAT I'D BE THE ONE TO EXACT THAT VENGEANCE.
FUEGO!
FWWOOOSSH

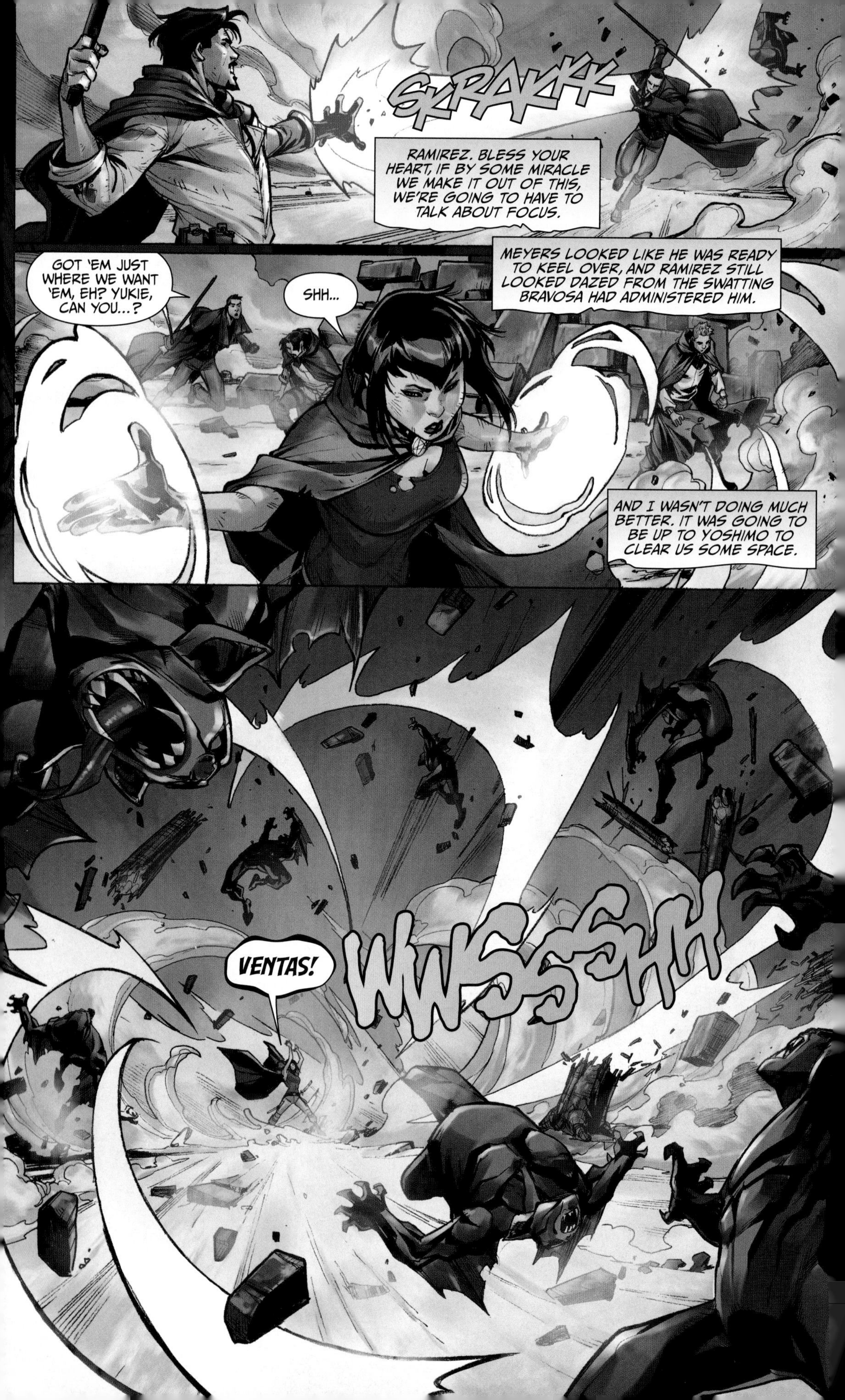
SKRAKKK
RAMIREZ. BLESS YOUR HEART, IF BY SOME MIRACLE WE MAKE IT OUT OF THIS, WE'RE GOING TO HAVE TO TALK ABOUT FOCUS.
GOT 'EM JUST WHERE WE WANT 'EM, EH? YUKIE, CAN YOU...?
SHH...
MEYERS LOOKED LIKE HE WAS READY TO KEEL OVER, AND RAMIREZ STILL LOOKED DAZED FROM THE SWATTING BRAVOSA HAD ADMINISTERED HIM.
AND I WASN'T DOING MUCH BETTER. IT WAS GOING TO BE UP TO YOSHIMO TO CLEAR US SOME SPACE.
VENTAS!
WWSSSHH

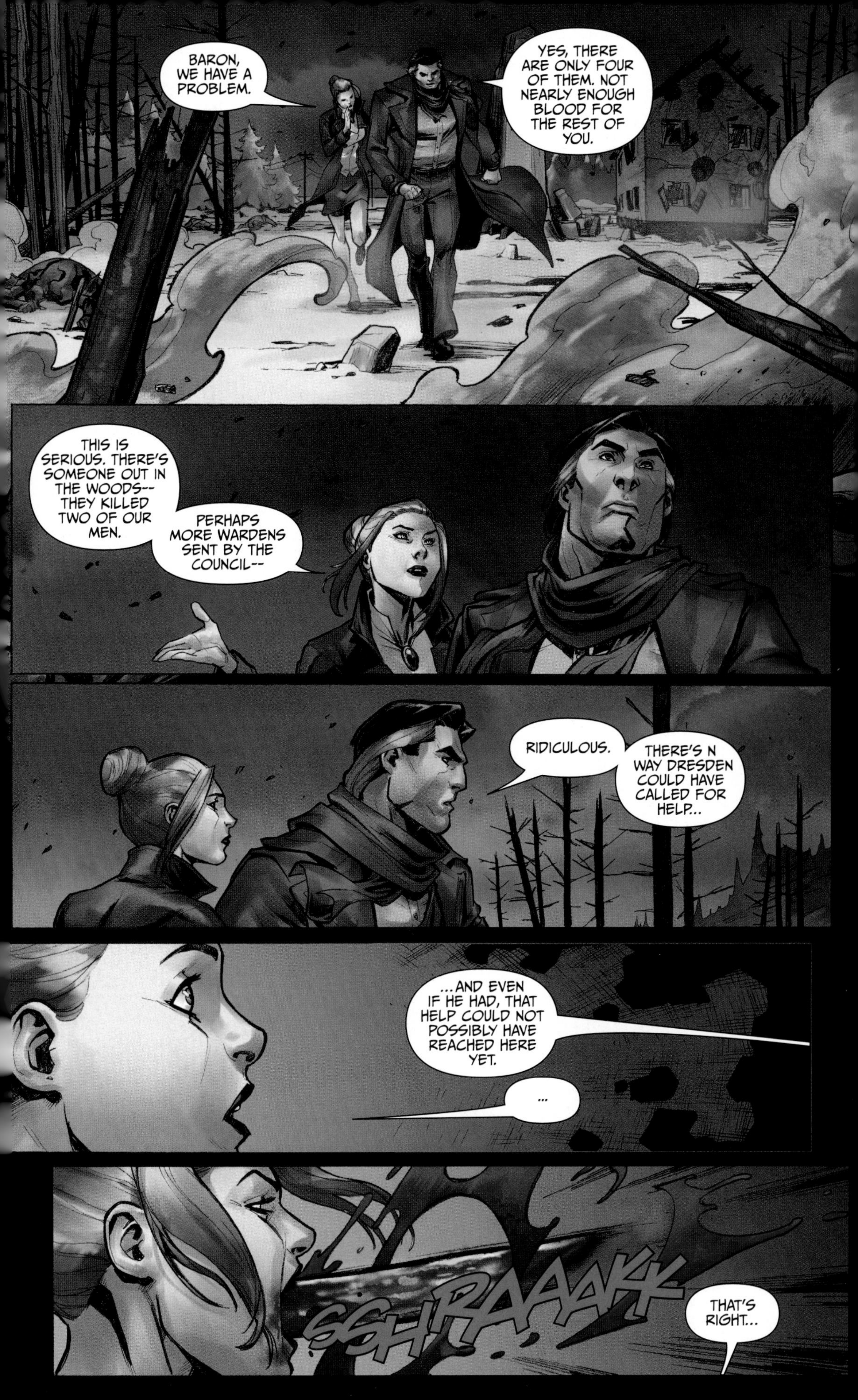
BARON, WE HAVE A PROBLEM.
YES, THERE ARE ONLY FOUR OF THEM. NOT NEARLY ENOUGH BLOOD FOR THE REST OF YOU.
THIS IS SERIOUS. THERE'S SOMEONE OUT IN THE WOODS-- THEY KILLED TWO OF OUR MEN.
PERHAPS MORE WARDENS SENT BY THE COUNCIL--
RIDICULOUS.
THERE'S N WAY DRESDEN COULD HAVE CALLED FOR HELP...
...AND EVEN IF HE HAD, THAT HELP COULD NOT POSSIBLY HAVE REACHED HERE YET.
...
SSHRAAAKK
THAT'S RIGHT...

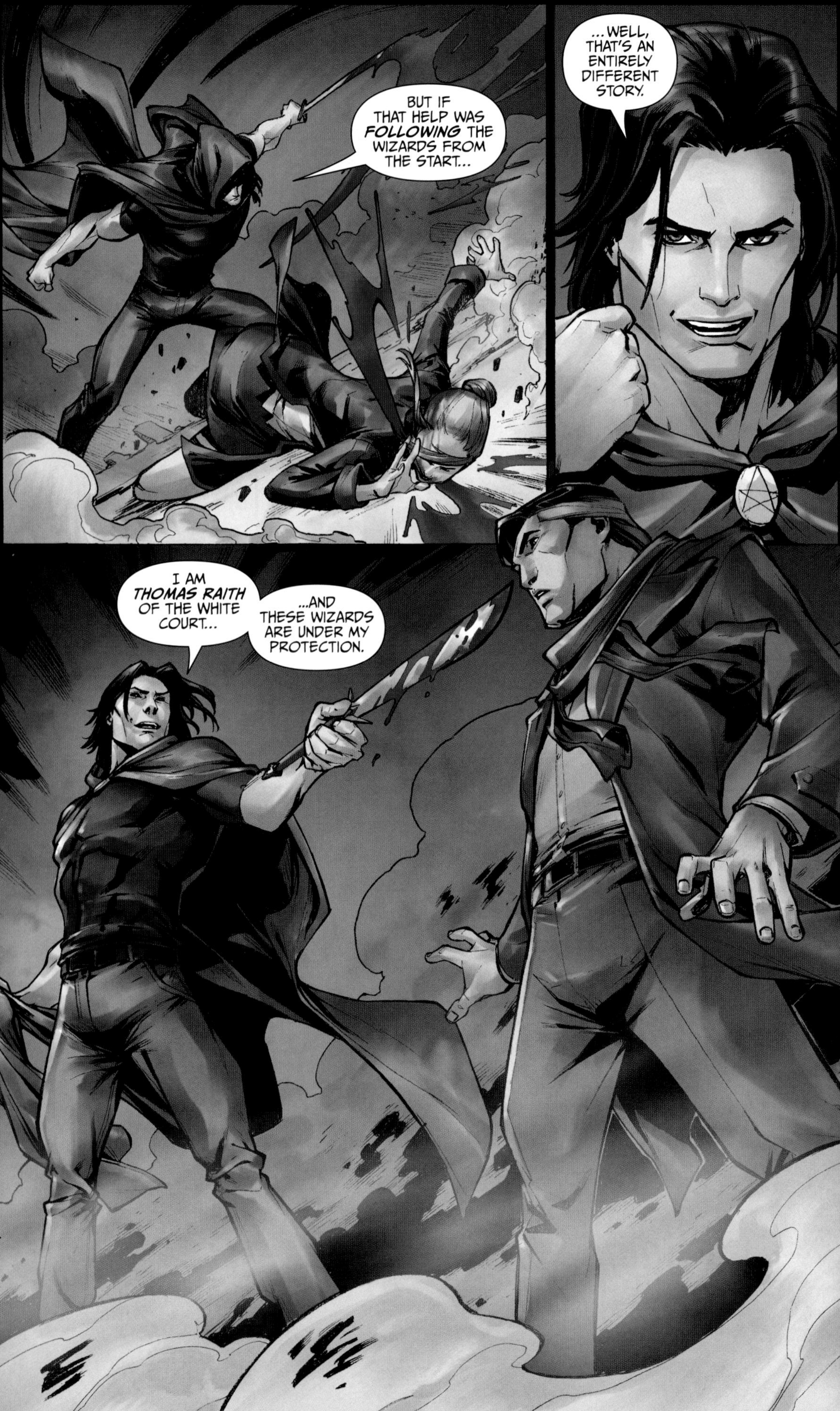
BUT IF THAT HELP WAS FOLLOWING THE WIZARDS FROM THE START...
...WELL, THAT'S AN ENTIRELY DIFFERENT STORY.
I AM THOMAS RAITH OF THE WHITE COURT...
...AND THESE WIZARDS ARE UNDER MY PROTECTION.

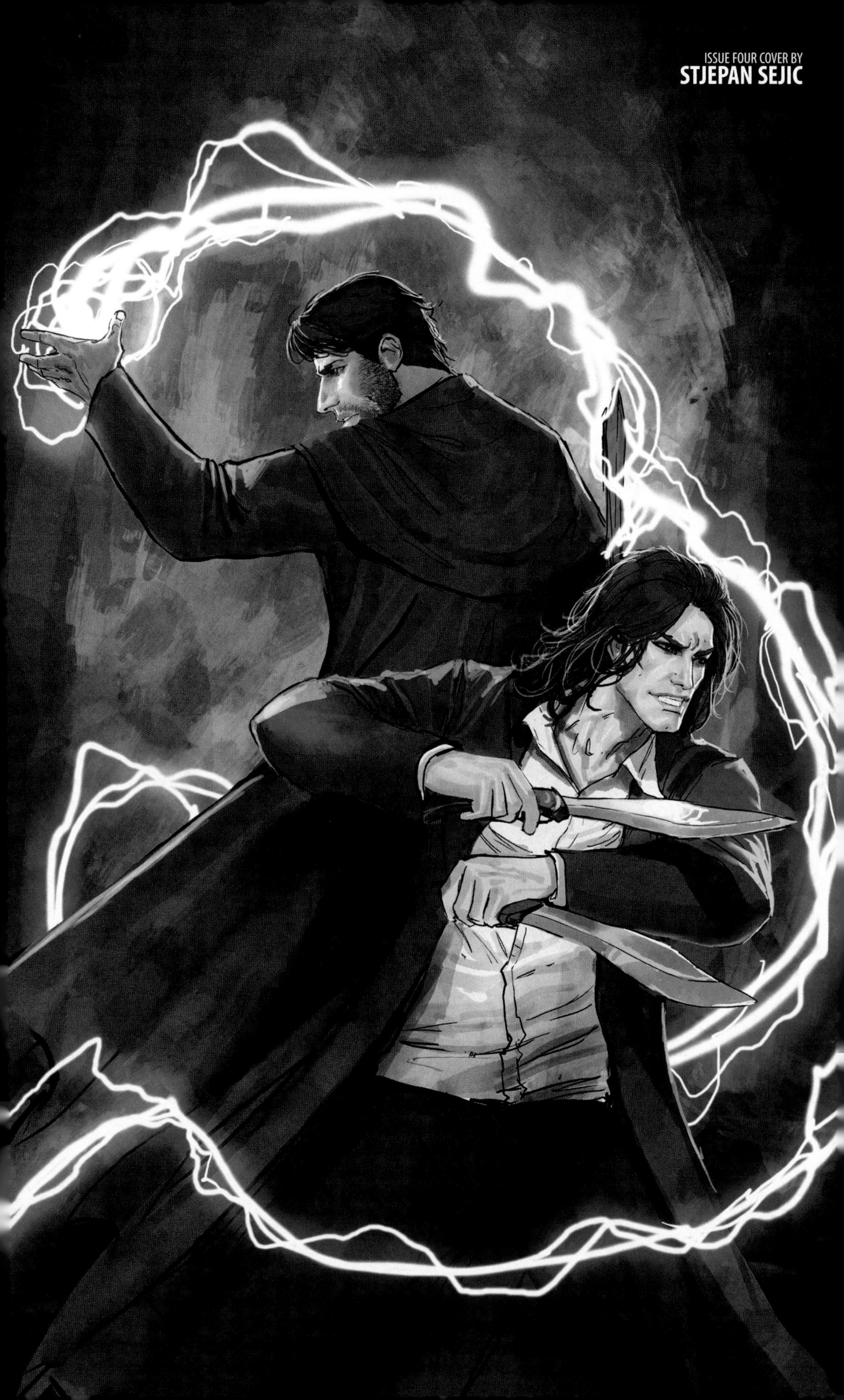

ISSUE FOUR COVER BY
STJEPAN SEJIC

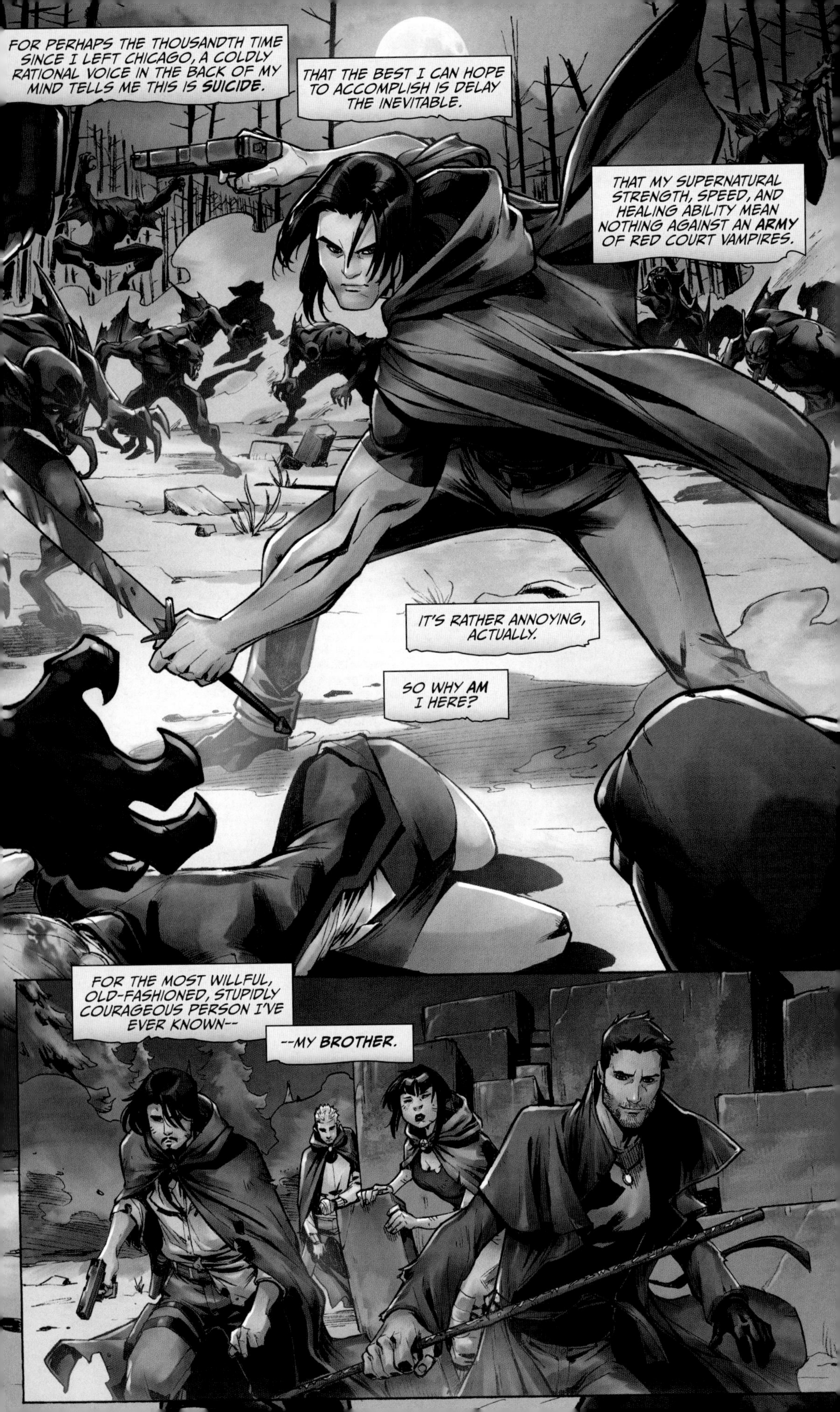
FOR PERHAPS THE THOUSANDTH TIME SINCE I LEFT CHICAGO, A COLDLY RATIONAL VOICE IN THE BACK OF MY MIND TELLS ME THIS IS SUICIDE.
THAT THE BEST I CAN HOPE TO ACCOMPLISH IS DELAY THE INEVITABLE.
THAT MY SUPERNATURAL STRENGTH, SPEED, AND HEALING ABILITY MEAN NOTHING AGAINST AN ARMY OF RED COURT VAMPIRES.
IT'S RATHER ANNOYING, ACTUALLY.
SO WHY AM I HERE?
FOR THE MOST WILLFUL, OLD-FASHIONED, STUPIDLY COURAGEOUS PERSON I'VE EVER KNOWN--
--MY BROTHER.

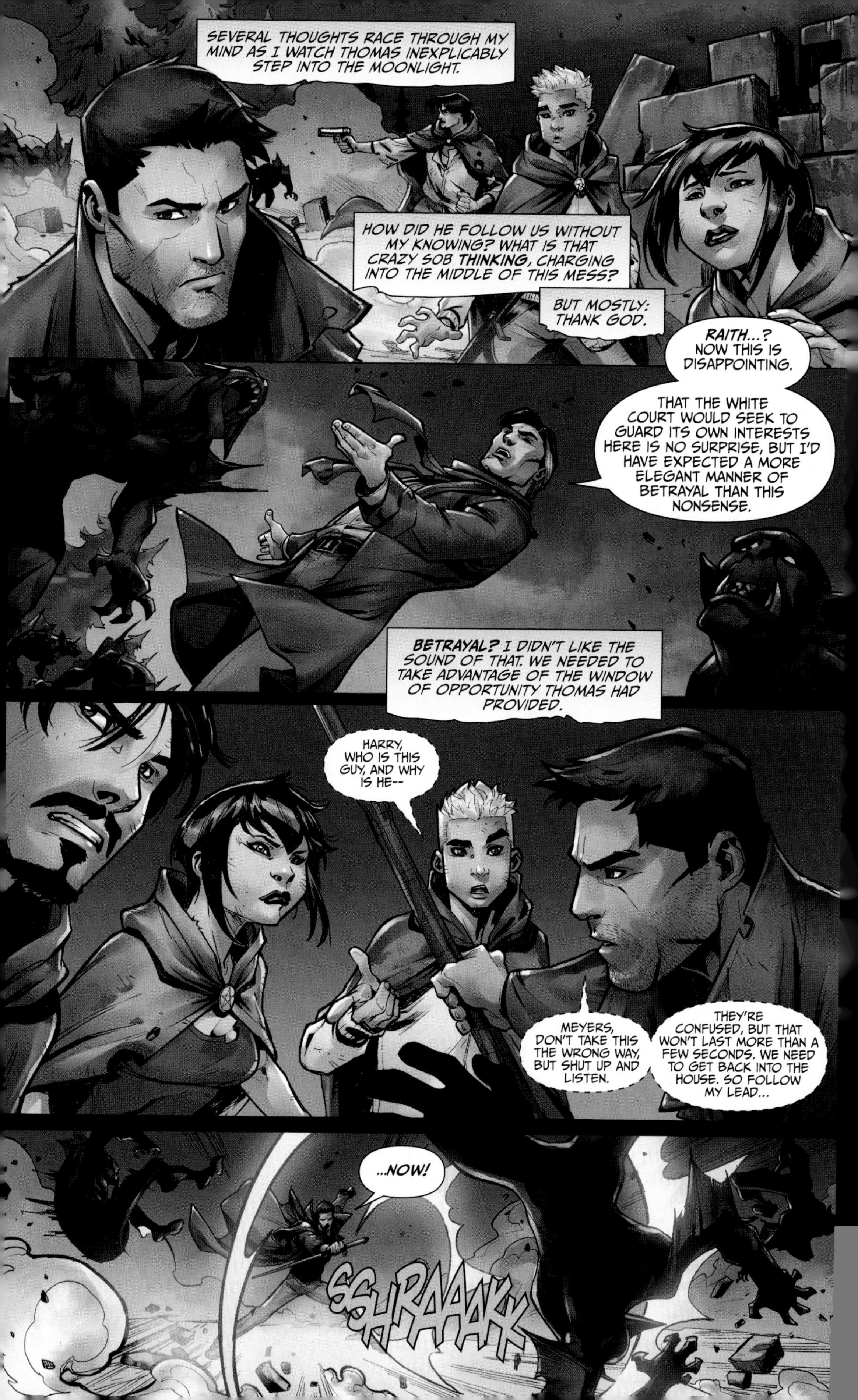

SEVERAL THOUGHTS RACE THROUGH MY MIND AS I WATCH THOMAS INEXPLICABLY STEP INTO THE MOONLIGHT.
HOW DID HE FOLLOW US WITHOUT MY KNOWING? WHAT IS THAT CRAZY SOB THINKING, CHARGING INTO THE MIDDLE OF THIS MESS?
BUT MOSTLY: THANK GOD.
RAITH...? NOW THIS IS DISAPPOINTING.
THAT THE WHITE COURT WOULD SEEK TO GUARD ITS OWN INTERESTS HERE IS NO SURPRISE, BUT I'D HAVE EXPECTED A MORE ELEGANT MANNER OF BETRAYAL THAN THIS NONSENSE.
BETRAYAL? I DIDN'T LIKE THE SOUND OF THAT. WE NEEDED TO TAKE ADVANTAGE OF THE WINDOW OF OPPORTUNITY THOMAS HAD PROVIDED.
HARRY, WHO IS THIS GUY, AND WHY IS HE--
MEYERS, DON'T TAKE THIS THE WRONG WAY, BUT SHUT UP AND LISTEN.
THEY'RE CONFUSED, BUT THAT WON'T LAST MORE THAN A FEW SECONDS. WE NEED TO GET BACK INTO THE HOUSE. SO FOLLOW MY LEAD...
...NOW!
SSHRAAAKK

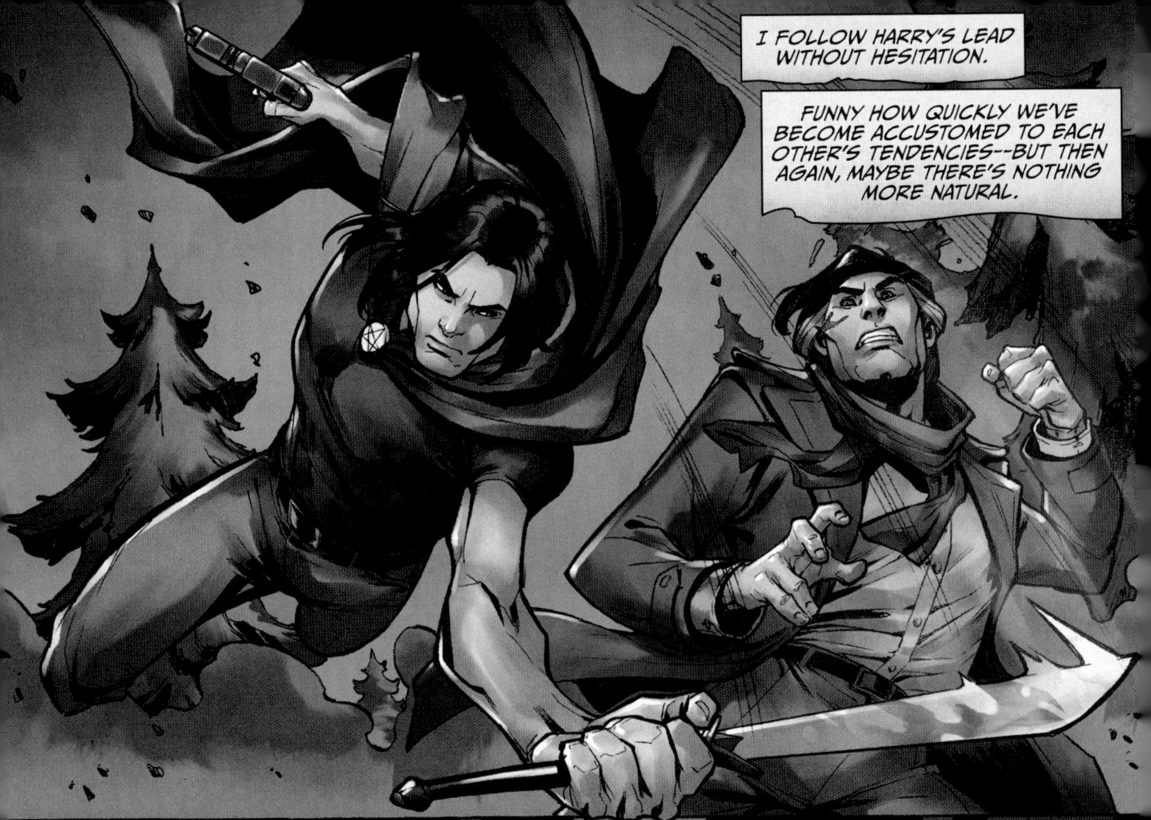
I FOLLOW HARRY'S LEAD WITHOUT HESITATION.
FUNNY HOW QUICKLY WE'VE BECOME ACCUSTOMED TO EACH OTHER'S TENDENCIES--BUT THEN AGAIN, MAYBE THERE'S NOTHING MORE NATURAL.
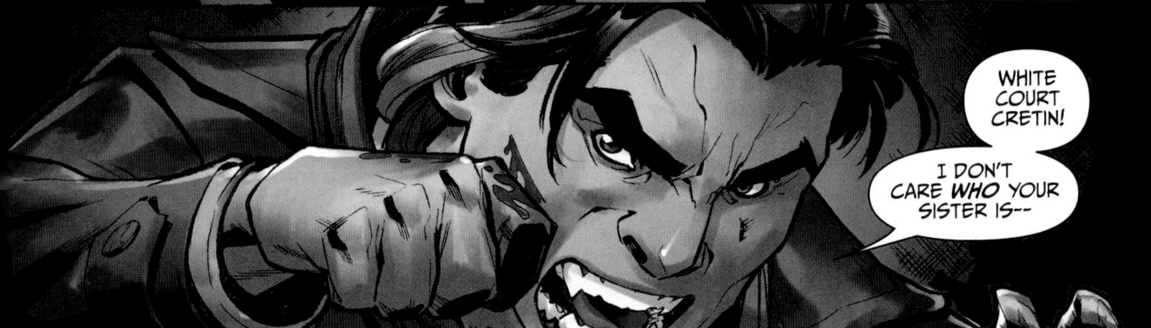
WHITE COURT CRETIN!
I DON'T CARE WHO YOUR SISTER IS--
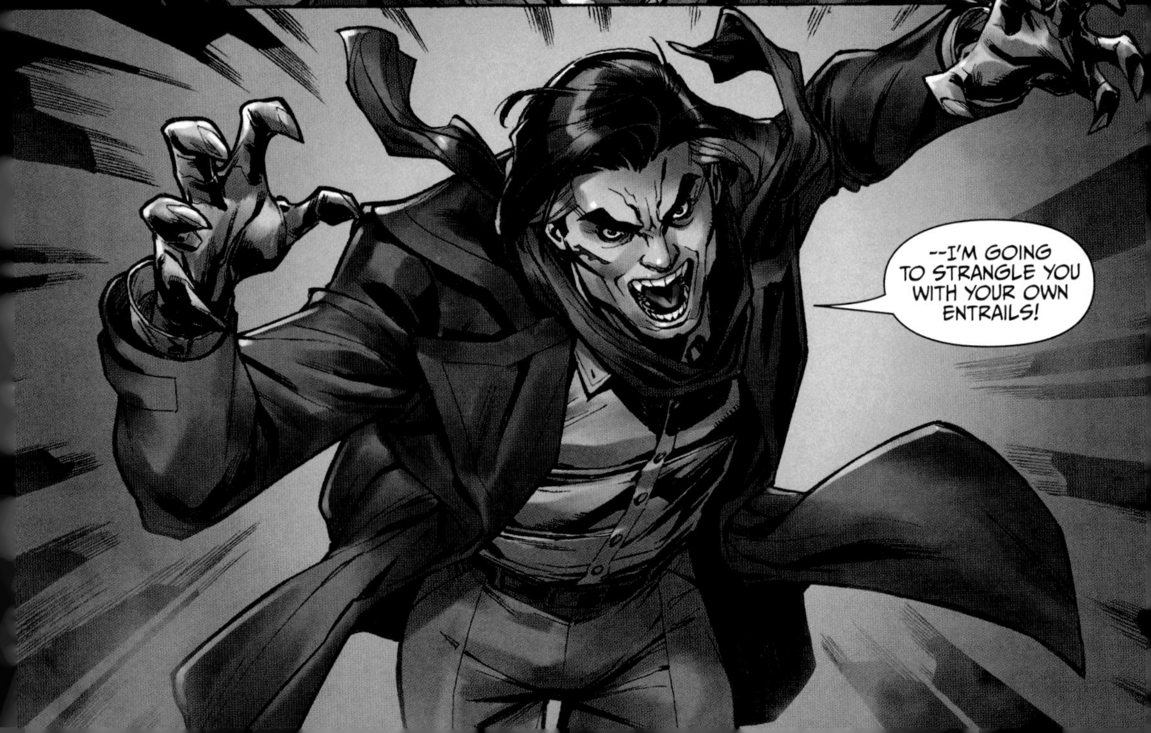
--I'M GOING TO STRANGLE YOU WITH YOUR OWN ENTRAILS!

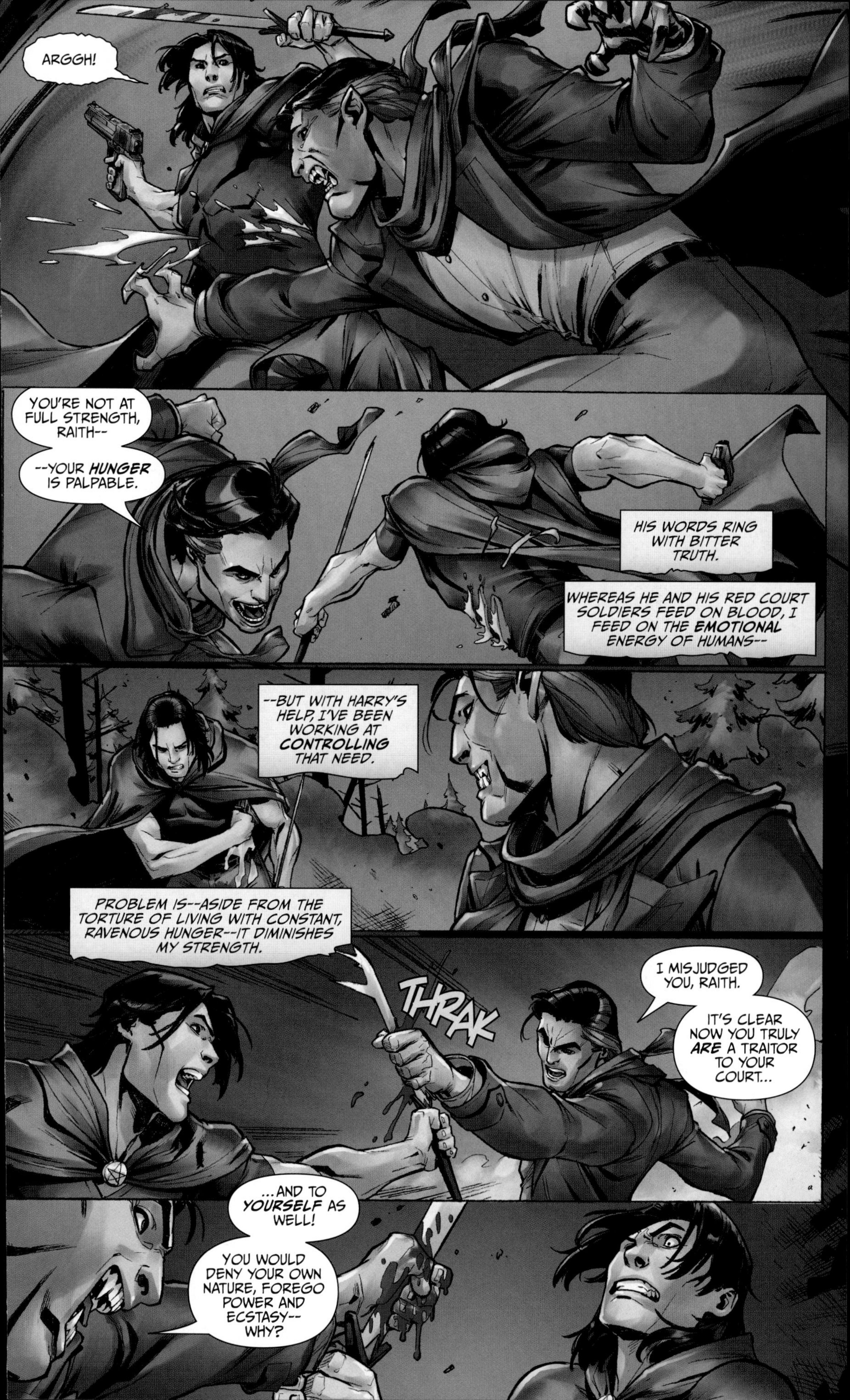
ARGGH!
YOU'RE NOT AT FULL STRENGTH, RAITH--
--YOUR **HUNGER** IS PALPABLE.
HIS WORDS RING WITH BITTER TRUTH.
WHEREAS HE AND HIS RED COURT SOLDIERS FEED ON BLOOD, I FEED ON THE **EMOTIONAL** ENERGY OF HUMANS--
--BUT WITH HARRY'S HELP, I'VE BEEN WORKING AT **CONTROLLING** THAT NEED.
PROBLEM IS--ASIDE FROM THE TORTURE OF LIVING WITH CONSTANT, RAVENOUS HUNGER--IT DIMINISHES MY STRENGTH.
THRAK
I MISJUDGED YOU, RAITH.
IT'S CLEAR NOW YOU TRULY **ARE** A TRAITOR TO YOUR COURT...
...AND TO **YOURSELF** AS WELL!
YOU WOULD DENY YOUR OWN NATURE, FOREGO POWER AND ECSTASY-- WHY?

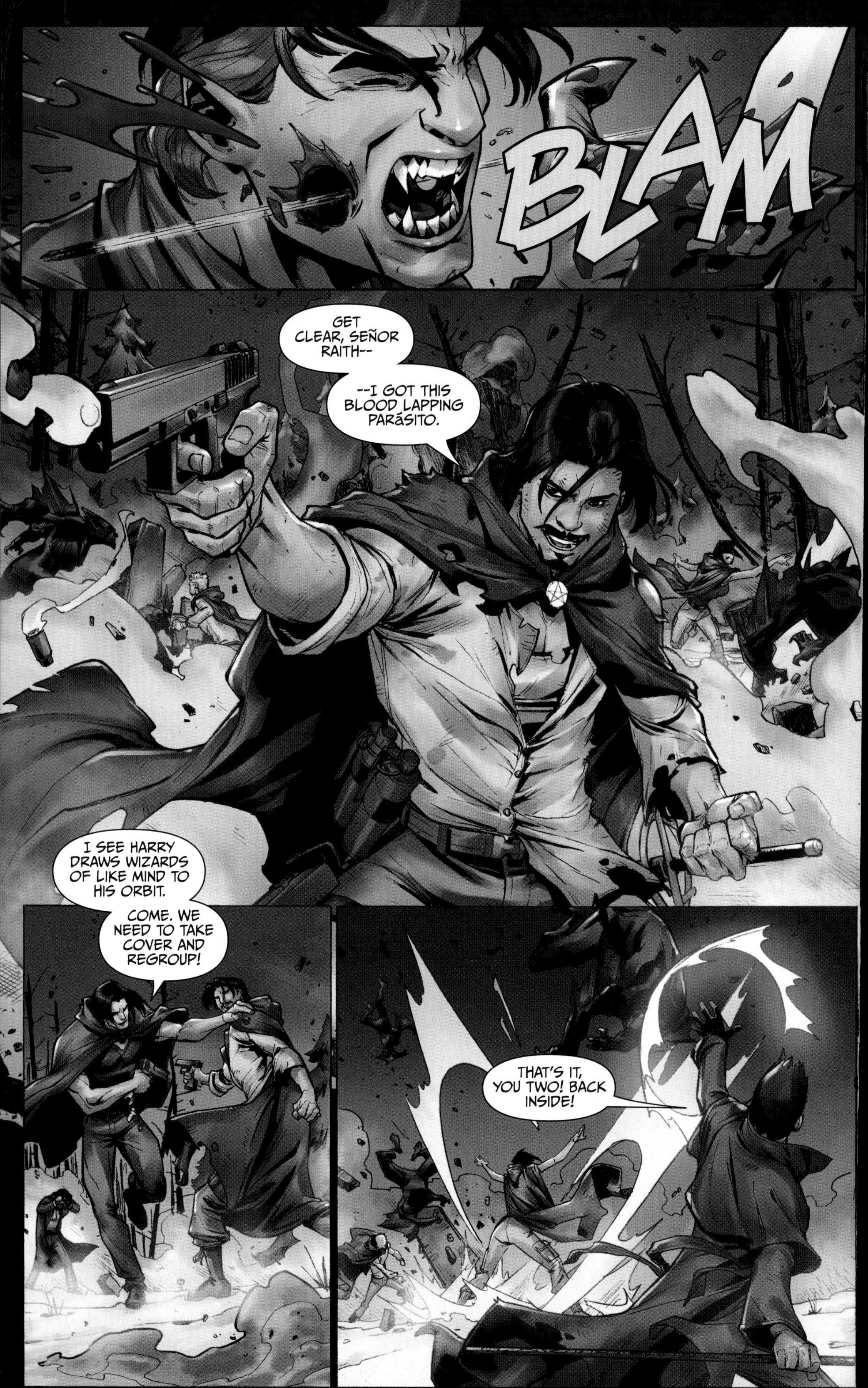
BLAM
GET CLEAR, SEÑOR RAITH--
--I GOT THIS BLOOD LAPPING PARÁSITO.
I SEE HARRY DRAWS WIZARDS OF LIKE MIND TO HIS ORBIT.
COME. WE NEED TO TAKE COVER AND REGROUP!
THAT'S IT, YOU TWO! BACK INSIDE!

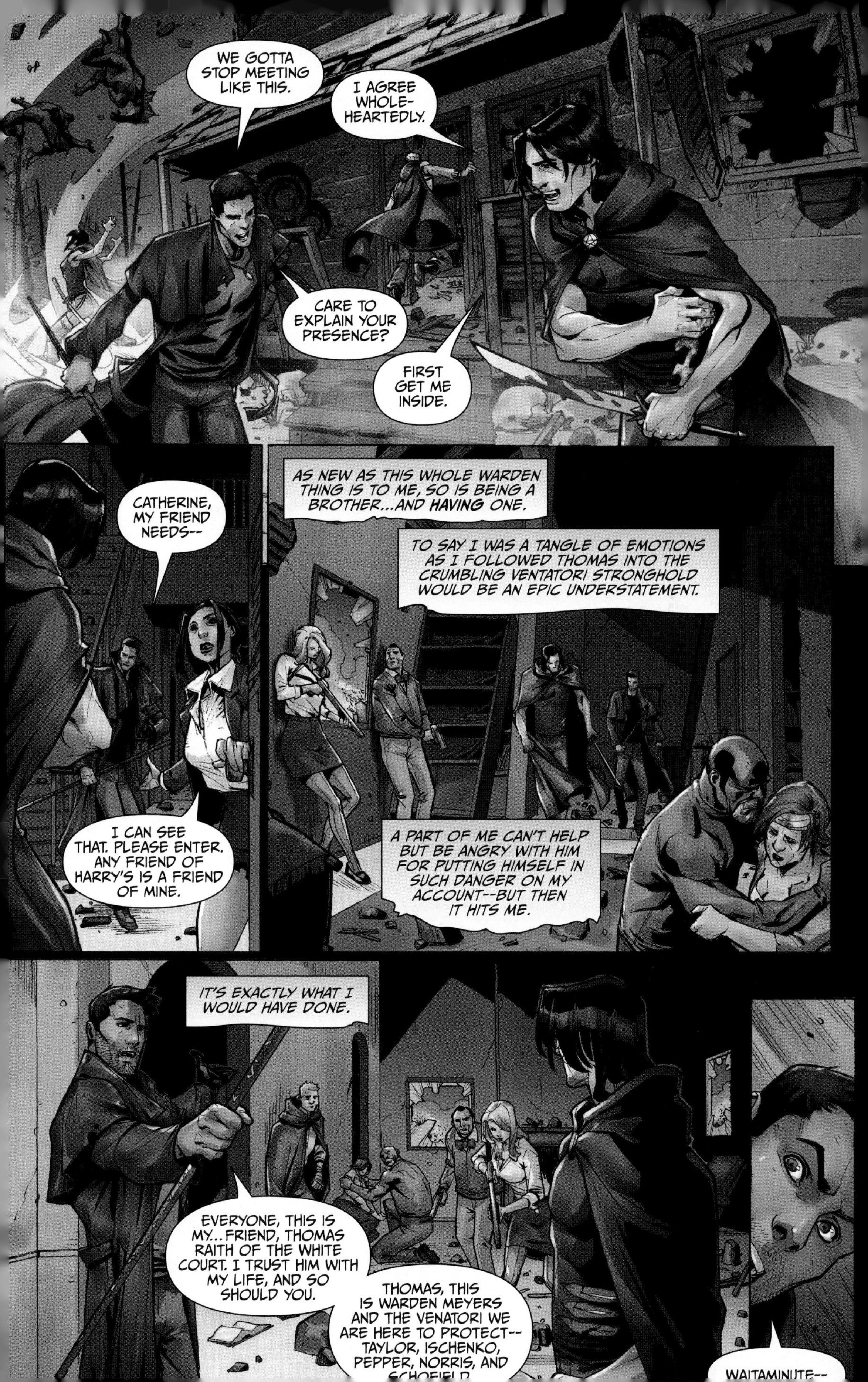
WE GOTTA STOP MEETING LIKE THIS.
I AGREE WHOLE-HEARTEDLY.
CARE TO EXPLAIN YOUR PRESENCE?
FIRST GET ME INSIDE.
CATHERINE, MY FRIEND NEEDS--
I CAN SEE THAT. PLEASE ENTER. ANY FRIEND OF HARRY'S IS A FRIEND OF MINE.
AS NEW AS THIS WHOLE WARDEN THING IS TO ME, SO IS BEING A BROTHER...AND HAVING ONE.
TO SAY I WAS A TANGLE OF EMOTIONS AS I FOLLOWED THOMAS INTO THE CRUMBLING VENTATORI STRONGHOLD WOULD BE AN EPIC UNDERSTATEMENT.
A PART OF ME CAN'T HELP BUT BE ANGRY WITH HIM FOR PUTTING HIMSELF IN SUCH DANGER ON MY ACCOUNT--BUT THEN IT HITS ME.
IT'S EXACTLY WHAT I WOULD HAVE DONE.
EVERYONE, THIS IS MY...FRIEND, THOMAS RAITH OF THE WHITE COURT. I TRUST HIM WITH MY LIFE, AND SO SHOULD YOU.
THOMAS, THIS IS WARDEN MEYERS AND THE VENATORI WE ARE HERE TO PROTECT-- TAYLOR, ISCHENKO, PEPPER, NORRIS, AND
WAITAMINUTE--

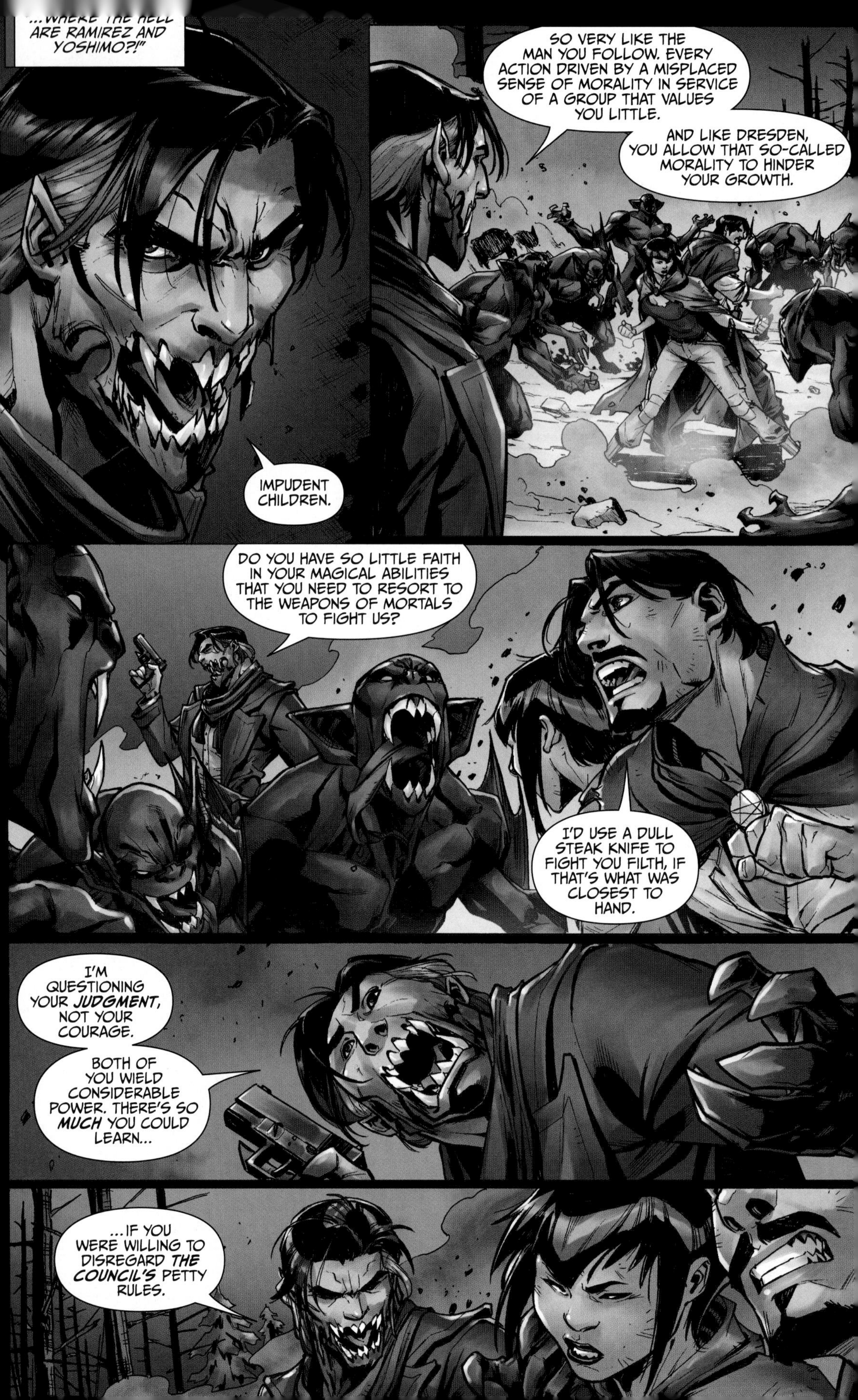
"...WHERE THE HELL ARE RAMIREZ AND YOSHIMO?!"
IMPUDENT CHILDREN.
SO VERY LIKE THE MAN YOU FOLLOW. EVERY ACTION DRIVEN BY A MISPLACED SENSE OF MORALITY IN SERVICE OF A GROUP THAT VALUES YOU LITTLE.
AND LIKE DRESDEN, YOU ALLOW THAT SO-CALLED MORALITY TO HINDER YOUR GROWTH.
DO YOU HAVE SO LITTLE FAITH IN YOUR MAGICAL ABILITIES THAT YOU NEED TO RESORT TO THE WEAPONS OF MORTALS TO FIGHT US?
I'D USE A DULL STEAK KNIFE TO FIGHT YOU FILTH, IF THAT'S WHAT WAS CLOSEST TO HAND.
I'M QUESTIONING YOUR *JUDGMENT*, NOT YOUR COURAGE.
BOTH OF YOU WIELD CONSIDERABLE POWER. THERE'S SO *MUCH* YOU COULD LEARN...
...IF YOU WERE WILLING TO DISREGARD *THE COUNCIL'S* PETTY RULES.

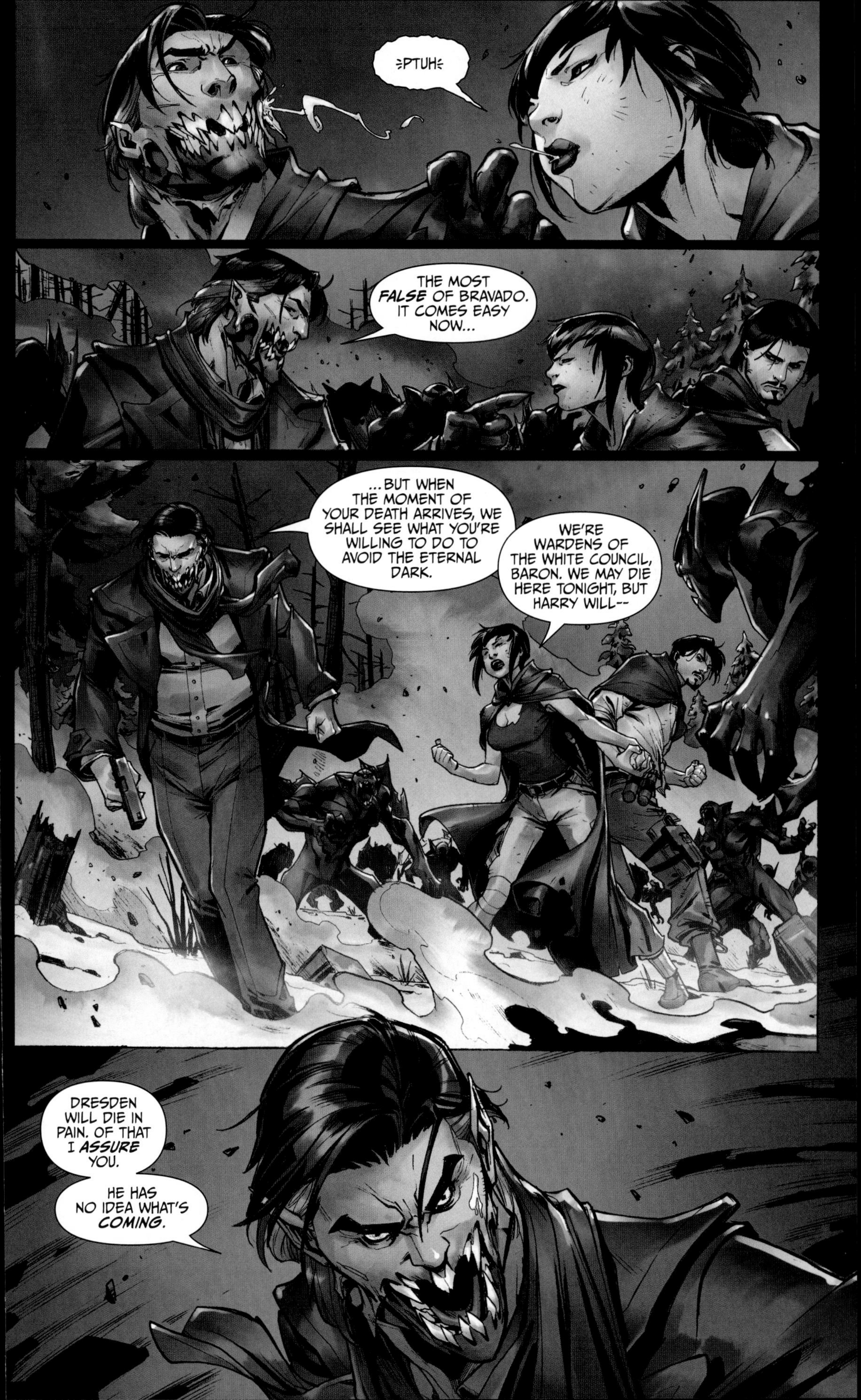

PTUH
THE MOST FALSE OF BRAVADO. IT COMES EASY NOW...
...BUT WHEN THE MOMENT OF YOUR DEATH ARRIVES, WE SHALL SEE WHAT YOU'RE WILLING TO DO TO AVOID THE ETERNAL DARK.
WE'RE WARDENS OF THE WHITE COUNCIL, BARON. WE MAY DIE HERE TONIGHT, BUT HARRY WILL--
DRESDEN WILL DIE IN PAIN. OF THAT I ASSURE YOU.
HE HAS NO IDEA WHAT'S COMING.

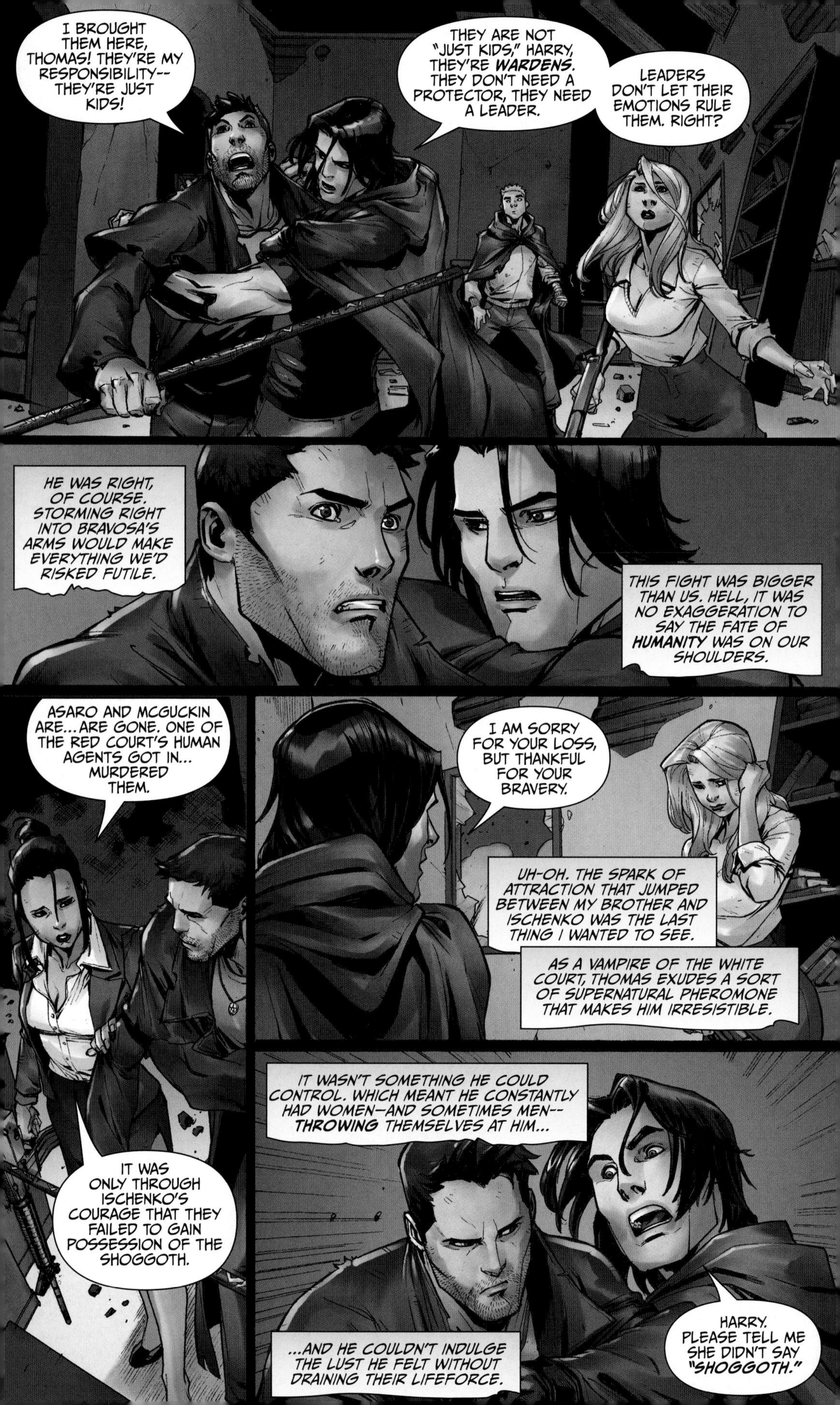

I BROUGHT THEM HERE, THOMAS! THEY'RE MY RESPONSIBILITY-- THEY'RE JUST KIDS!
THEY ARE NOT "JUST KIDS," HARRY, THEY'RE WARDENS. THEY DON'T NEED A PROTECTOR, THEY NEED A LEADER.
LEADERS DON'T LET THEIR EMOTIONS RULE THEM. RIGHT?
HE WAS RIGHT, OF COURSE. STORMING RIGHT INTO BRAVOSA'S ARMS WOULD MAKE EVERYTHING WE'D RISKED FUTILE.
THIS FIGHT WAS BIGGER THAN US. HELL, IT WAS NO EXAGGERATION TO SAY THE FATE OF HUMANITY WAS ON OUR SHOULDERS.
ASARO AND MCGUCKIN ARE...ARE GONE. ONE OF THE RED COURT'S HUMAN AGENTS GOT IN... MURDERED THEM.
IT WAS ONLY THROUGH ISCHENKO'S COURAGE THAT THEY FAILED TO GAIN POSSESSION OF THE SHOGGOTH.
I AM SORRY FOR YOUR LOSS, BUT THANKFUL FOR YOUR BRAVERY.
UH-OH. THE SPARK OF ATTRACTION THAT JUMPED BETWEEN MY BROTHER AND ISCHENKO WAS THE LAST THING I WANTED TO SEE.
AS A VAMPIRE OF THE WHITE COURT, THOMAS EXUDES A SORT OF SUPERNATURAL PHEROMONE THAT MAKES HIM IRRESISTIBLE.
IT WASN'T SOMETHING HE COULD CONTROL. WHICH MEANT HE CONSTANTLY HAD WOMEN--AND SOMETIMES MEN-- THROWING THEMSELVES AT HIM...
...AND HE COULDN'T INDULGE THE LUST HE FELT WITHOUT DRAINING THEIR LIFEFORCE.
HARRY. PLEASE TELL ME SHE DIDN'T SAY "SHOGGOTH."

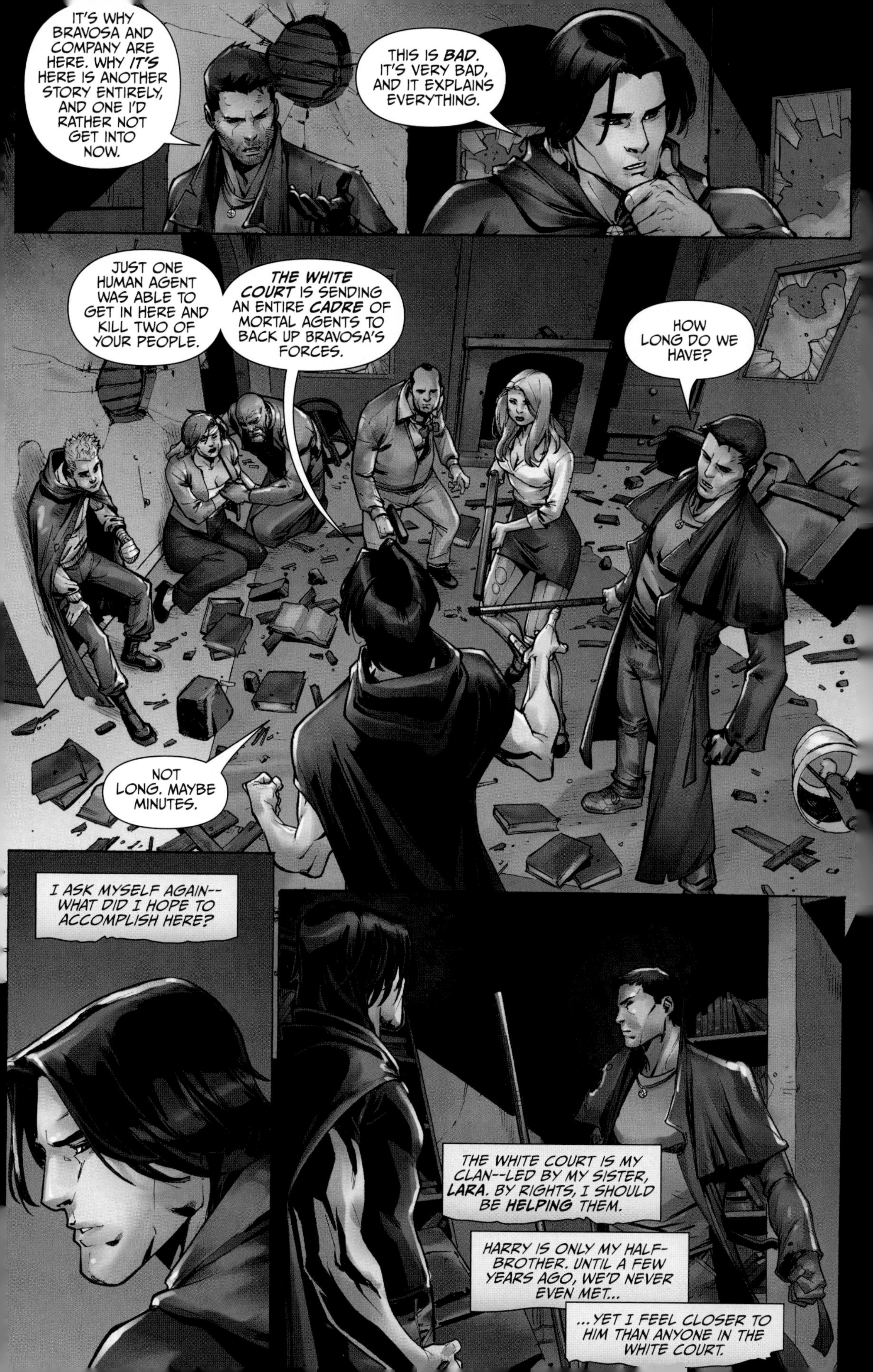
IT'S WHY BRAVOSA AND COMPANY ARE HERE. WHY *IT'S* HERE IS ANOTHER STORY ENTIRELY, AND ONE I'D RATHER NOT GET INTO NOW.
THIS IS *BAD*. IT'S VERY BAD, AND IT EXPLAINS EVERYTHING.
JUST ONE HUMAN AGENT WAS ABLE TO GET IN HERE AND KILL TWO OF YOUR PEOPLE.
THE WHITE COURT IS SENDING AN ENTIRE *CADRE* OF MORTAL AGENTS TO BACK UP BRAVOSA'S FORCES.
HOW LONG DO WE HAVE?
NOT LONG. MAYBE MINUTES.
I ASK MYSELF AGAIN-- WHAT DID I HOPE TO ACCOMPLISH HERE?
THE WHITE COURT IS MY CLAN--LED BY MY SISTER, **LARA**. BY RIGHTS, I SHOULD BE **HELPING** THEM.
HARRY IS ONLY MY HALF-BROTHER. UNTIL A FEW YEARS AGO, WE'D NEVER EVEN MET...
...YET I FEEL CLOSER TO HIM THAN ANYONE IN THE WHITE COURT.

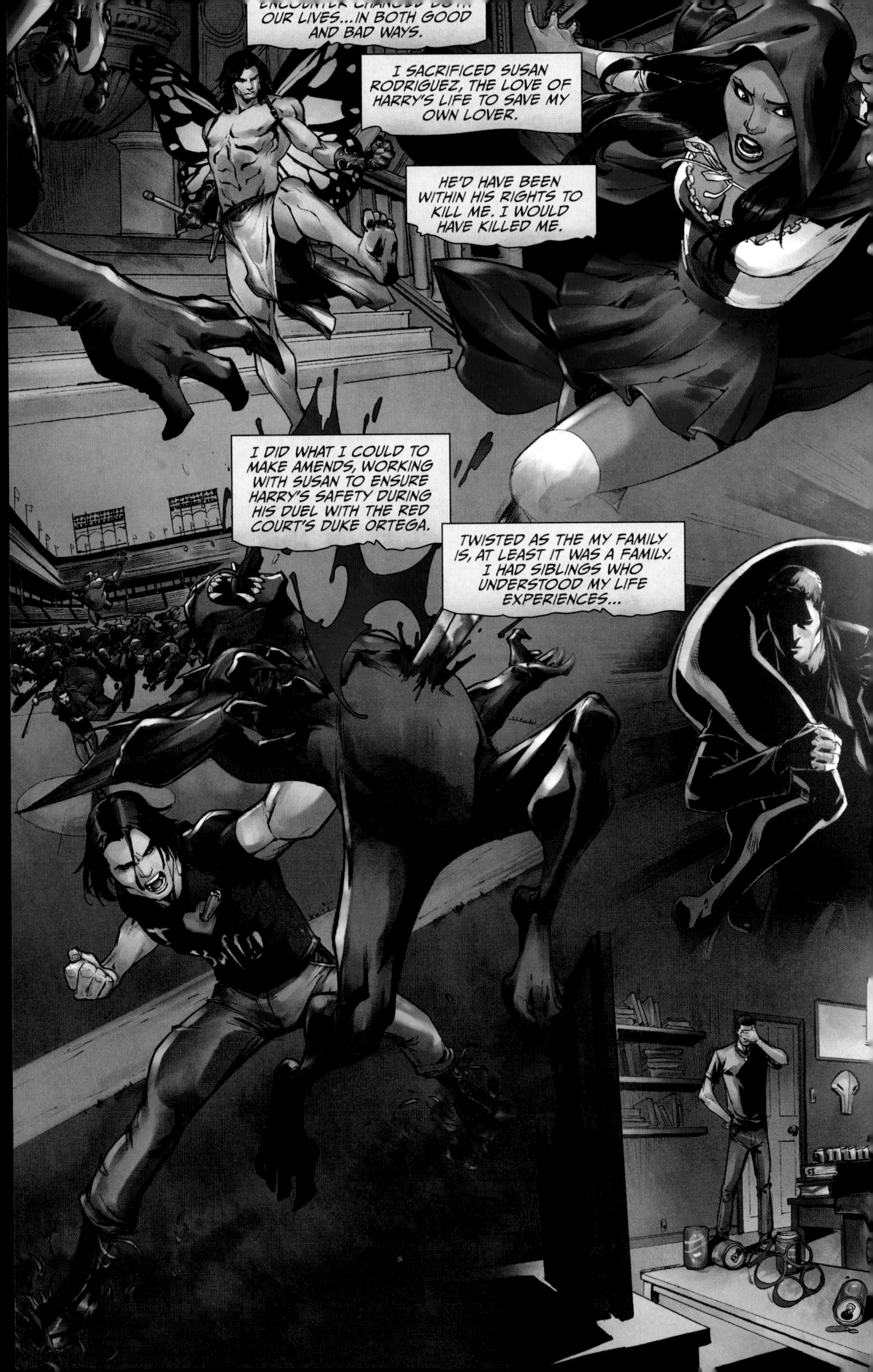
OUR LIVES...IN BOTH GOOD AND BAD WAYS.
I SACRIFICED SUSAN RODRIGUEZ, THE LOVE OF HARRY'S LIFE TO SAVE MY OWN LOVER.
HE'D HAVE BEEN WITHIN HIS RIGHTS TO KILL ME. I WOULD HAVE KILLED ME.
I DID WHAT I COULD TO MAKE AMENDS, WORKING WITH SUSAN TO ENSURE HARRY'S SAFETY DURING HIS DUEL WITH THE RED COURT'S DUKE ORTEGA.
TWISTED AS THE MY FAMILY IS, AT LEAST IT WAS A FAMILY. I HAD SIBLINGS WHO UNDERSTOOD MY LIFE EXPERIENCES...

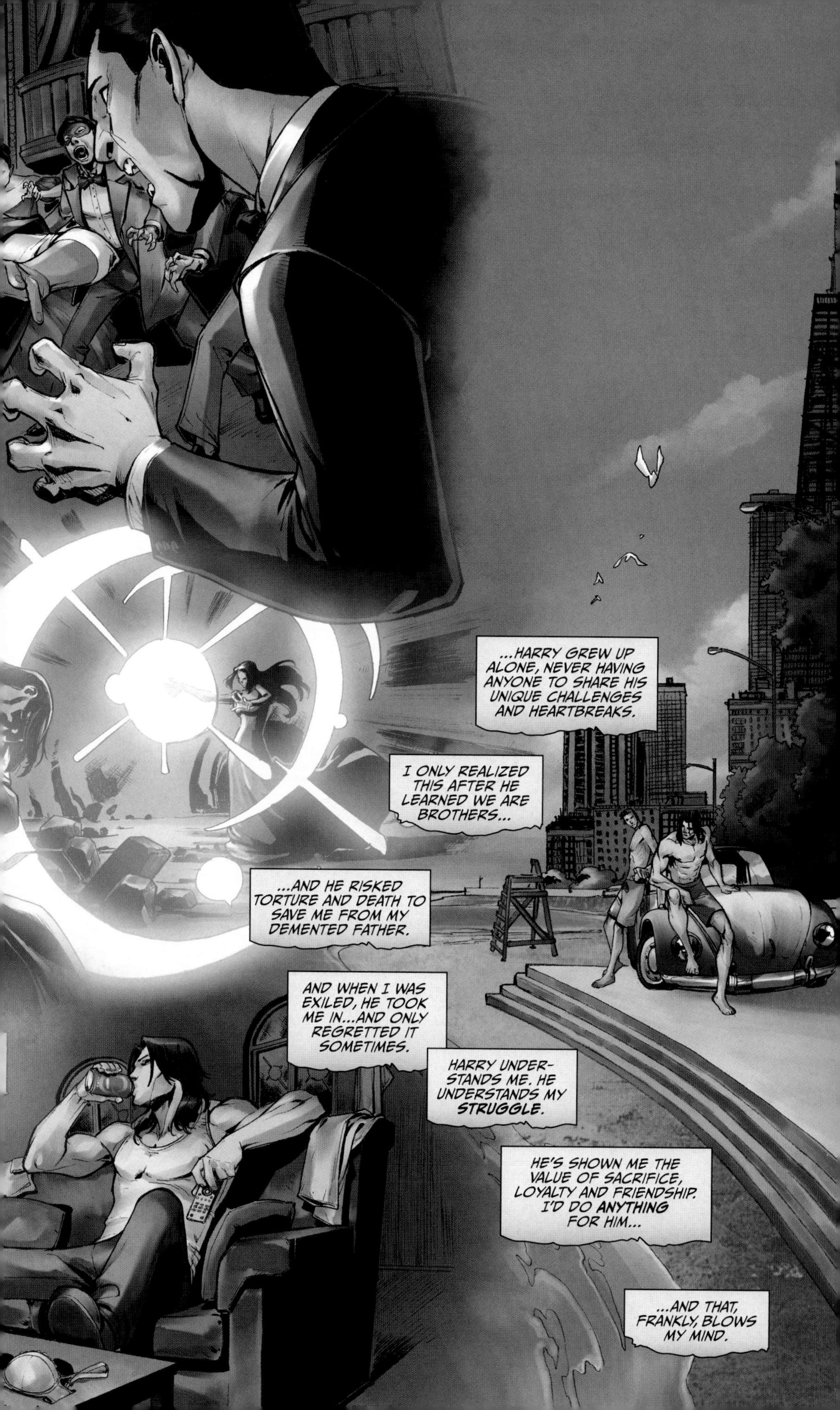
...HARRY GREW UP ALONE, NEVER HAVING ANYONE TO SHARE HIS UNIQUE CHALLENGES AND HEARTBREAKS.
I ONLY REALIZED THIS AFTER HE LEARNED WE ARE BROTHERS...
...AND HE RISKED TORTURE AND DEATH TO SAVE ME FROM MY DEMENTED FATHER.
AND WHEN I WAS EXILED, HE TOOK ME IN...AND ONLY REGRETTED IT SOMETIMES.
HARRY UNDERSTANDS ME. HE UNDERSTANDS MY **STRUGGLE**.
HE'S SHOWN ME THE VALUE OF SACRIFICE, LOYALTY AND FRIENDSHIP. I'D DO **ANYTHING** FOR HIM...
...AND THAT, FRANKLY, BLOWS MY MIND.

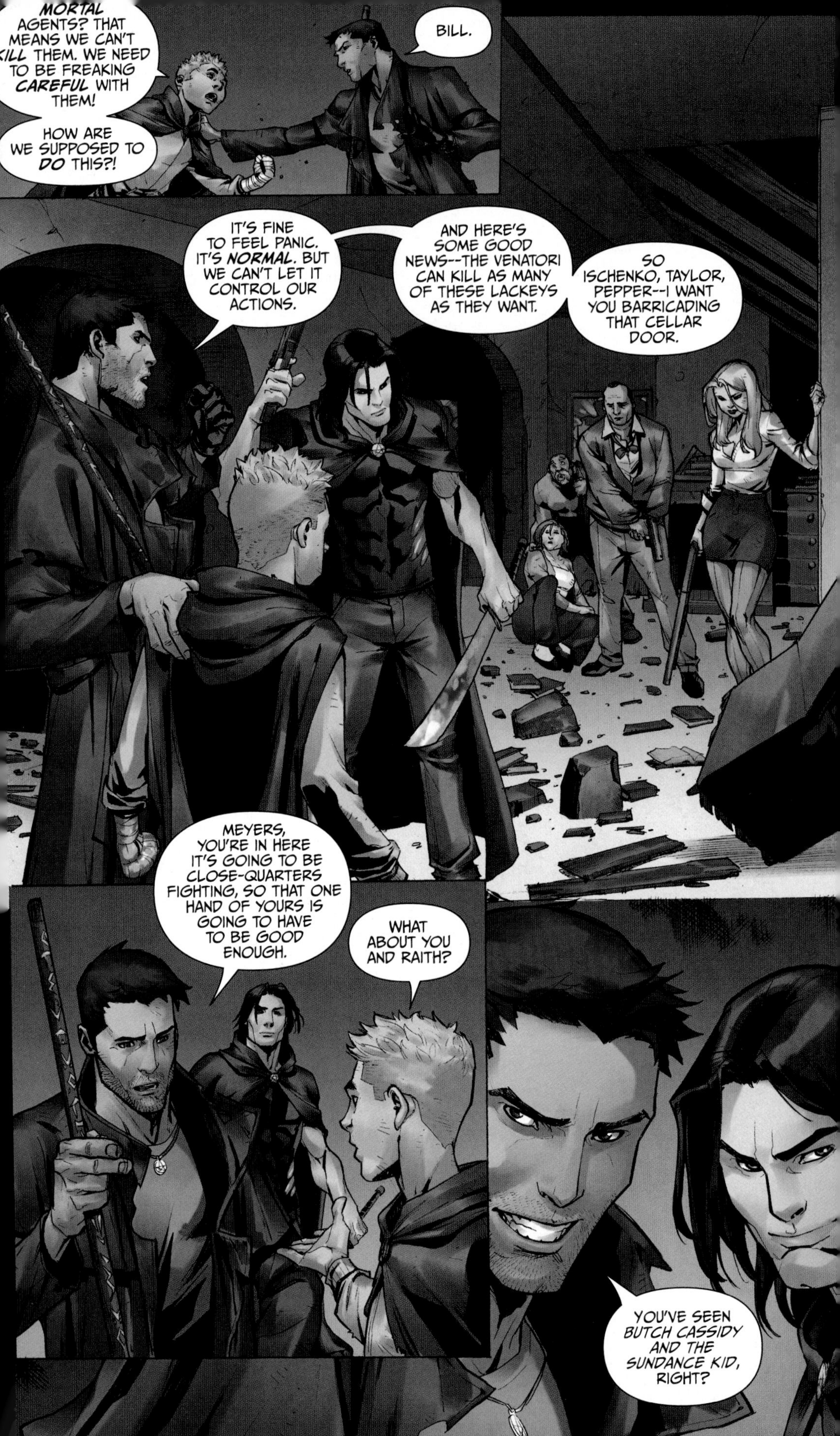
MORTAL AGENTS? THAT MEANS WE CAN'T KILL THEM. WE NEED TO BE FREAKING CAREFUL WITH THEM!
HOW ARE WE SUPPOSED TO DO THIS?!
BILL.
IT'S FINE TO FEEL PANIC. IT'S NORMAL. BUT WE CAN'T LET IT CONTROL OUR ACTIONS.
AND HERE'S SOME GOOD NEWS--THE VENATORI CAN KILL AS MANY OF THESE LACKEYS AS THEY WANT.
SO ISCHENKO, TAYLOR, PEPPER--I WANT YOU BARRICADING THAT CELLAR DOOR.
MEYERS, YOU'RE IN HERE IT'S GOING TO BE CLOSE-QUARTERS FIGHTING, SO THAT ONE HAND OF YOURS IS GOING TO HAVE TO BE GOOD ENOUGH.
WHAT ABOUT YOU AND RAITH?
YOU'VE SEEN BUTCH CASSIDY AND THE SUNDANCE KID, RIGHT?

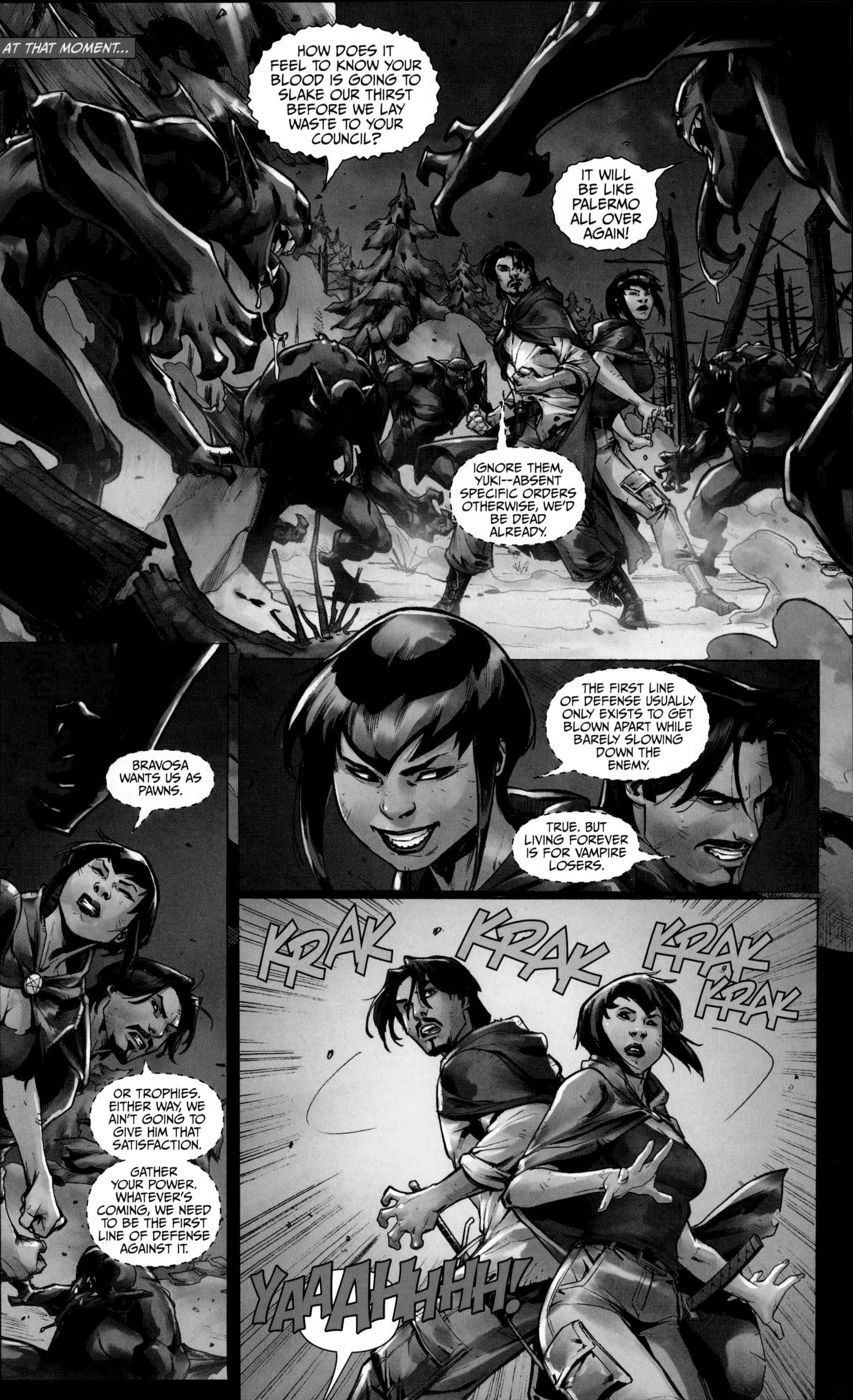
AT THAT MOMENT...
HOW DOES IT FEEL TO KNOW YOUR BLOOD IS GOING TO SLAKE OUR THIRST BEFORE WE LAY WASTE TO YOUR COUNCIL?
IT WILL BE LIKE PALERMO ALL OVER AGAIN!
IGNORE THEM, YUKI--ABSENT SPECIFIC ORDERS OTHERWISE, WE'D BE DEAD ALREADY.
BRAVOSA WANTS US AS PAWNS.
OR TROPHIES. EITHER WAY, WE AIN'T GOING TO GIVE HIM THAT SATISFACTION.
GATHER YOUR POWER. WHATEVER'S COMING, WE NEED TO BE THE FIRST LINE OF DEFENSE AGAINST IT.
THE FIRST LINE OF DEFENSE USUALLY ONLY EXISTS TO GET BLOWN APART WHILE BARELY SLOWING DOWN THE ENEMY.
TRUE. BUT LIVING FOREVER IS FOR VAMPIRE LOSERS.
KRAK KRAK KRAK KRAK
YAAAHHHH!

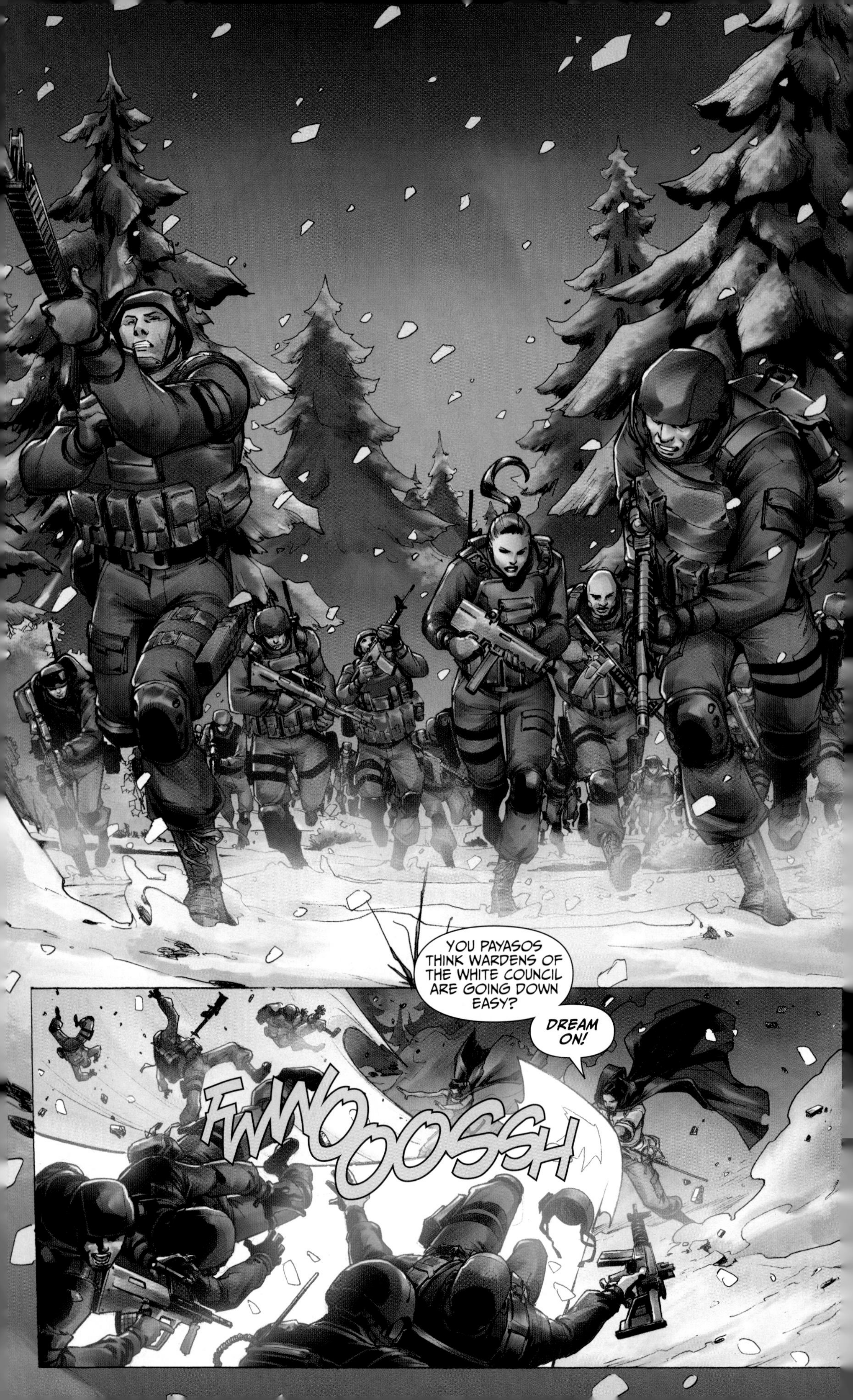
YOU PAYASOS THINK WARDENS OF THE WHITE COUNCIL ARE GOING DOWN EASY?
DREAM ON!
FWWOOOSSH

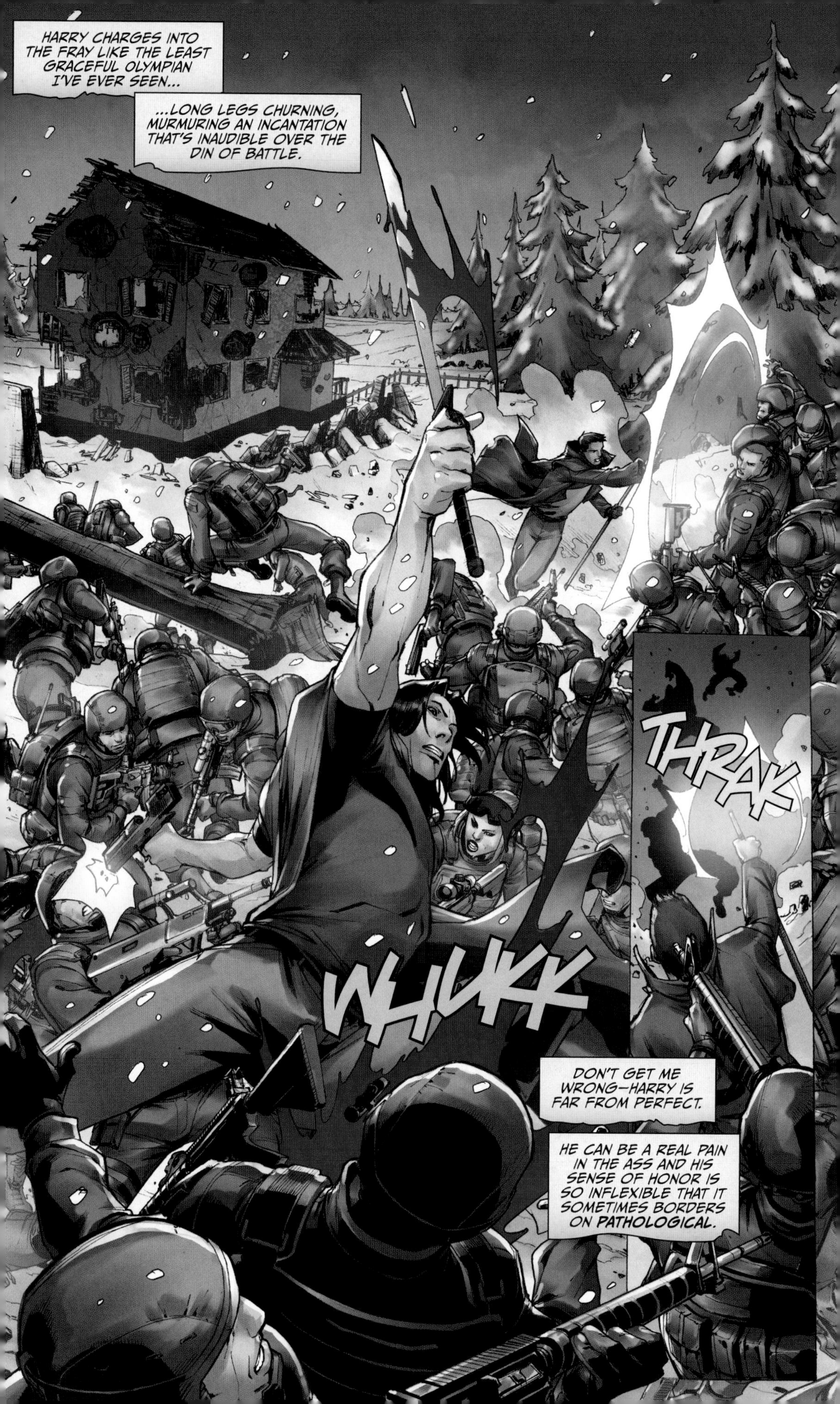
HARRY CHARGES INTO THE FRAY LIKE THE LEAST GRACEFUL OLYMPIAN I'VE EVER SEEN...
...LONG LEGS CHURNING, MURMURING AN INCANTATION THAT'S INAUDIBLE OVER THE DIN OF BATTLE.
THRAK
WHUKK
DON'T GET ME WRONG—HARRY IS FAR FROM PERFECT.
HE CAN BE A REAL PAIN IN THE ASS AND HIS SENSE OF HONOR IS SO INFLEXIBLE THAT IT SOMETIMES BORDERS ON **PATHOLOGICAL**.

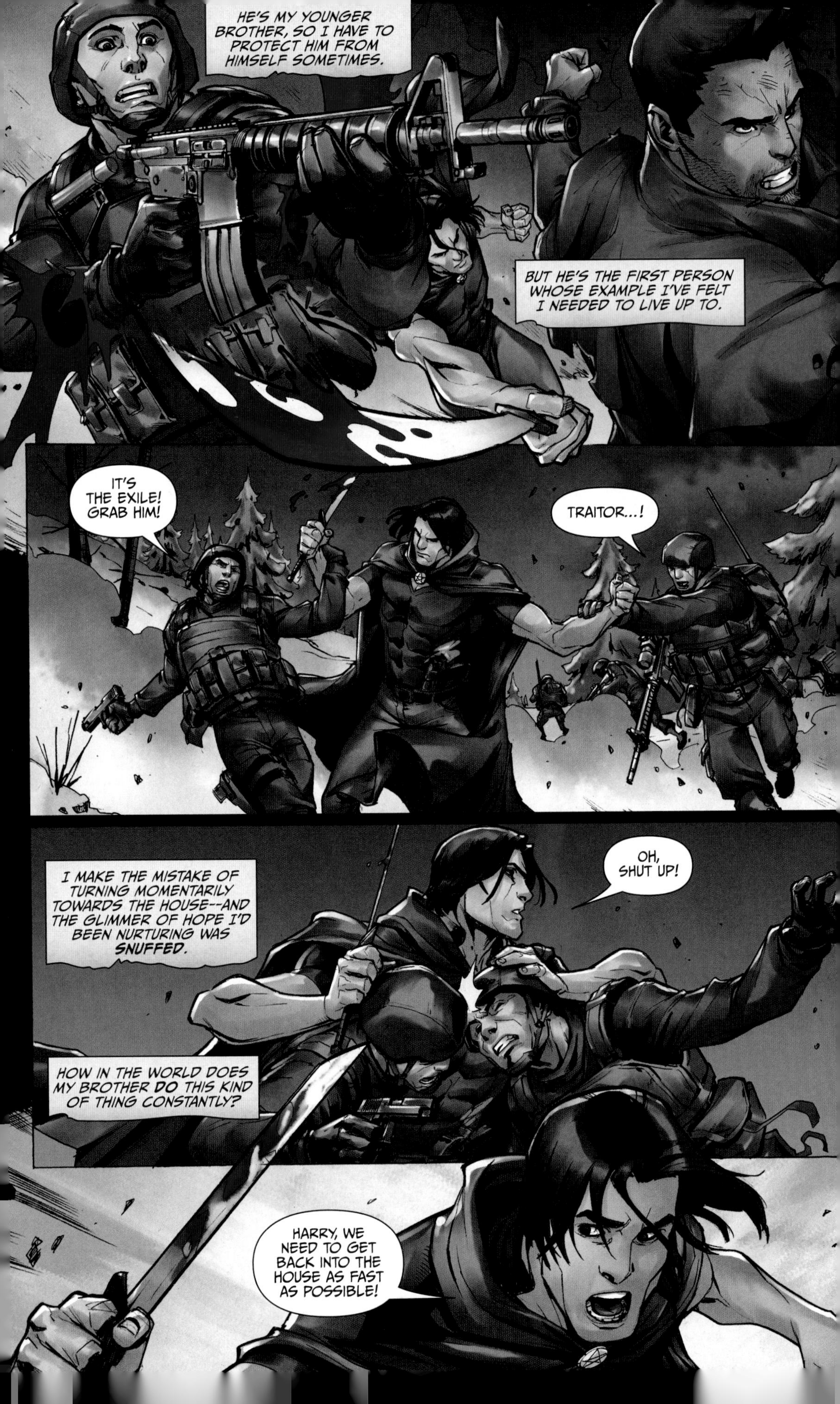

HE'S MY YOUNGER BROTHER, SO I HAVE TO PROTECT HIM FROM HIMSELF SOMETIMES.
BUT HE'S THE FIRST PERSON WHOSE EXAMPLE I'VE FELT I NEEDED TO LIVE UP TO.
IT'S THE EXILE! GRAB HIM!
TRAITOR...!
I MAKE THE MISTAKE OF TURNING MOMENTARILY TOWARDS THE HOUSE--AND THE GLIMMER OF HOPE I'D BEEN NURTURING WAS SNUFFED.
OH, SHUT UP!
HOW IN THE WORLD DOES MY BROTHER DO THIS KIND OF THING CONSTANTLY?
HARRY, WE NEED TO GET BACK INTO THE HOUSE AS FAST AS POSSIBLE!

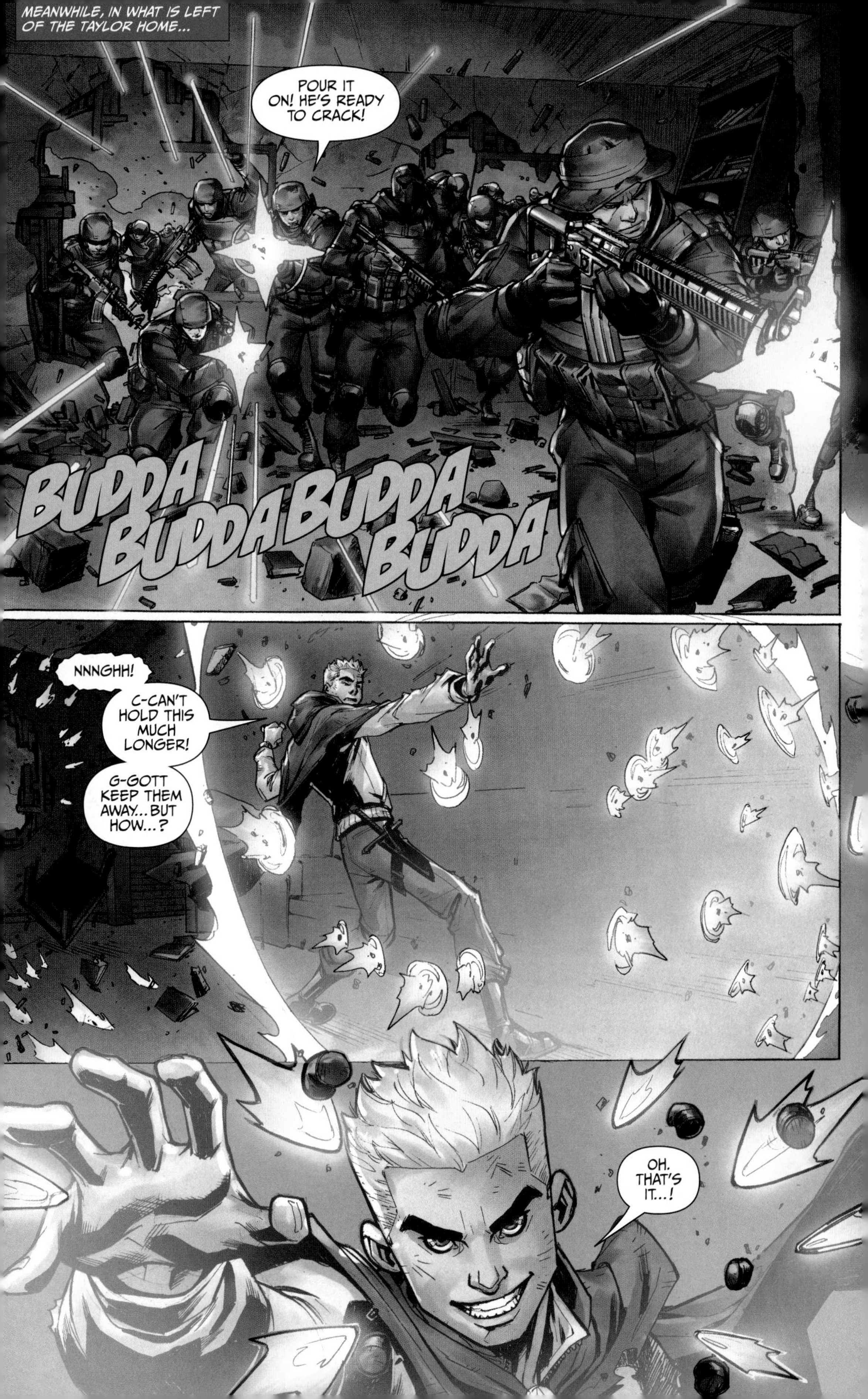
MEANWHILE, IN WHAT IS LEFT OF THE TAYLOR HOME...
POUR IT ON! HE'S READY TO CRACK!
BUDDA BUDDA BUDDA BUDDA
NNNGHH!
C-CAN'T HOLD THIS MUCH LONGER!
G-GOTT KEEP THEM AWAY...BUT HOW...?
OH. THAT'S IT...!

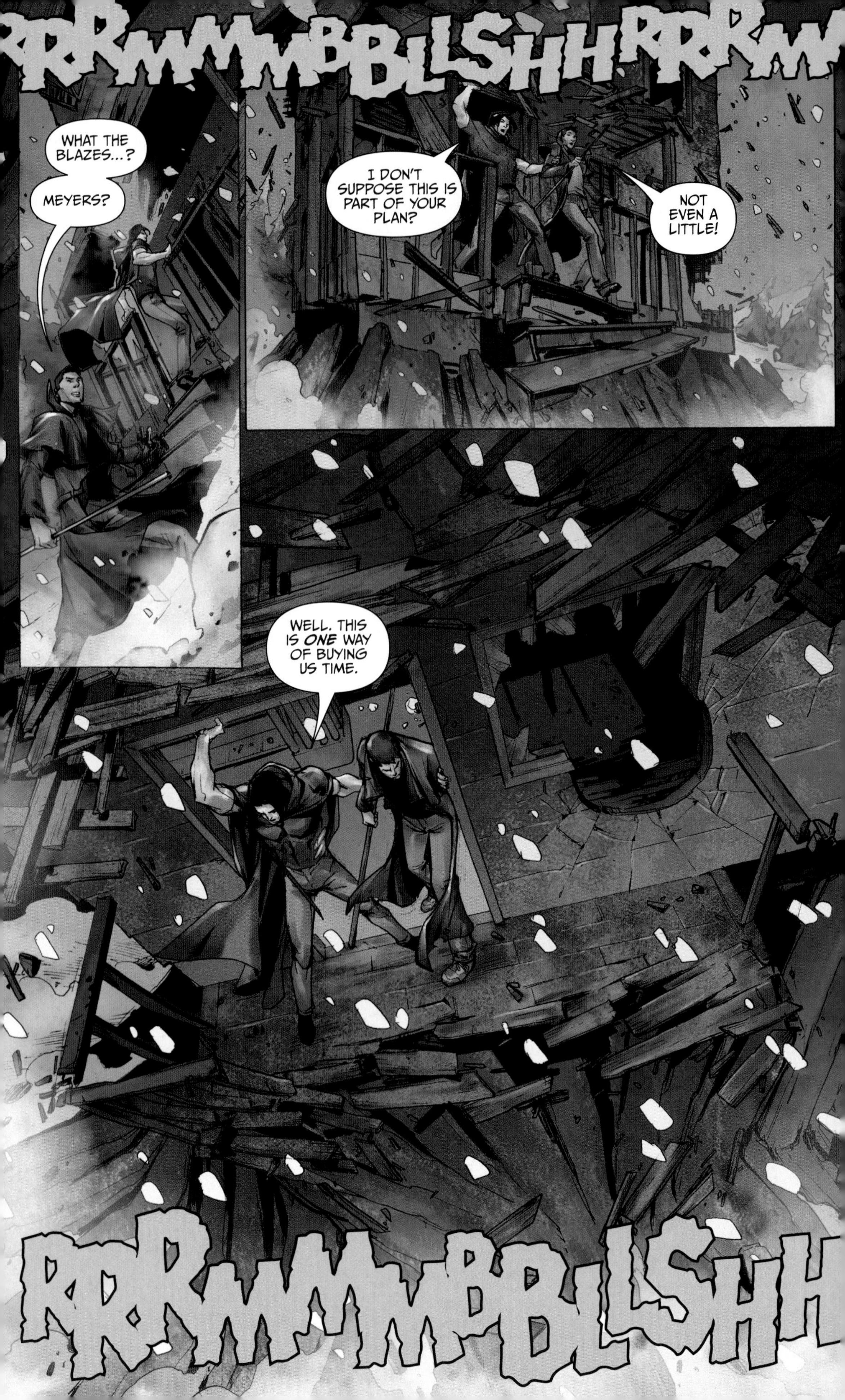
RRRWMMBBLLSHHRRRW
WHAT THE BLAZES...?
MEYERS?
I DON'T SUPPOSE THIS IS PART OF YOUR PLAN?
NOT EVEN A LITTLE!
WELL. THIS IS *ONE* WAY OF BUYING US TIME.
RRRWMMBBLLSHH

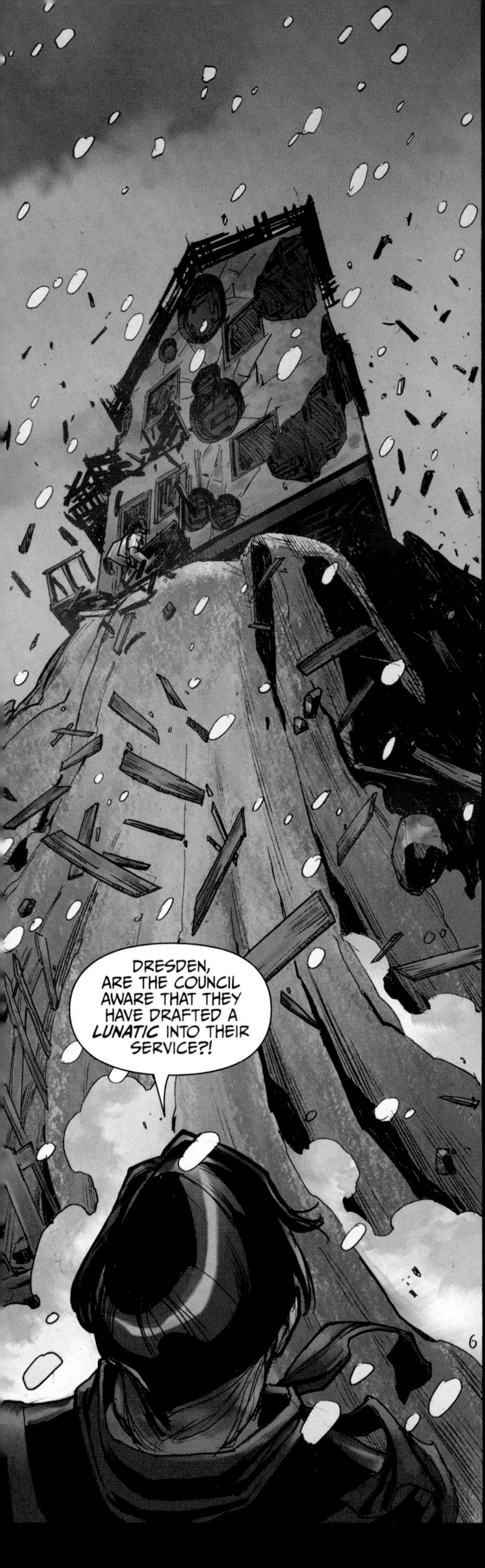
DRESDEN, ARE THE COUNCIL AWARE THAT THEY HAVE DRAFTED A *LUNATIC* INTO THEIR SERVICE?!

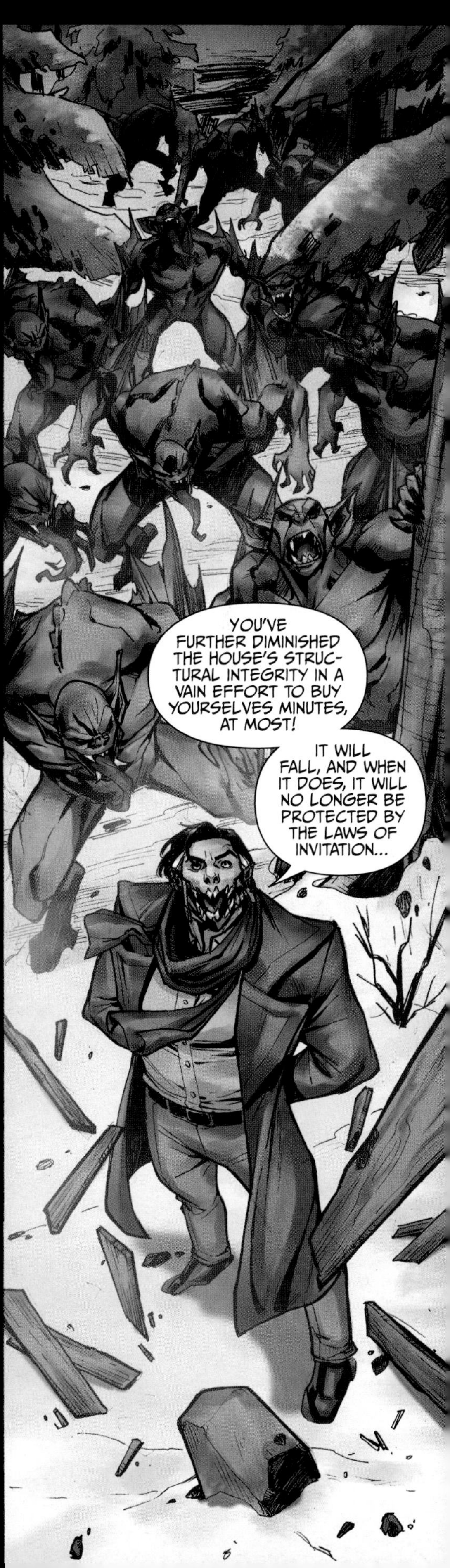
YOU'VE FURTHER DIMINISHED THE HOUSE'S STRUC-TURAL INTEGRITY IN A VAIN EFFORT TO BUY YOURSELVES MINUTES, AT MOST!
IT WILL FALL, AND WHEN IT DOES, IT WILL NO LONGER BE PROTECTED BY THE LAWS OF INVITATION...

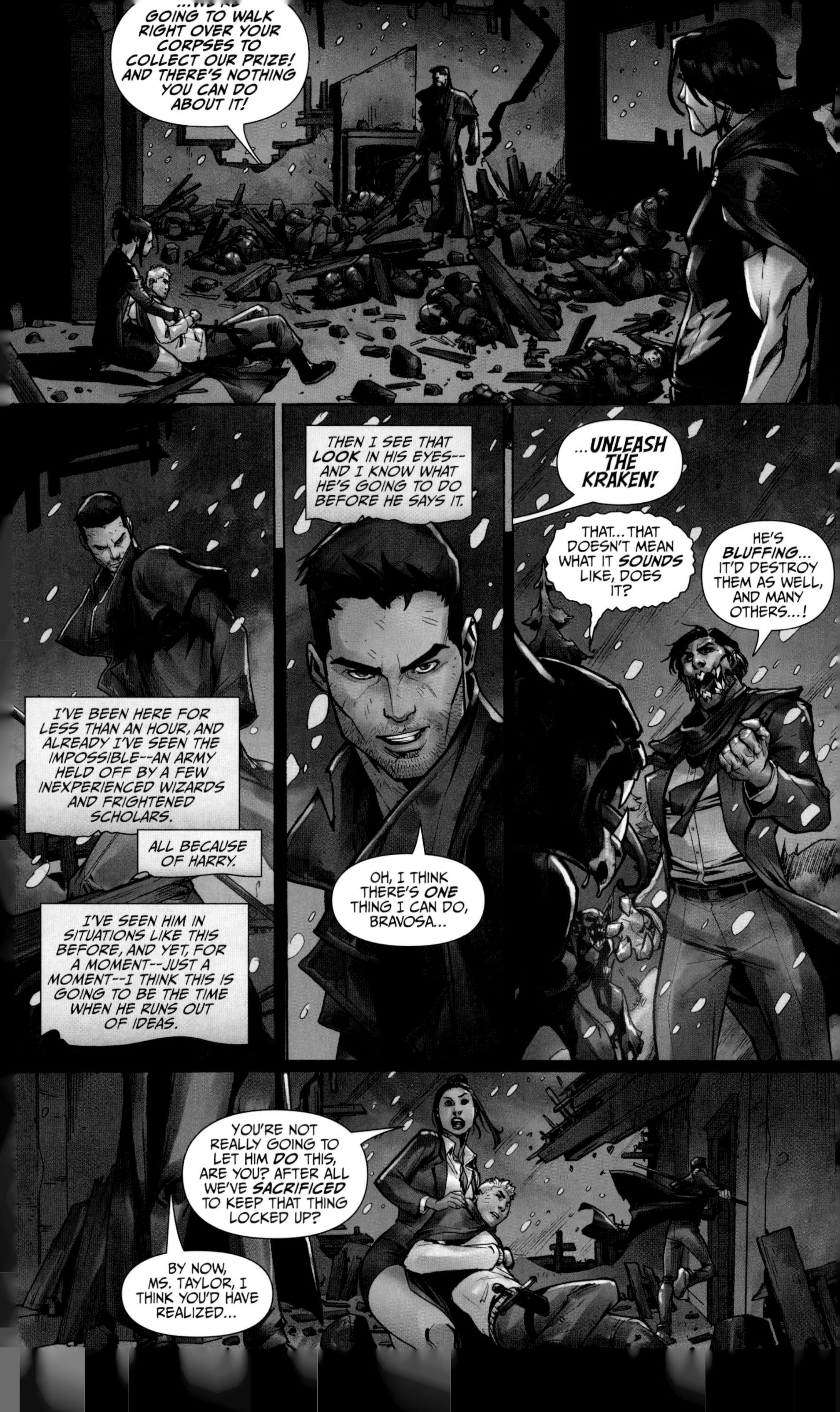
...WE'RE GOING TO WALK RIGHT OVER YOUR CORPSES TO COLLECT OUR PRIZE! AND THERE'S NOTHING YOU CAN DO ABOUT IT!
I'VE BEEN HERE FOR LESS THAN AN HOUR, AND ALREADY I'VE SEEN THE IMPOSSIBLE--AN ARMY HELD OFF BY A FEW INEXPERIENCED WIZARDS AND FRIGHTENED SCHOLARS.
ALL BECAUSE OF HARRY.
I'VE SEEN HIM IN SITUATIONS LIKE THIS BEFORE, AND YET, FOR A MOMENT--JUST A MOMENT--I THINK THIS IS GOING TO BE THE TIME WHEN HE RUNS OUT OF IDEAS.
THEN I SEE THAT LOOK IN HIS EYES-- AND I KNOW WHAT HE'S GOING TO DO BEFORE HE SAYS IT.
OH, I THINK THERE'S ONE THING I CAN DO, BRAVOSA...
...UNLEASH THE KRAKEN!
THAT... THAT DOESN'T MEAN WHAT IT SOUNDS LIKE, DOES IT?
HE'S BLUFFING... IT'D DESTROY THEM AS WELL, AND MANY OTHERS...!
YOU'RE NOT REALLY GOING TO LET HIM DO THIS, ARE YOU? AFTER ALL WE'VE SACRIFICED TO KEEP THAT THING LOCKED UP?
BY NOW, MS. TAYLOR, I THINK YOU'D HAVE REALIZED...

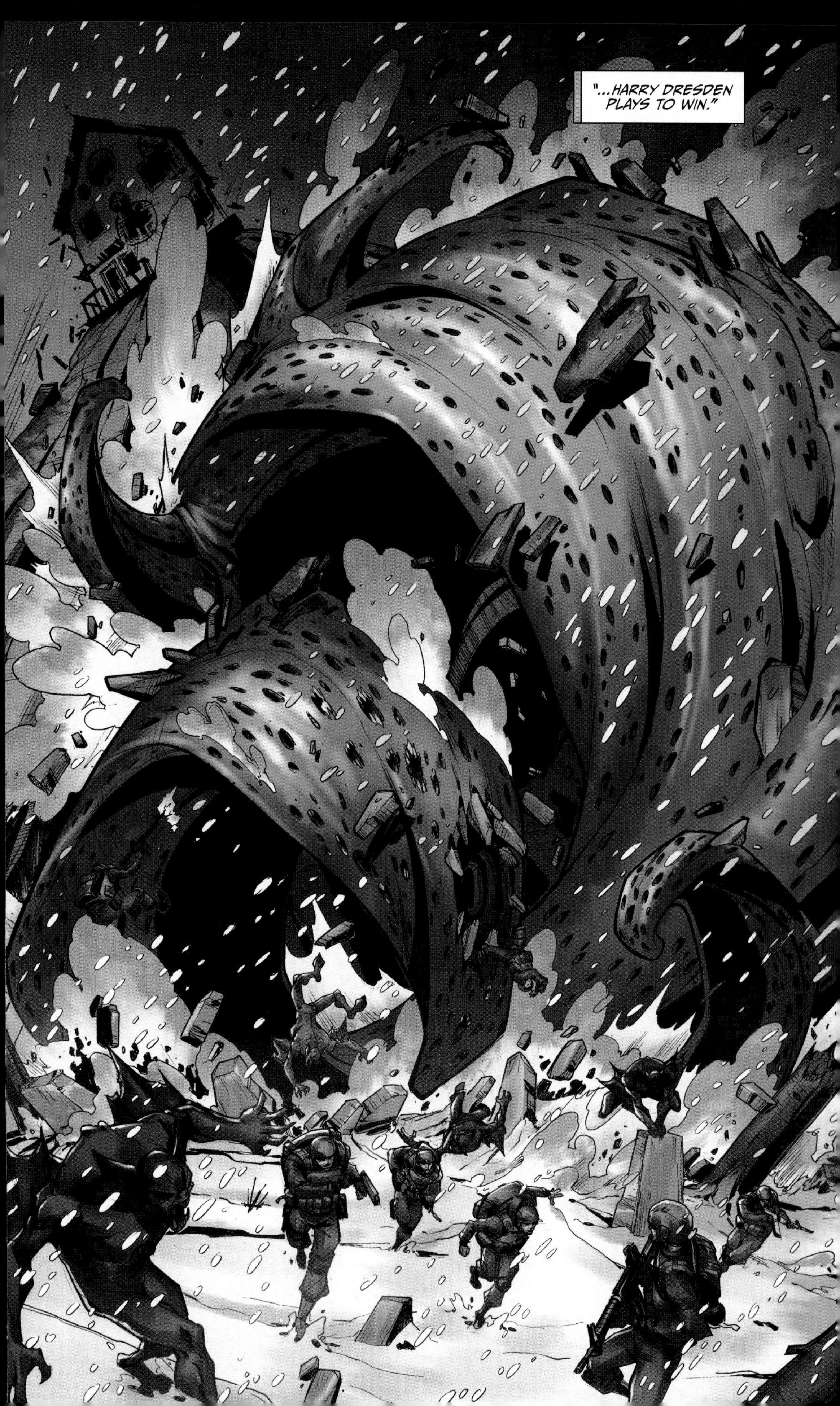
"...HARRY DRESDEN PLAYS TO WIN."

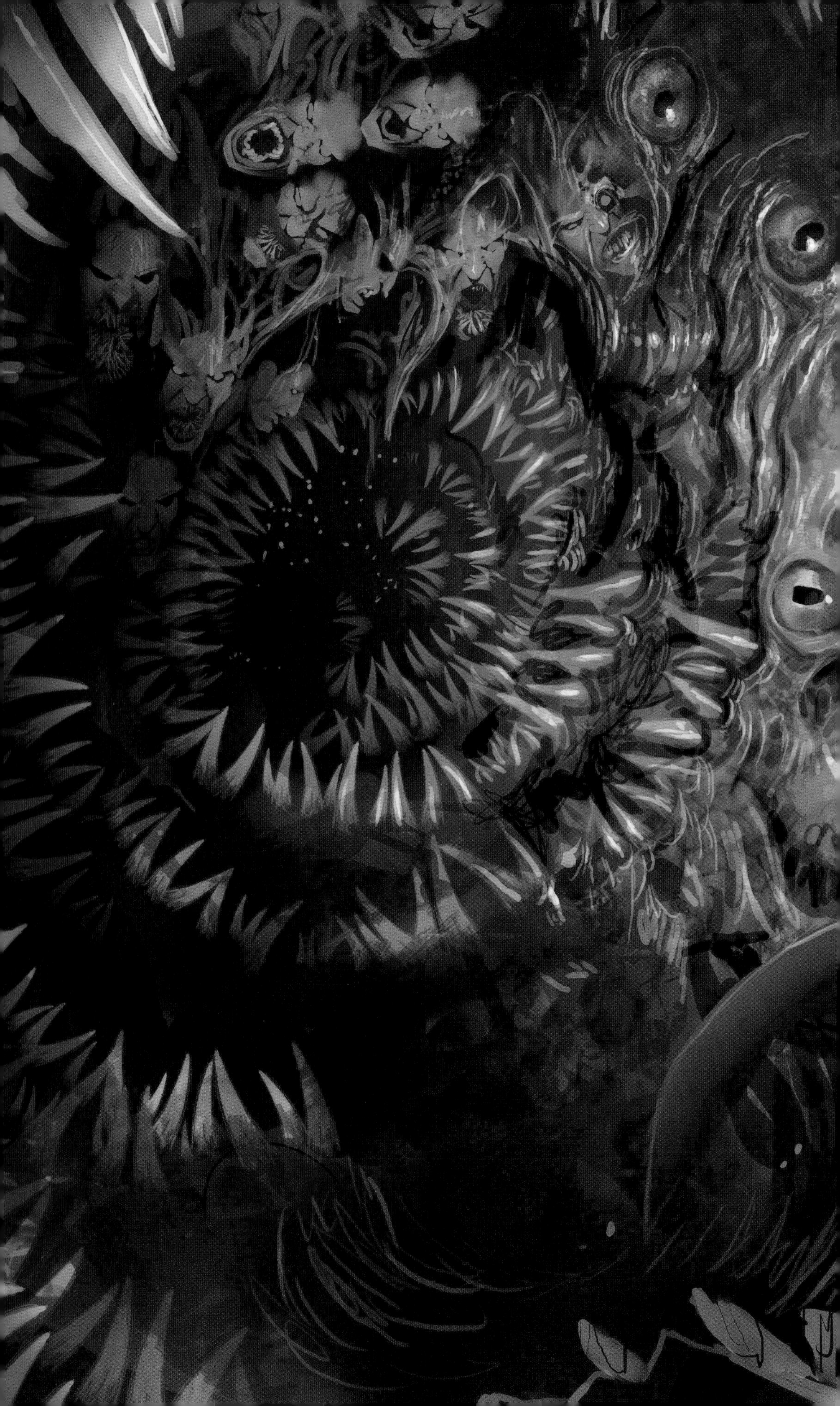

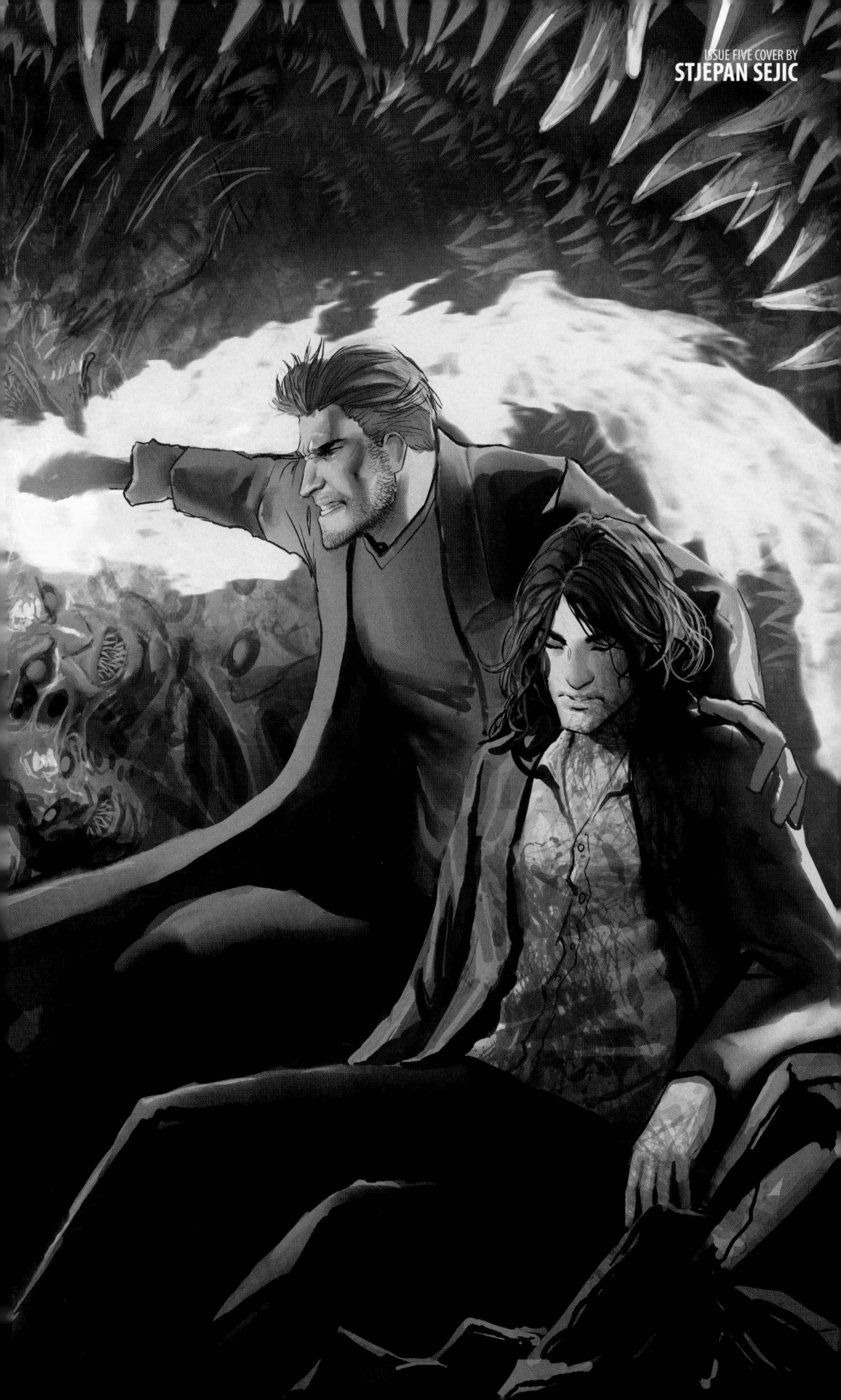
ISSUE FIVE COVER BY
STJEPAN SEJIC

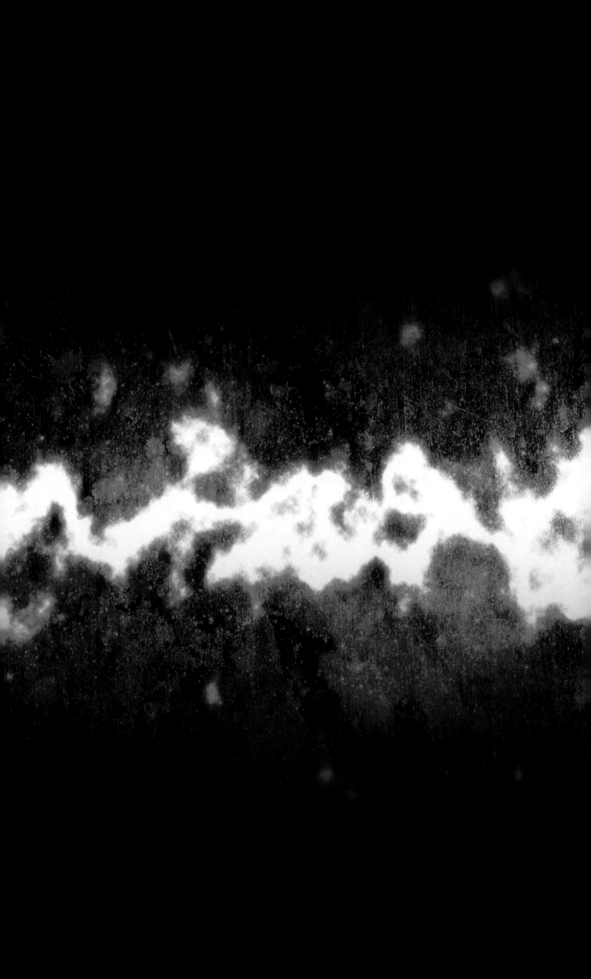

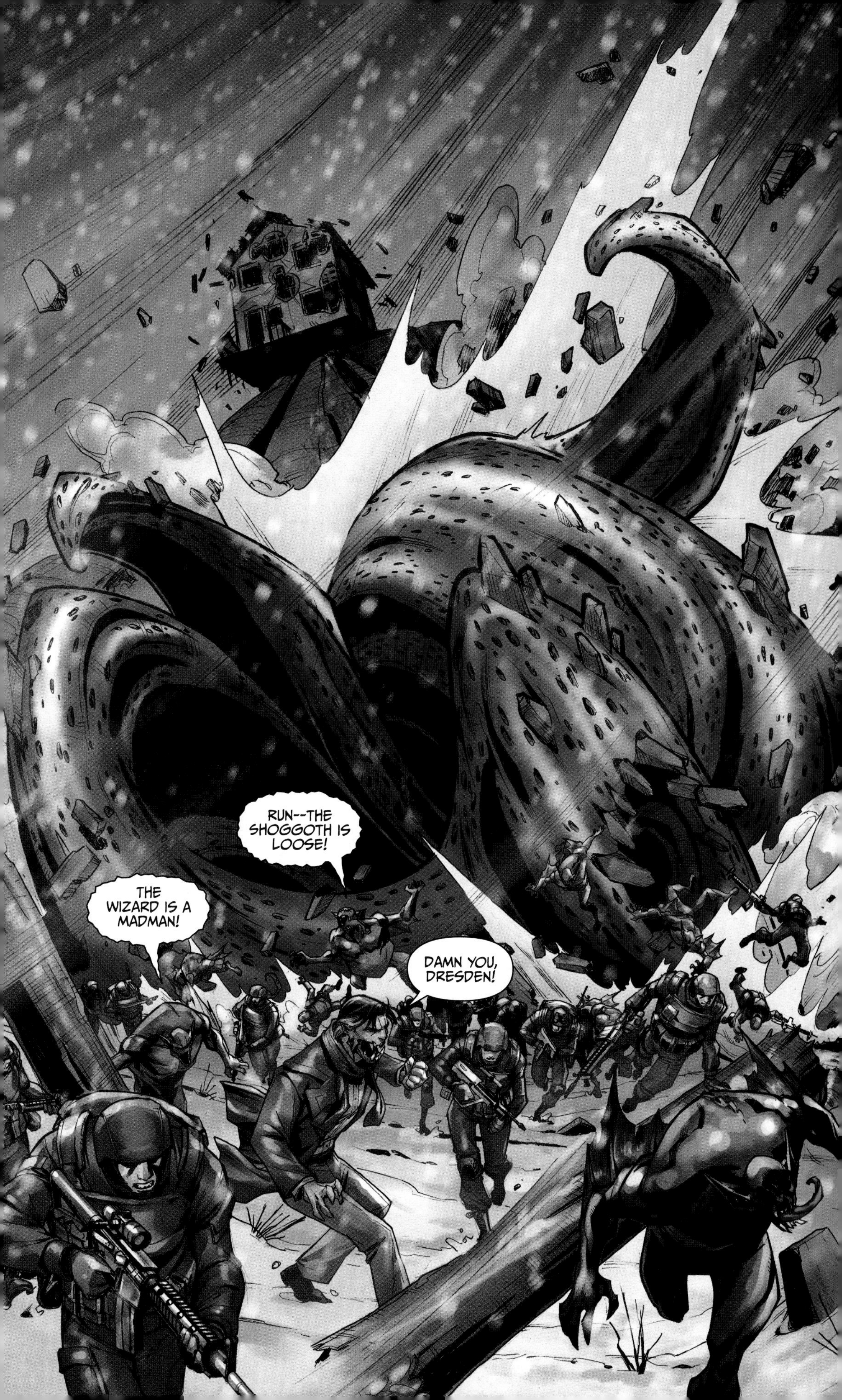
RUN--THE SHOGGOTH IS LOOSE!
THE WIZARD IS A MADMAN!
DAMN YOU, DRESDEN!

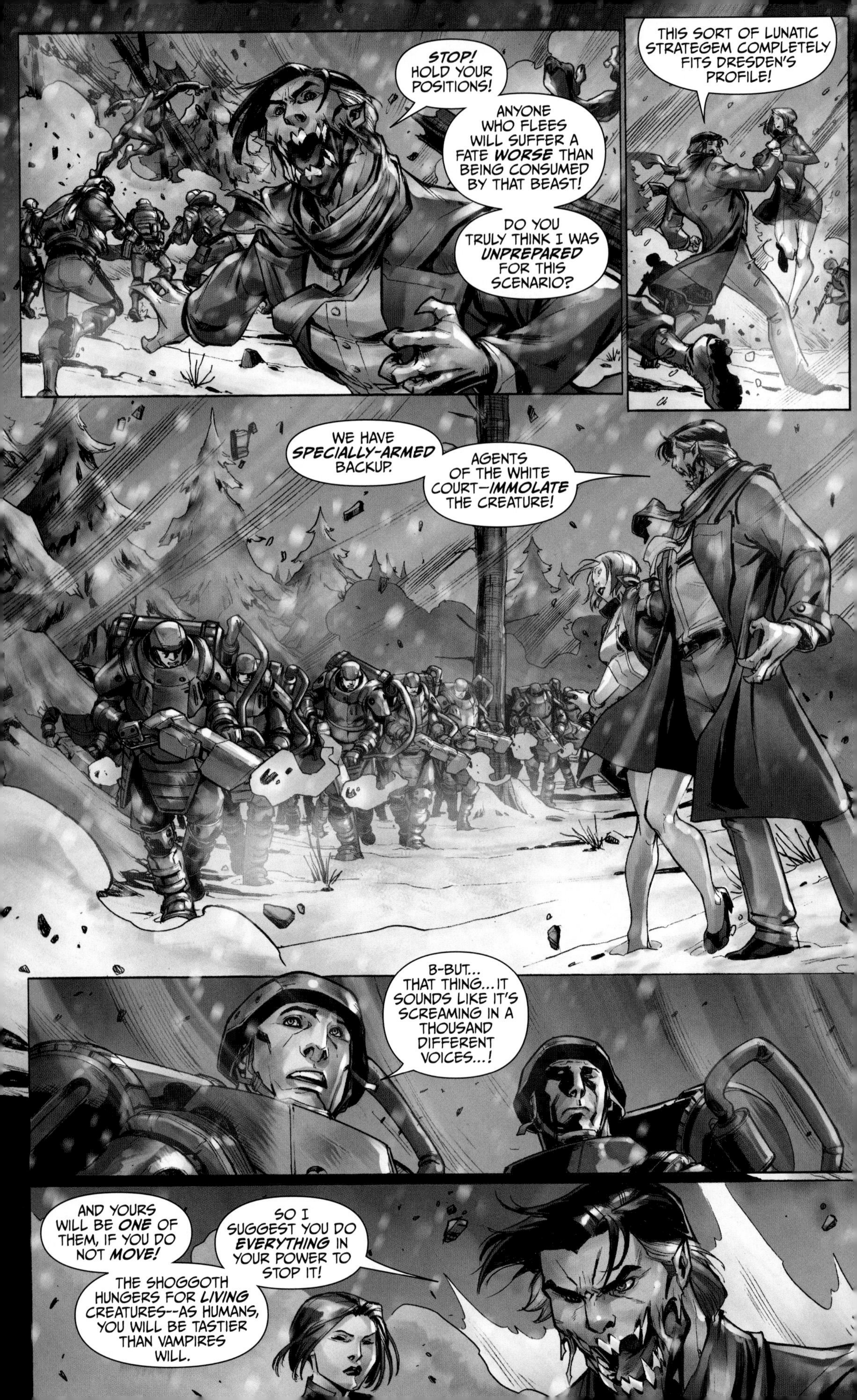
STOP! HOLD YOUR POSITIONS!
ANYONE WHO FLEES WILL SUFFER A FATE WORSE THAN BEING CONSUMED BY THAT BEAST!
DO YOU TRULY THINK I WAS UNPREPARED FOR THIS SCENARIO?
THIS SORT OF LUNATIC STRATEGEM COMPLETELY FITS DRESDEN'S PROFILE!
WE HAVE SPECIALLY-ARMED BACKUP.
AGENTS OF THE WHITE COURT—IMMOLATE THE CREATURE!
B-BUT... THAT THING... IT SOUNDS LIKE IT'S SCREAMING IN A THOUSAND DIFFERENT VOICES...!
AND YOURS WILL BE ONE OF THEM, IF YOU DO NOT MOVE!
THE SHOGGOTH HUNGERS FOR LIVING CREATURES--AS HUMANS, YOU WILL BE TASTIER THAN VAMPIRES WILL.
SO I SUGGEST YOU DO EVERYTHING IN YOUR POWER TO STOP IT!

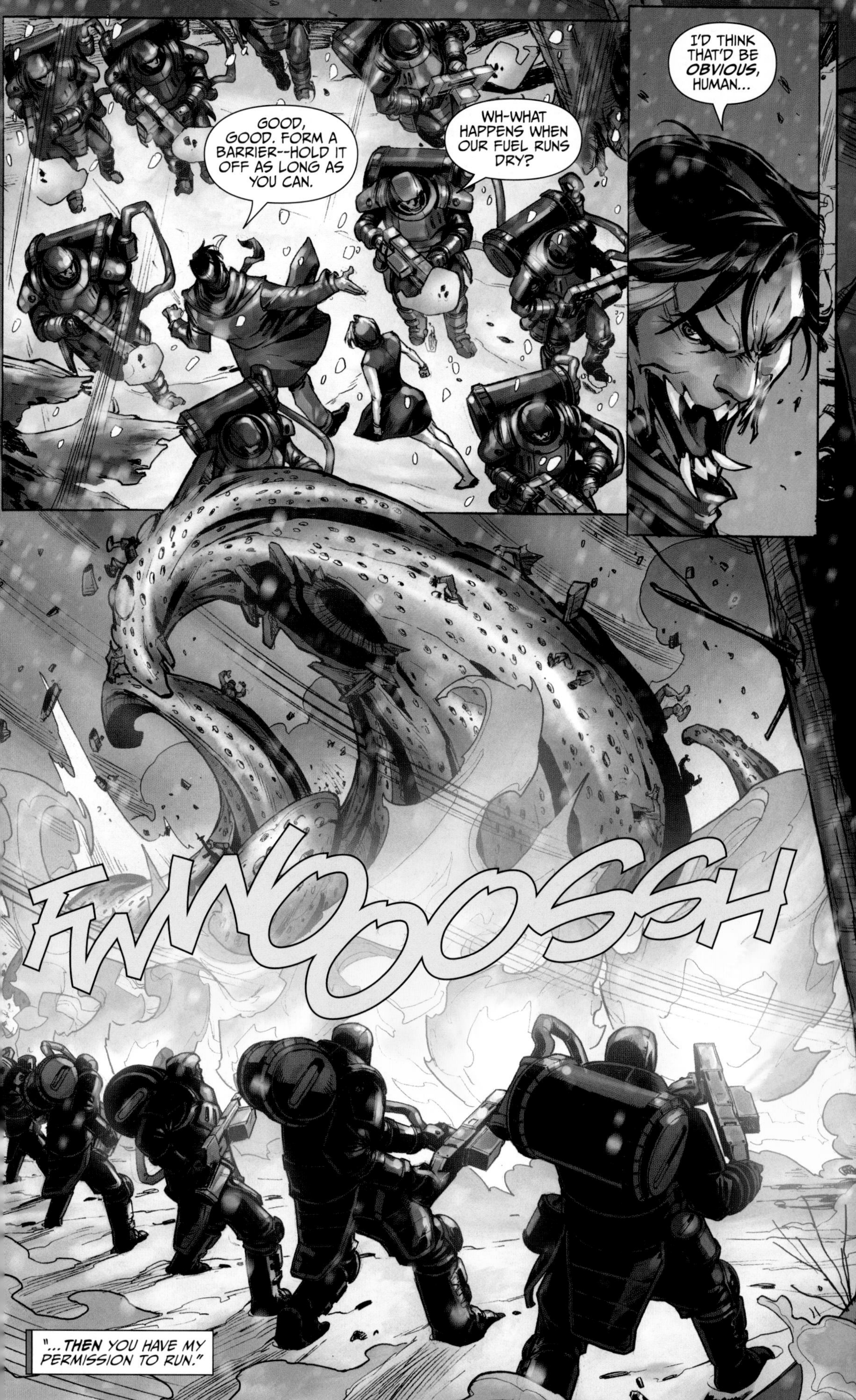
GOOD, GOOD. FORM A BARRIER--HOLD IT OFF AS LONG AS YOU CAN.
WH-WHAT HAPPENS WHEN OUR FUEL RUNS DRY?
I'D THINK THAT'D BE *OBVIOUS*, HUMAN...
FWOOOOSH
"...**THEN** YOU HAVE MY PERMISSION TO RUN."

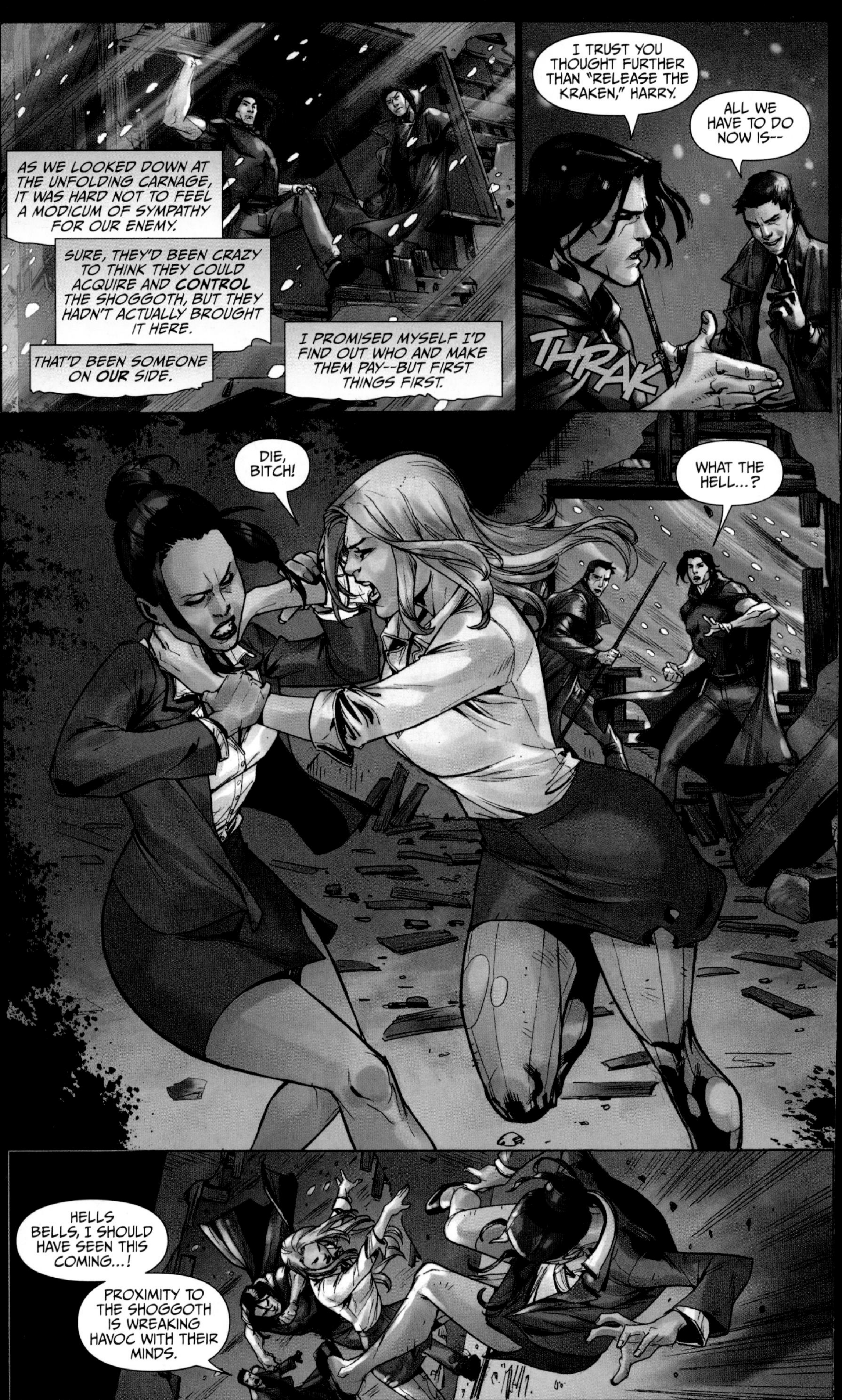
AS WE LOOKED DOWN AT THE UNFOLDING CARNAGE, IT WAS HARD NOT TO FEEL A MODICUM OF SYMPATHY FOR OUR ENEMY.
SURE, THEY'D BEEN CRAZY TO THINK THEY COULD ACQUIRE AND CONTROL THE SHOGGOTH, BUT THEY HADN'T ACTUALLY BROUGHT IT HERE.
THAT'D BEEN SOMEONE ON OUR SIDE.
I PROMISED MYSELF I'D FIND OUT WHO AND MAKE THEM PAY--BUT FIRST THINGS FIRST.
I TRUST YOU THOUGHT FURTHER THAN "RELEASE THE KRAKEN," HARRY.
ALL WE HAVE TO DO NOW IS--
THRAK
DIE, BITCH!
WHAT THE HELL...?
HELLS BELLS, I SHOULD HAVE SEEN THIS COMING...!
PROXIMITY TO THE SHOGGOTH IS WREAKING HAVOC WITH THEIR MINDS.

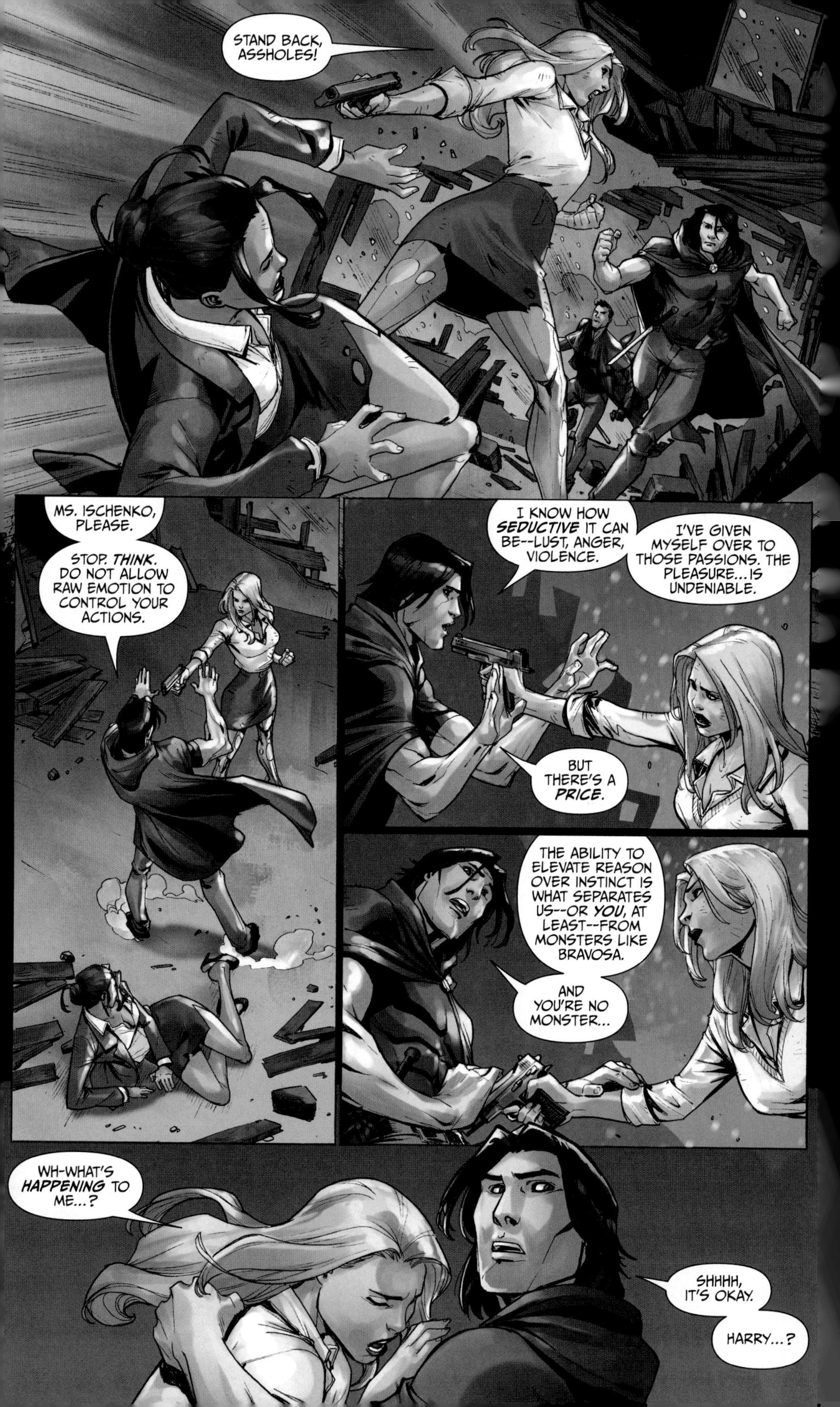

STAND BACK, ASSHOLES!
MS. ISCHENKO, PLEASE.
STOP. *THINK.* DO NOT ALLOW RAW EMOTION TO CONTROL YOUR ACTIONS.
I KNOW HOW *SEDUCTIVE* IT CAN BE--LUST, ANGER, VIOLENCE.
I'VE GIVEN MYSELF OVER TO THOSE PASSIONS. THE PLEASURE... IS UNDENIABLE.
BUT THERE'S A *PRICE*.
THE ABILITY TO ELEVATE REASON OVER INSTINCT IS WHAT SEPARATES US--OR *YOU*, AT LEAST--FROM MONSTERS LIKE BRAVOSA.
AND YOU'RE NO MONSTER...
WH-WHAT'S *HAPPENING* TO ME...?
SHHHH, IT'S OKAY.
HARRY...?

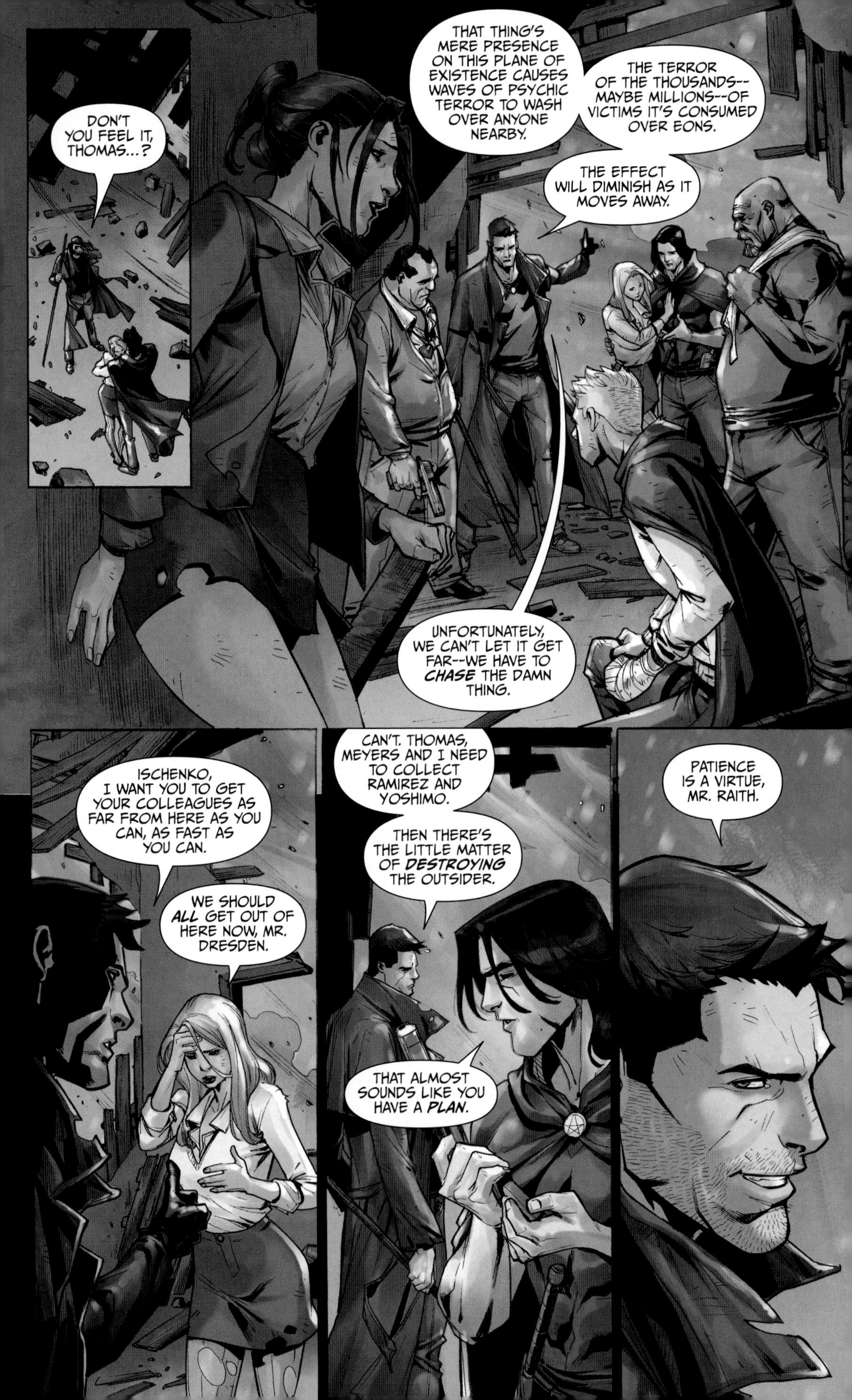
DON'T YOU FEEL IT, THOMAS...?
THAT THING'S MERE PRESENCE ON THIS PLANE OF EXISTENCE CAUSES WAVES OF PSYCHIC TERROR TO WASH OVER ANYONE NEARBY.
THE TERROR OF THE THOUSANDS--MAYBE MILLIONS--OF VICTIMS IT'S CONSUMED OVER EONS.
THE EFFECT WILL DIMINISH AS IT MOVES AWAY.
UNFORTUNATELY, WE CAN'T LET IT GET FAR--WE HAVE TO *CHASE* THE DAMN THING.
ISCHENKO, I WANT YOU TO GET YOUR COLLEAGUES AS FAR FROM HERE AS YOU CAN, AS FAST AS YOU CAN.
WE SHOULD *ALL* GET OUT OF HERE NOW, MR. DRESDEN.
CAN'T. THOMAS, MEYERS AND I NEED TO COLLECT RAMIREZ AND YOSHIMO.
THEN THERE'S THE LITTLE MATTER OF *DESTROYING* THE OUTSIDER.
THAT ALMOST SOUNDS LIKE YOU HAVE A *PLAN*.
PATIENCE IS A VIRTUE, MR. RAITH.

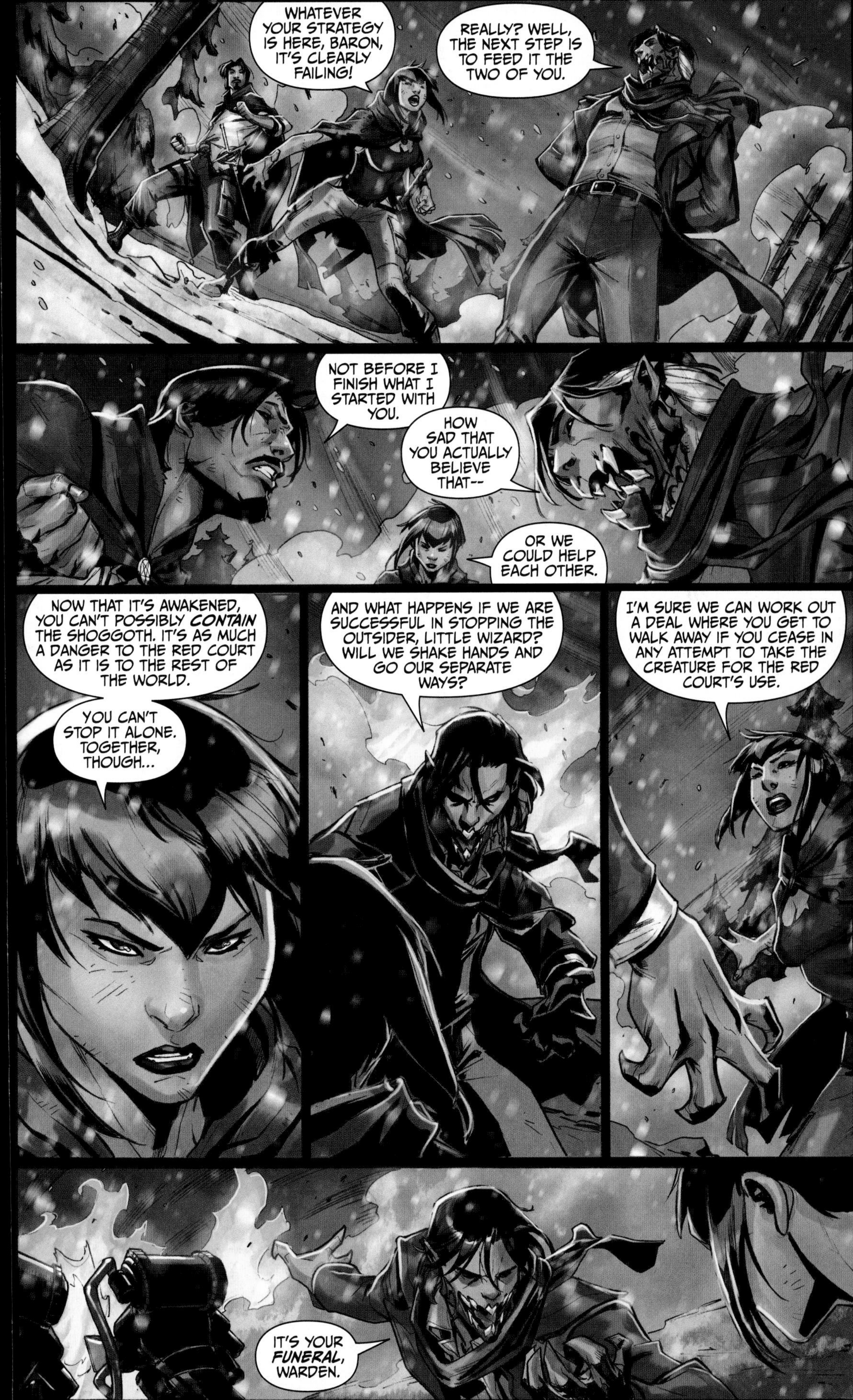
WHATEVER YOUR STRATEGY IS HERE, BARON, IT'S CLEARLY FAILING!
REALLY? WELL, THE NEXT STEP IS TO FEED IT THE TWO OF YOU.
NOT BEFORE I FINISH WHAT I STARTED WITH YOU.
HOW SAD THAT YOU ACTUALLY BELIEVE THAT--
OR WE COULD HELP EACH OTHER.
NOW THAT IT'S AWAKENED, YOU CAN'T POSSIBLY *CONTAIN* THE SHOGGOTH. IT'S AS MUCH A DANGER TO THE RED COURT AS IT IS TO THE REST OF THE WORLD.
YOU CAN'T STOP IT ALONE. TOGETHER, THOUGH...
AND WHAT HAPPENS IF WE ARE SUCCESSFUL IN STOPPING THE OUTSIDER, LITTLE WIZARD? WILL WE SHAKE HANDS AND GO OUR SEPARATE WAYS?
I'M SURE WE CAN WORK OUT A DEAL WHERE YOU GET TO WALK AWAY IF YOU CEASE IN ANY ATTEMPT TO TAKE THE CREATURE FOR THE RED COURT'S USE.
IT'S YOUR *FUNERAL*, WARDEN.

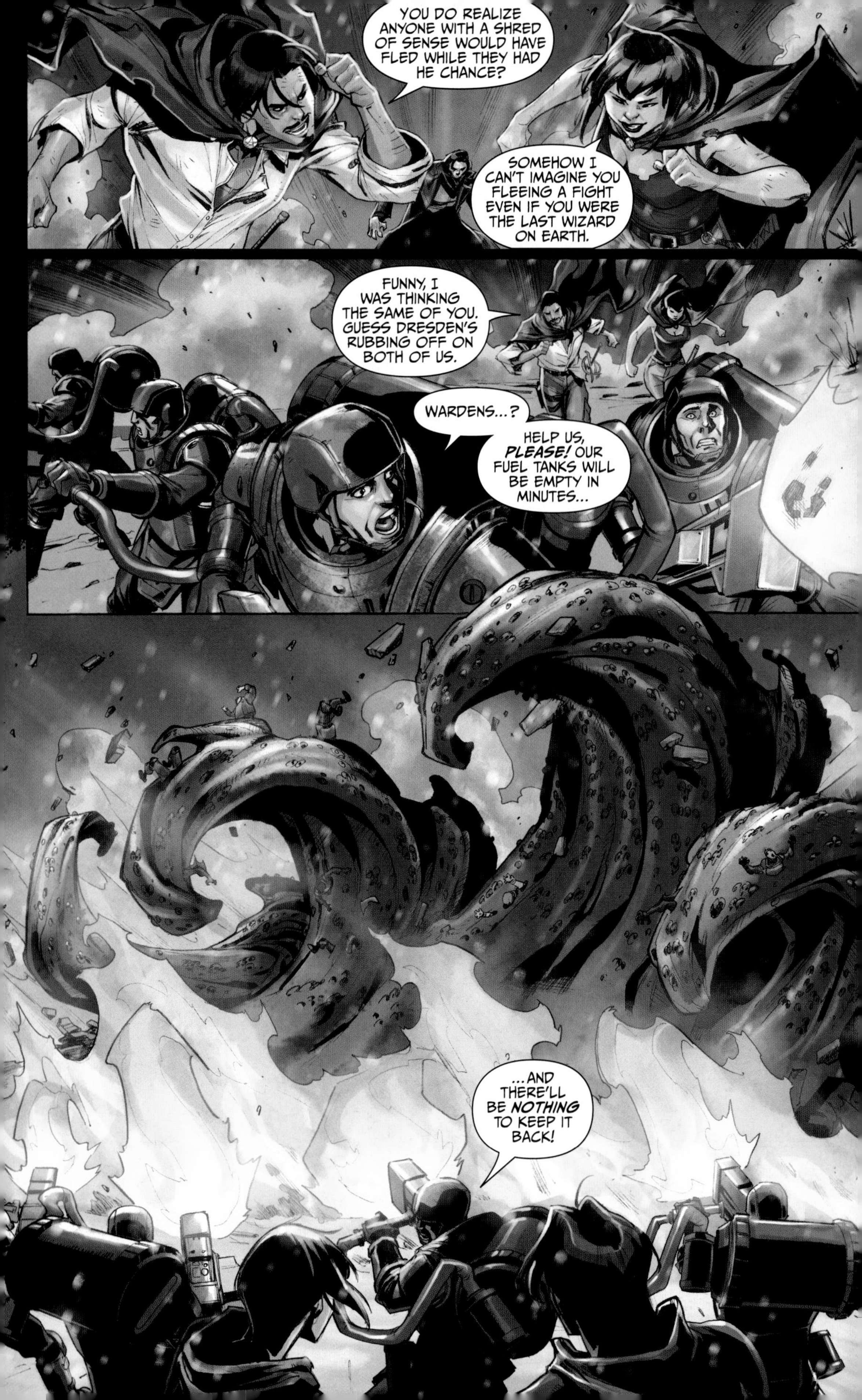
YOU DO REALIZE ANYONE WITH A SHRED OF SENSE WOULD HAVE FLED WHILE THEY HAD HE CHANCE?
SOMEHOW I CAN'T IMAGINE YOU FLEEING A FIGHT EVEN IF YOU WERE THE LAST WIZARD ON EARTH.
FUNNY, I WAS THINKING THE SAME OF YOU. GUESS DRESDEN'S RUBBING OFF ON BOTH OF US.
WARDENS...?
HELP US, ***PLEASE!*** OUR FUEL TANKS WILL BE EMPTY IN MINUTES...
...AND THERE'LL BE ***NOTHING*** TO KEEP IT BACK!

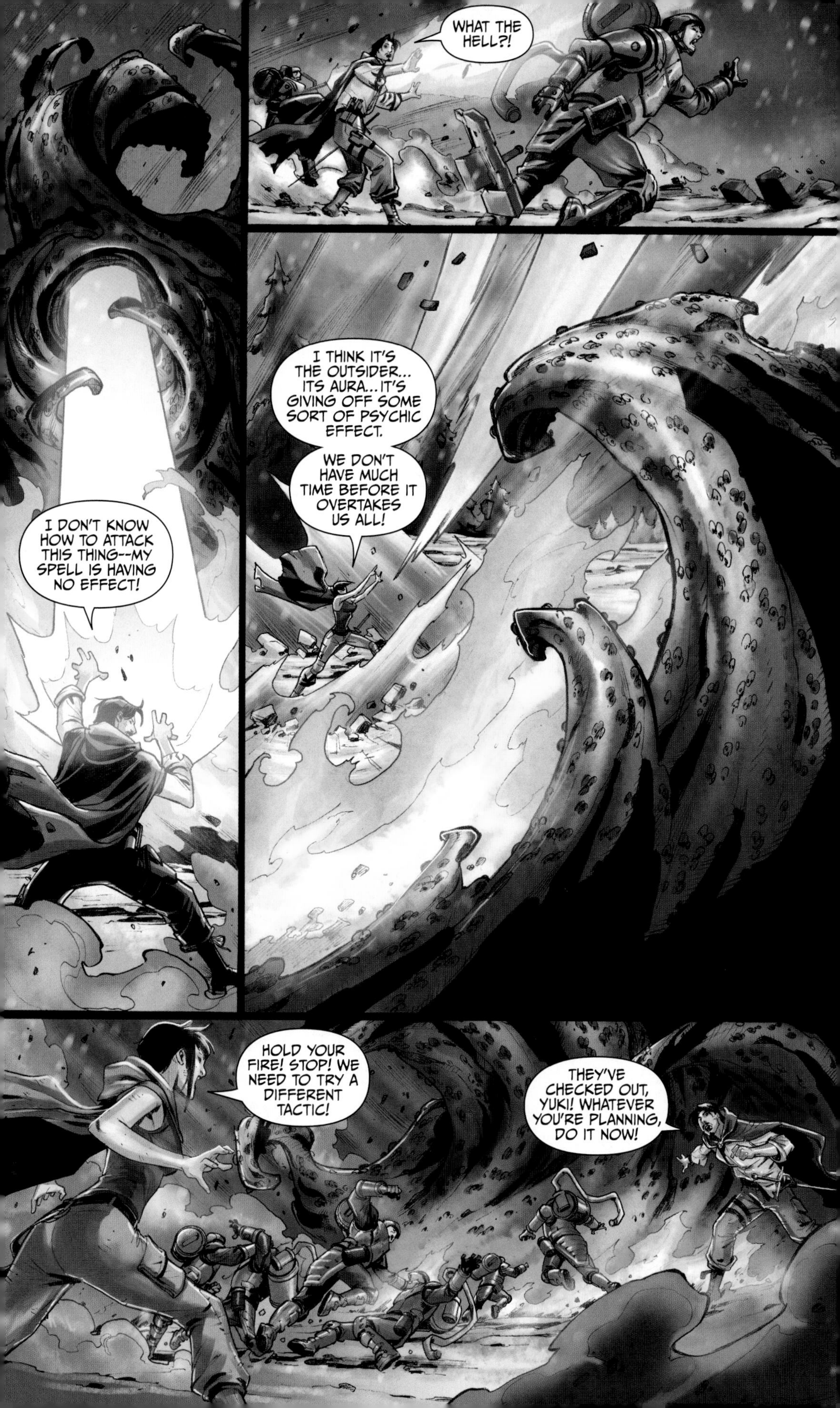
WHAT THE HELL?!
I THINK IT'S THE OUTSIDER... ITS AURA... IT'S GIVING OFF SOME SORT OF PSYCHIC EFFECT.
WE DON'T HAVE MUCH TIME BEFORE IT OVERTAKES US ALL!
I DON'T KNOW HOW TO ATTACK THIS THING--MY SPELL IS HAVING NO EFFECT!
HOLD YOUR FIRE! STOP! WE NEED TO TRY A DIFFERENT TACTIC!
THEY'VE CHECKED OUT, YUKI! WHATEVER YOU'RE PLANNING, DO IT NOW!

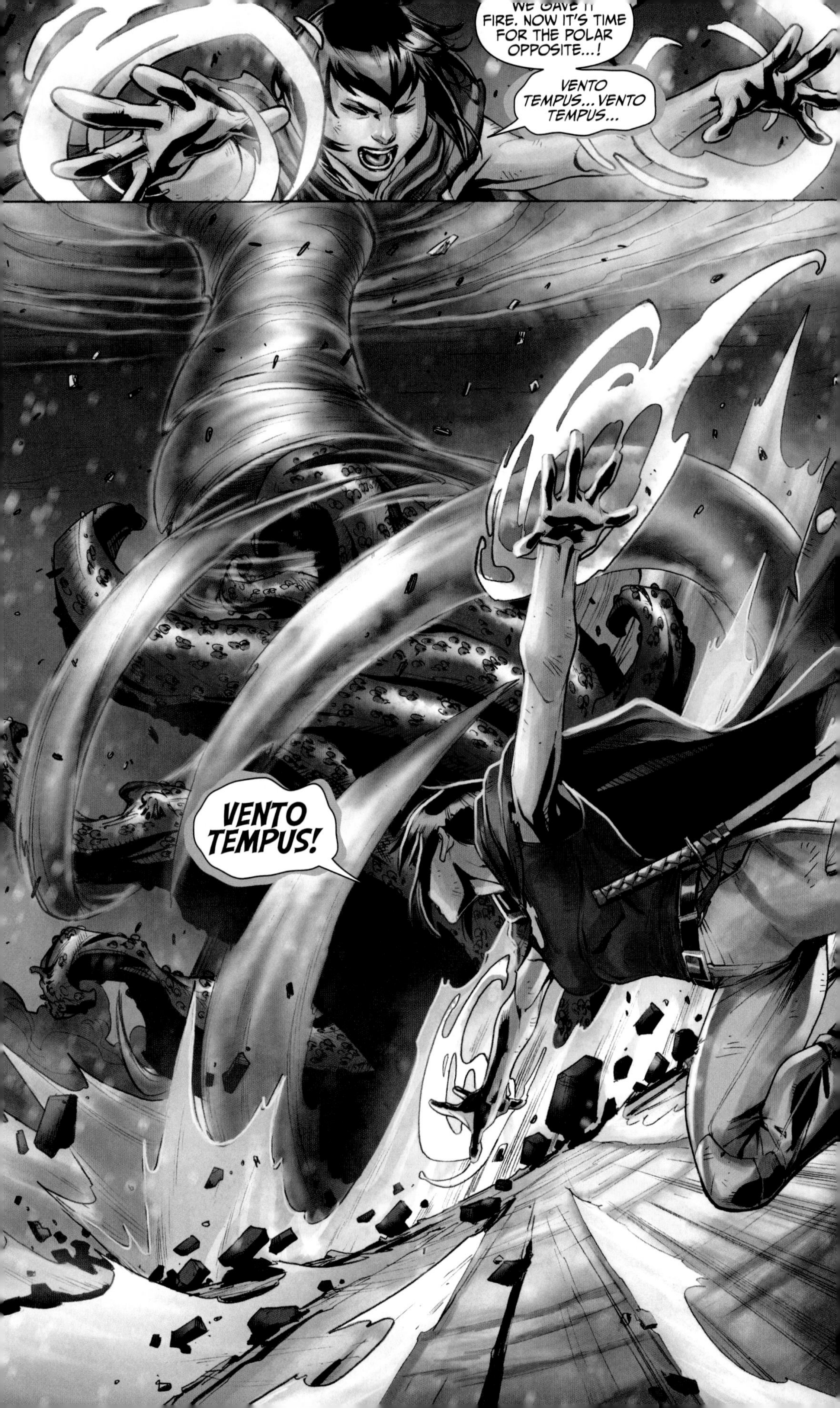
WE GAVE IT FIRE. NOW IT'S TIME FOR THE POLAR OPPOSITE...!
VENTO TEMPUS...VENTO TEMPUS...
VENTO TEMPUS!

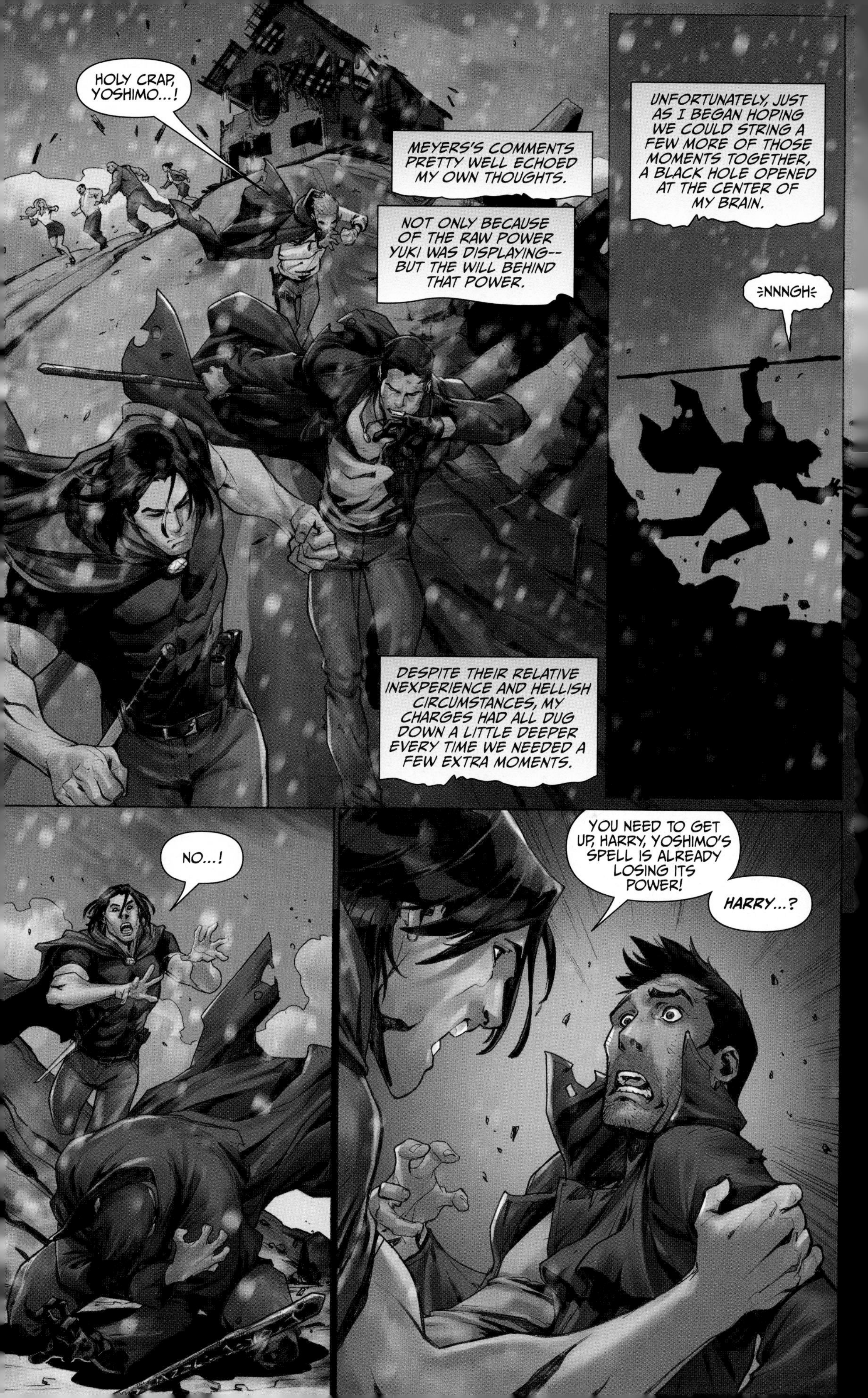
HOLY CRAP, YOSHIMO...!
MEYERS'S COMMENTS PRETTY WELL ECHOED MY OWN THOUGHTS.
NOT ONLY BECAUSE OF THE RAW POWER YUKI WAS DISPLAYING--BUT THE WILL BEHIND THAT POWER.
DESPITE THEIR RELATIVE INEXPERIENCE AND HELLISH CIRCUMSTANCES, MY CHARGES HAD ALL DUG DOWN A LITTLE DEEPER EVERY TIME WE NEEDED A FEW EXTRA MOMENTS.
UNFORTUNATELY, JUST AS I BEGAN HOPING WE COULD STRING A FEW MORE OF THOSE MOMENTS TOGETHER, A BLACK HOLE OPENED AT THE CENTER OF MY BRAIN.
NNNGH
NO...!
YOU NEED TO GET UP, HARRY, YOSHIMO'S SPELL IS ALREADY LOSING ITS POWER!
HARRY...?

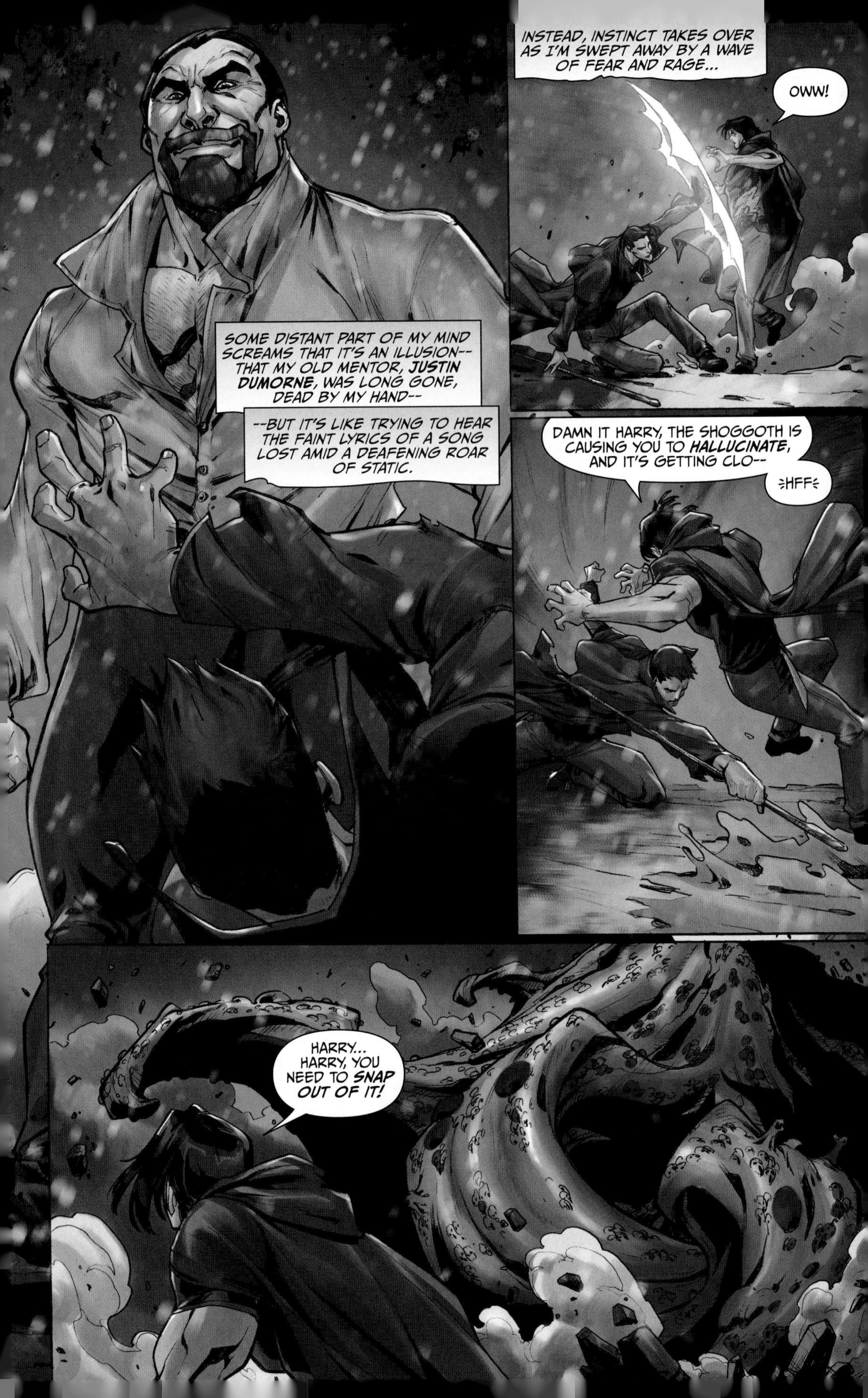

SOME DISTANT PART OF MY MIND SCREAMS THAT IT'S AN ILLUSION--THAT MY OLD MENTOR, JUSTIN DUMORNE, WAS LONG GONE, DEAD BY MY HAND--
--BUT IT'S LIKE TRYING TO HEAR THE FAINT LYRICS OF A SONG LOST AMID A DEAFENING ROAR OF STATIC.
INSTEAD, INSTINCT TAKES OVER AS I'M SWEPT AWAY BY A WAVE OF FEAR AND RAGE...
OWW!
DAMN IT HARRY, THE SHOGGOTH IS CAUSING YOU TO HALLUCINATE, AND IT'S GETTING CLO--
HFF
HARRY... HARRY, YOU NEED TO SNAP OUT OF IT!

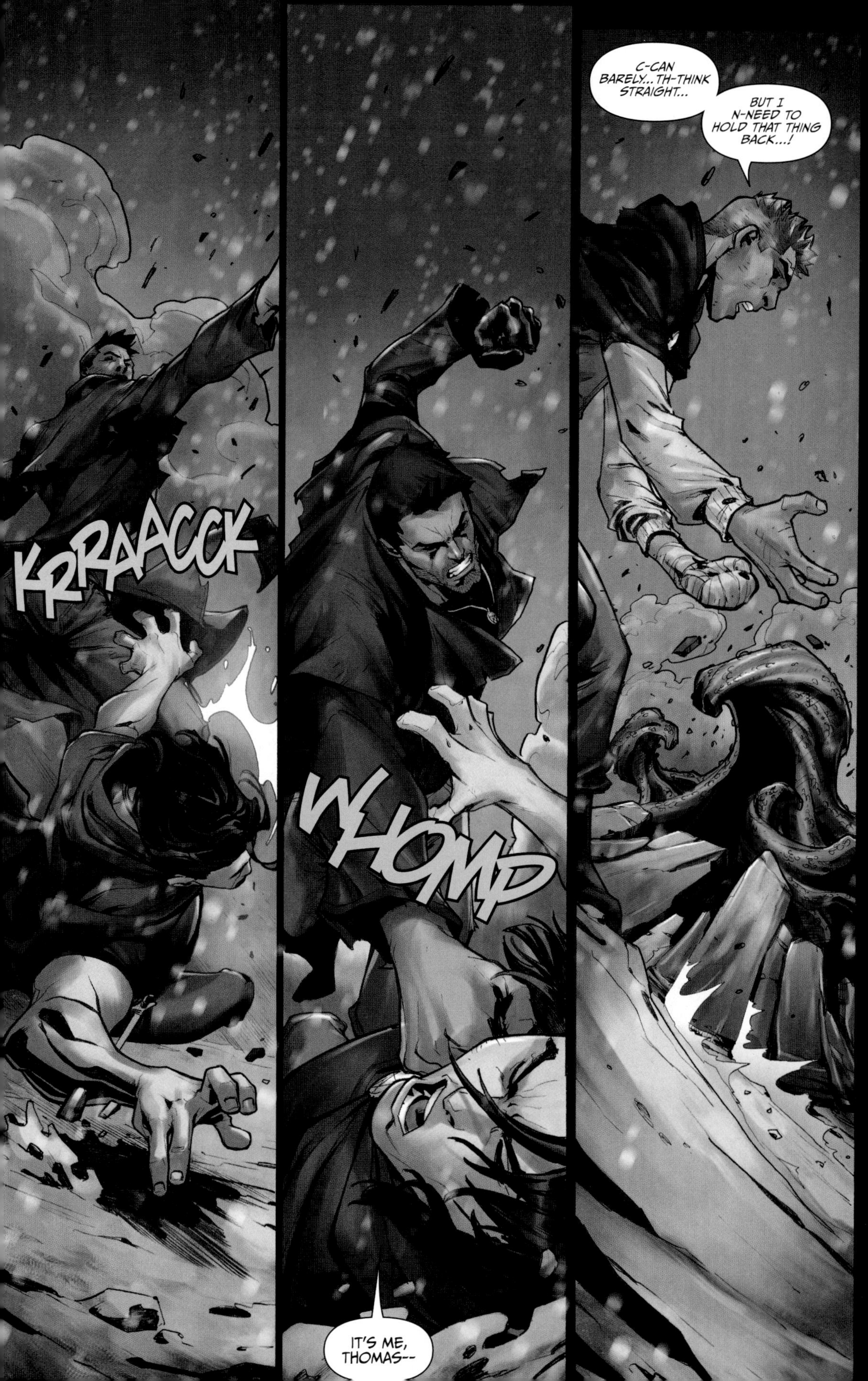
KRRAACCK
WHOMP
IT'S ME, THOMAS--
C-CAN BARELY...TH-THINK STRAIGHT...
BUT I N-NEED TO HOLD THAT THING BACK...!

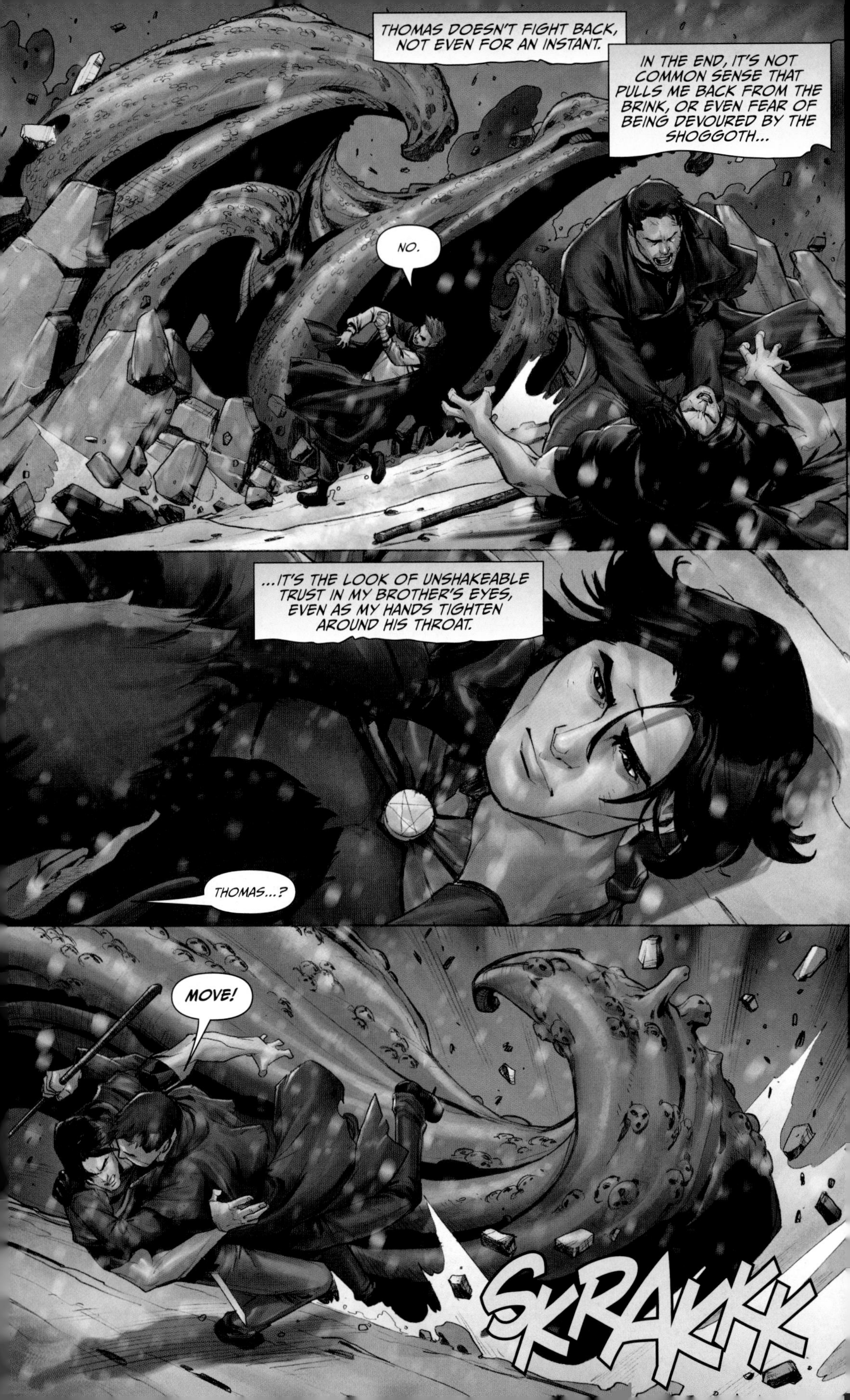
THOMAS DOESN'T FIGHT BACK, NOT EVEN FOR AN INSTANT.
IN THE END, IT'S NOT COMMON SENSE THAT PULLS ME BACK FROM THE BRINK, OR EVEN FEAR OF BEING DEVOURED BY THE SHOGGOTH...
NO.
...IT'S THE LOOK OF UNSHAKEABLE TRUST IN MY BROTHER'S EYES, EVEN AS MY HANDS TIGHTEN AROUND HIS THROAT.
THOMAS...?
MOVE!
SKRAKK

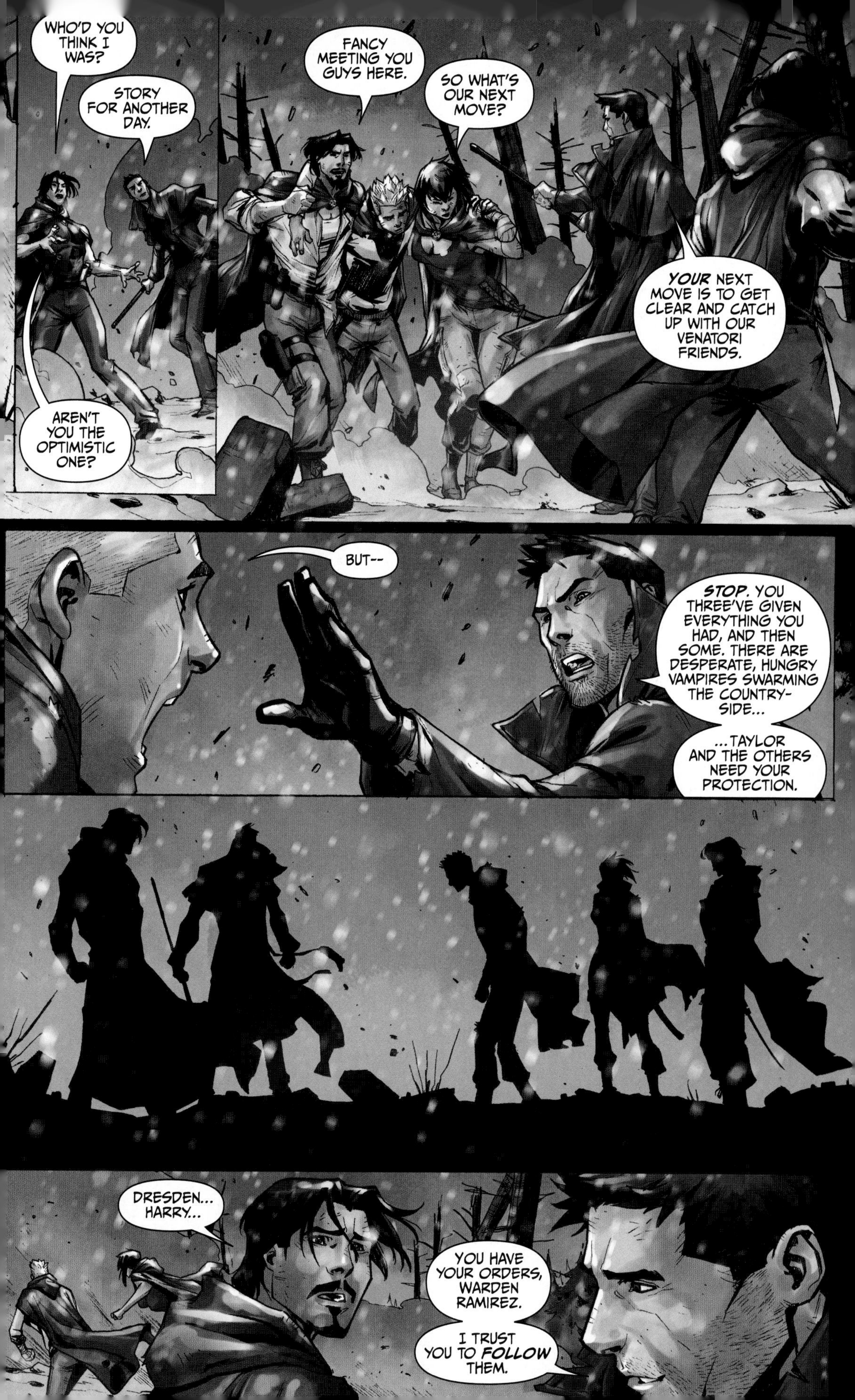
WHO'D YOU THINK I WAS?
STORY FOR ANOTHER DAY.
AREN'T YOU THE OPTIMISTIC ONE?
FANCY MEETING YOU GUYS HERE.
SO WHAT'S OUR NEXT MOVE?
YOUR NEXT MOVE IS TO GET CLEAR AND CATCH UP WITH OUR VENATORI FRIENDS.
BUT--
STOP. YOU THREE'VE GIVEN EVERYTHING YOU HAD, AND THEN SOME. THERE ARE DESPERATE, HUNGRY VAMPIRES SWARMING THE COUNTRY-SIDE...
...TAYLOR AND THE OTHERS NEED YOUR PROTECTION.
DRESDEN... HARRY...
YOU HAVE YOUR ORDERS, WARDEN RAMIREZ.
I TRUST YOU TO FOLLOW THEM.

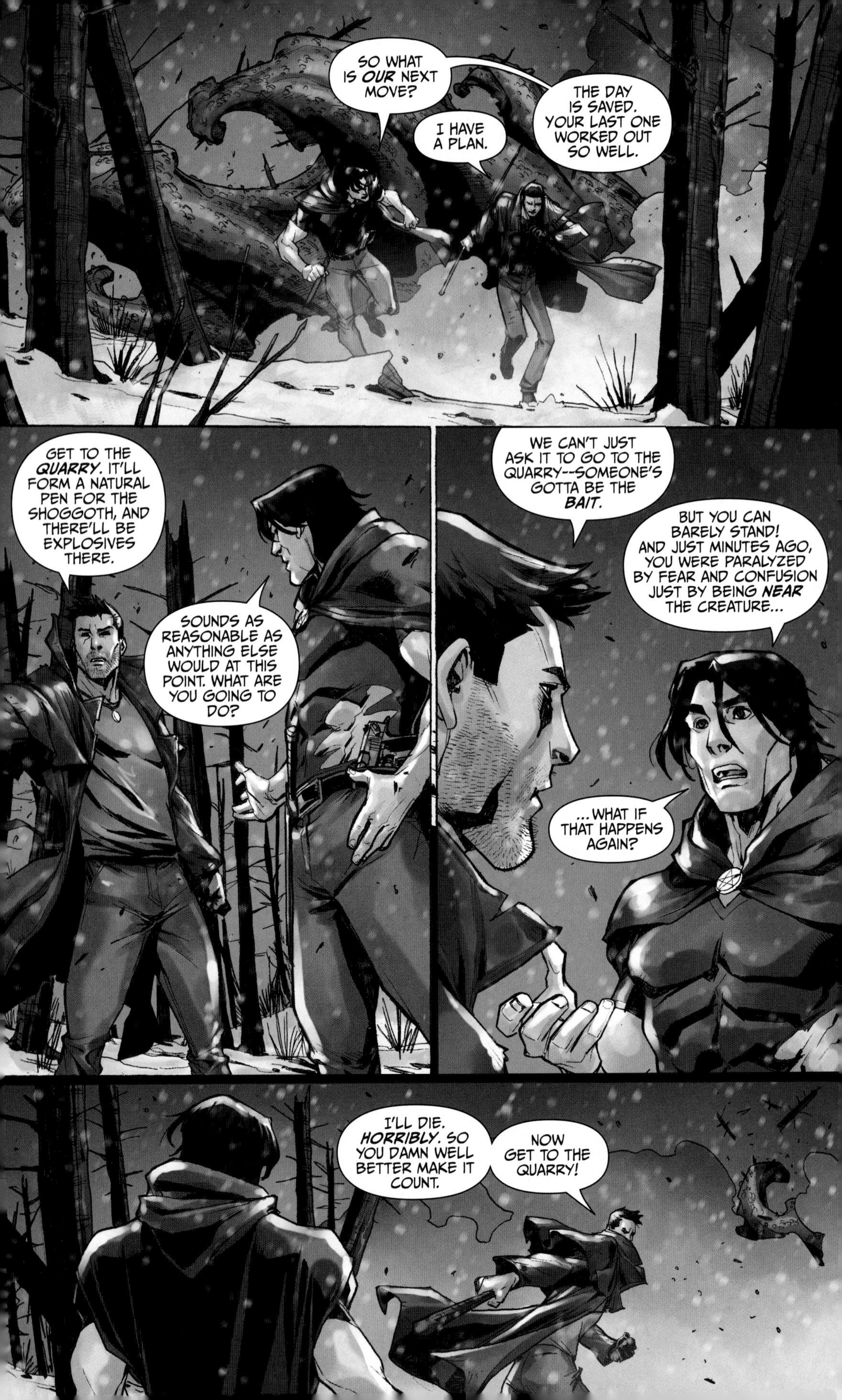
SO WHAT IS OUR NEXT MOVE?
I HAVE A PLAN.
THE DAY IS SAVED. YOUR LAST ONE WORKED OUT SO WELL.
GET TO THE QUARRY. IT'LL FORM A NATURAL PEN FOR THE SHOGGOTH, AND THERE'LL BE EXPLOSIVES THERE.
SOUNDS AS REASONABLE AS ANYTHING ELSE WOULD AT THIS POINT. WHAT ARE YOU GOING TO DO?
WE CAN'T JUST ASK IT TO GO TO THE QUARRY--SOMEONE'S GOTTA BE THE BAIT.
BUT YOU CAN BARELY STAND! AND JUST MINUTES AGO, YOU WERE PARALYZED BY FEAR AND CONFUSION JUST BY BEING NEAR THE CREATURE...
...WHAT IF THAT HAPPENS AGAIN?
I'LL DIE. HORRIBLY. SO YOU DAMN WELL BETTER MAKE IT COUNT.
NOW GET TO THE QUARRY!

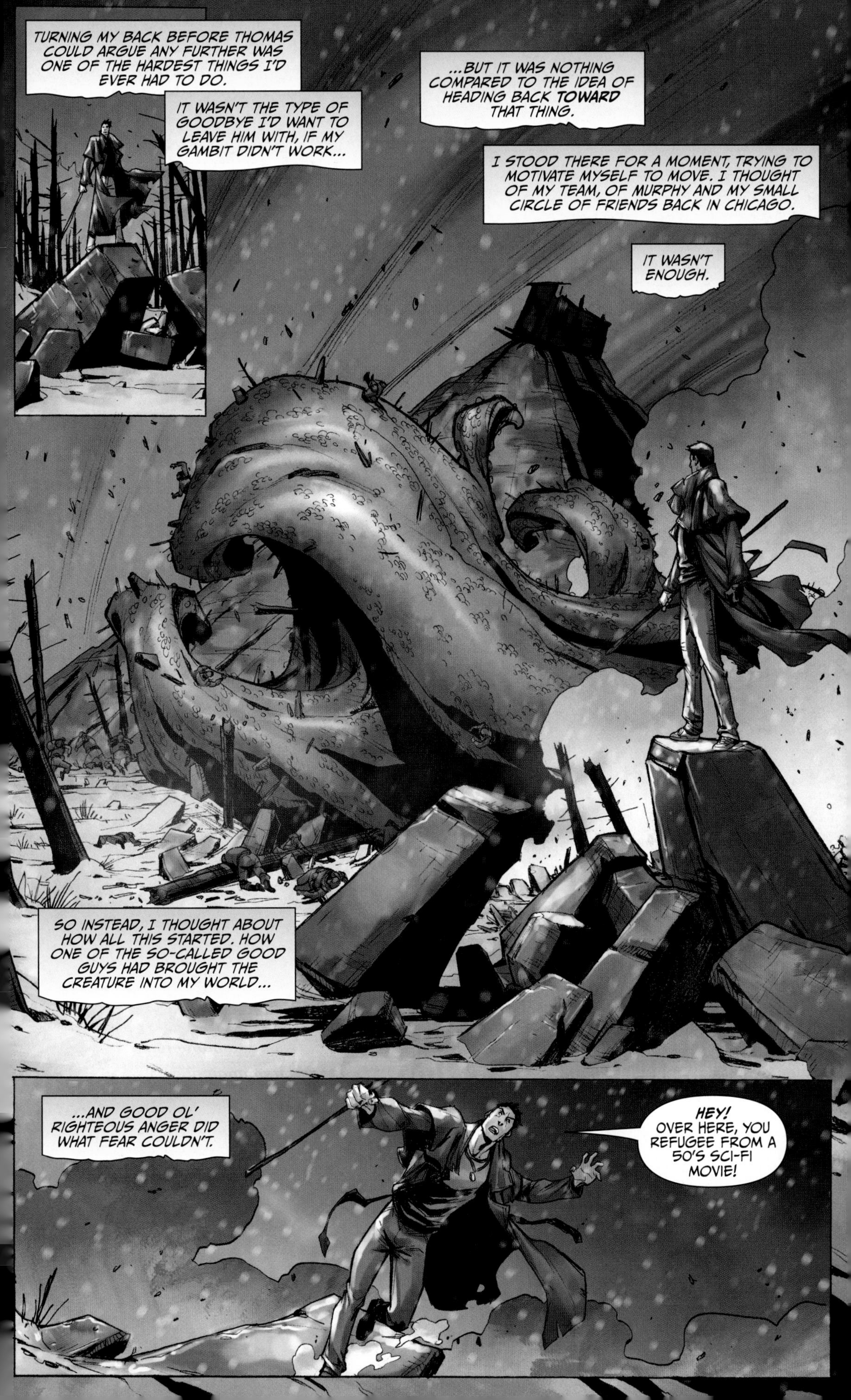
TURNING MY BACK BEFORE THOMAS COULD ARGUE ANY FURTHER WAS ONE OF THE HARDEST THINGS I'D EVER HAD TO DO.
IT WASN'T THE TYPE OF GOODBYE I'D WANT TO LEAVE HIM WITH, IF MY GAMBIT DIDN'T WORK...
...BUT IT WAS NOTHING COMPARED TO THE IDEA OF HEADING BACK **TOWARD** THAT THING.
I STOOD THERE FOR A MOMENT, TRYING TO MOTIVATE MYSELF TO MOVE. I THOUGHT OF MY TEAM, OF MURPHY AND MY SMALL CIRCLE OF FRIENDS BACK IN CHICAGO.
IT WASN'T ENOUGH.
SO INSTEAD, I THOUGHT ABOUT HOW ALL THIS STARTED. HOW ONE OF THE SO-CALLED GOOD GUYS HAD BROUGHT THE CREATURE INTO MY WORLD...
...AND GOOD OL' RIGHTEOUS ANGER DID WHAT FEAR COULDN'T.
HEY! OVER HERE, YOU REFUGEE FROM A 50'S SCI-FI MOVIE!

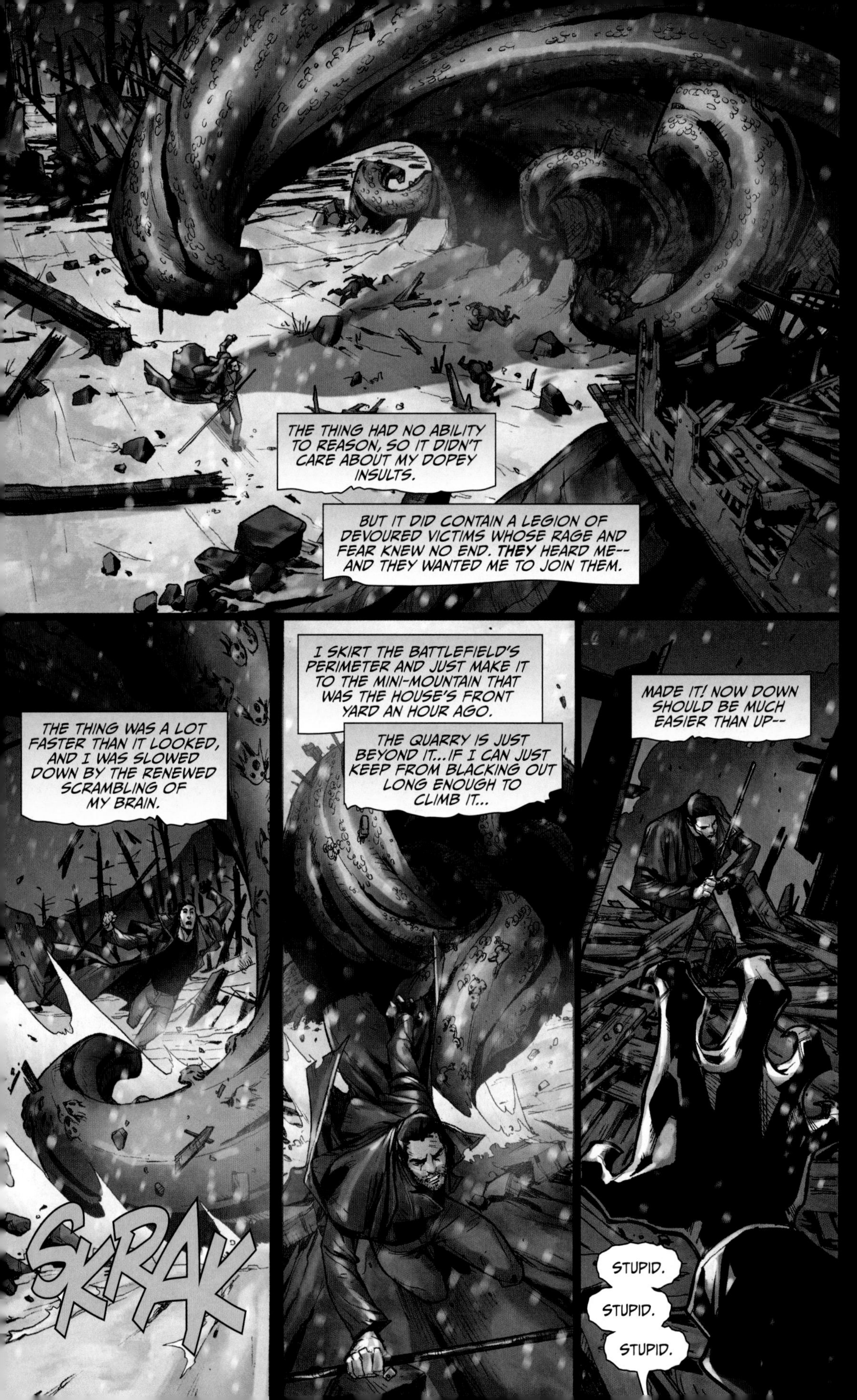
THE THING HAD NO ABILITY TO REASON, SO IT DIDN'T CARE ABOUT MY DOPEY INSULTS.
BUT IT DID CONTAIN A LEGION OF DEVOURED VICTIMS WHOSE RAGE AND FEAR KNEW NO END. THEY HEARD ME-- AND THEY WANTED ME TO JOIN THEM.
THE THING WAS A LOT FASTER THAN IT LOOKED, AND I WAS SLOWED DOWN BY THE RENEWED SCRAMBLING OF MY BRAIN.
SKRAK
I SKIRT THE BATTLEFIELD'S PERIMETER AND JUST MAKE IT TO THE MINI-MOUNTAIN THAT WAS THE HOUSE'S FRONT YARD AN HOUR AGO.
THE QUARRY IS JUST BEYOND IT...IF I CAN JUST KEEP FROM BLACKING OUT LONG ENOUGH TO CLIMB IT...
MADE IT! NOW DOWN SHOULD BE MUCH EASIER THAN UP--
STUPID.
STUPID.
STUPID.

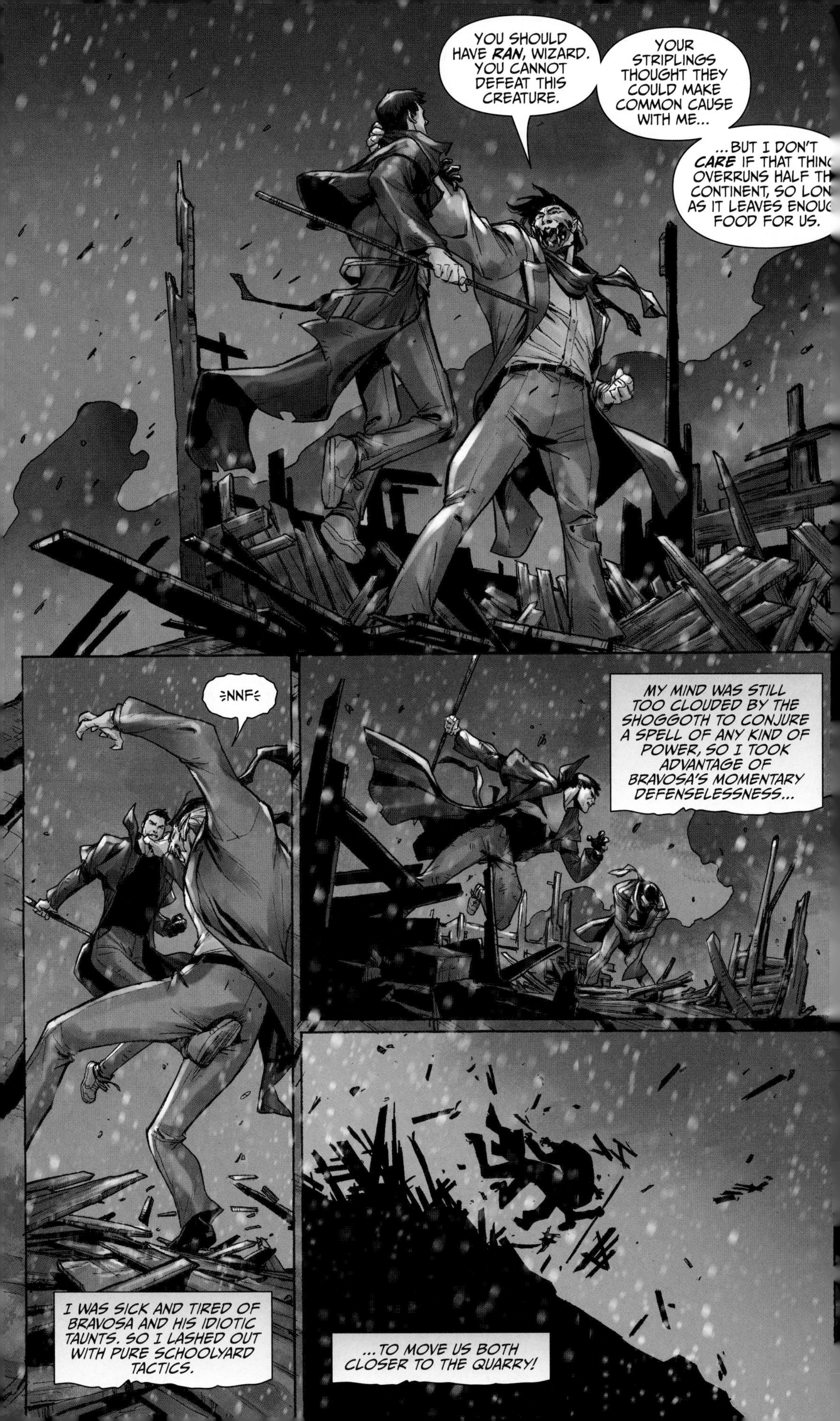
YOU SHOULD HAVE *RAN*, WIZARD. YOU CANNOT DEFEAT THIS CREATURE.
YOUR STRIPLINGS THOUGHT THEY COULD MAKE COMMON CAUSE WITH ME...
...BUT I DON'T *CARE* IF THAT THING OVERRUNS HALF TH CONTINENT, SO LON AS IT LEAVES ENOUG FOOD FOR US.
NNF
I WAS SICK AND TIRED OF BRAVOSA AND HIS IDIOTIC TAUNTS. SO I LASHED OUT WITH PURE SCHOOLYARD TACTICS.
MY MIND WAS STILL TOO CLOUDED BY THE SHOGGOTH TO CONJURE A SPELL OF ANY KIND OF POWER, SO I TOOK ADVANTAGE OF BRAVOSA'S MOMENTARY DEFENSELESSNESS...
...TO MOVE US BOTH CLOSER TO THE QUARRY!

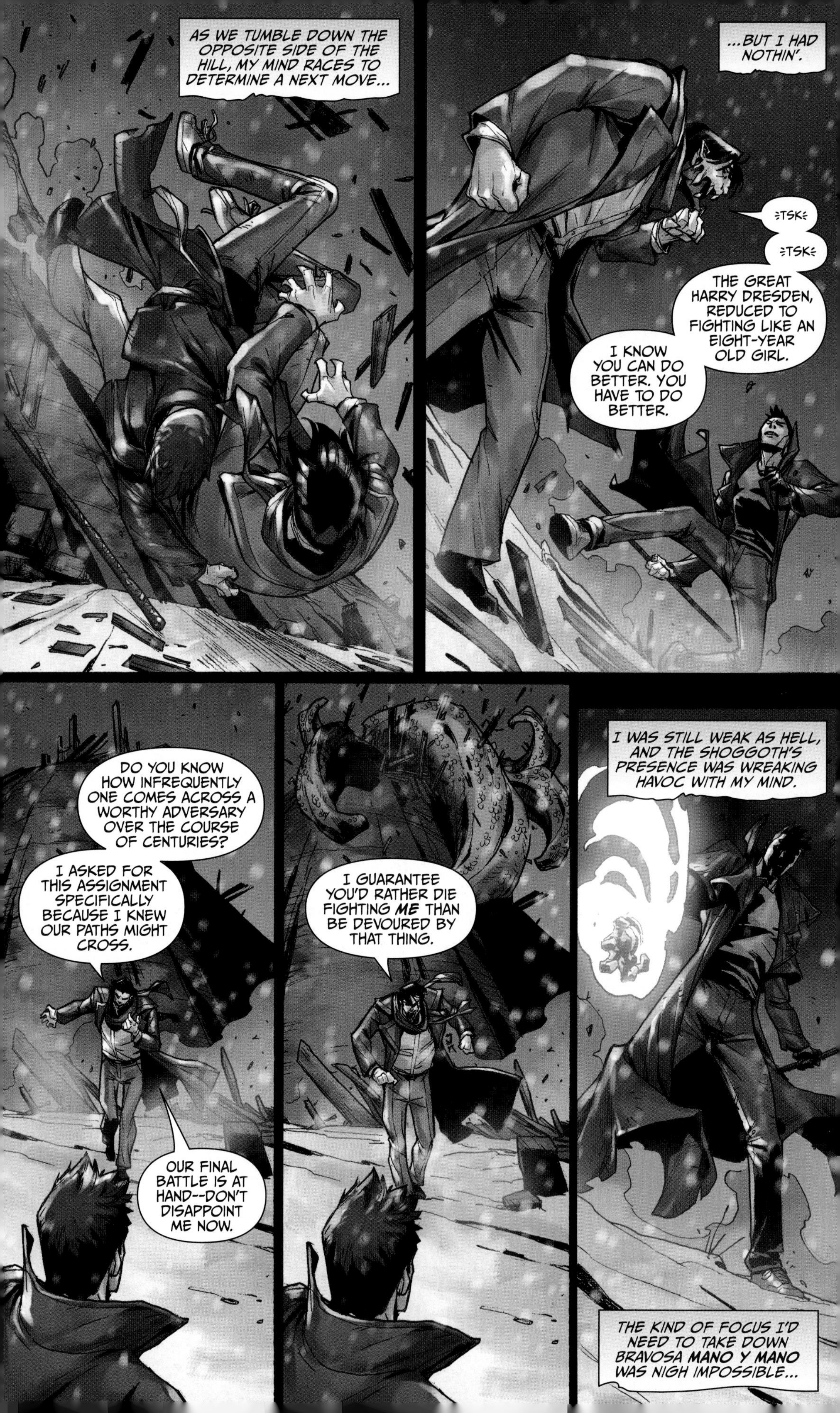
AS WE TUMBLE DOWN THE OPPOSITE SIDE OF THE HILL, MY MIND RACES TO DETERMINE A NEXT MOVE...
...BUT I HAD NOTHIN'.
TSK
TSK
THE GREAT HARRY DRESDEN, REDUCED TO FIGHTING LIKE AN EIGHT-YEAR OLD GIRL.
I KNOW YOU CAN DO BETTER. YOU HAVE TO DO BETTER.
DO YOU KNOW HOW INFREQUENTLY ONE COMES ACROSS A WORTHY ADVERSARY OVER THE COURSE OF CENTURIES?
I ASKED FOR THIS ASSIGNMENT SPECIFICALLY BECAUSE I KNEW OUR PATHS MIGHT CROSS.
OUR FINAL BATTLE IS AT HAND--DON'T DISAPPOINT ME NOW.
I GUARANTEE YOU'D RATHER DIE FIGHTING *ME* THAN BE DEVOURED BY THAT THING.
I WAS STILL WEAK AS HELL, AND THE SHOGGOTH'S PRESENCE WAS WREAKING HAVOC WITH MY MIND.
THE KIND OF FOCUS I'D NEED TO TAKE DOWN BRAVOSA **MANO Y MANO** WAS NIGH IMPOSSIBLE...

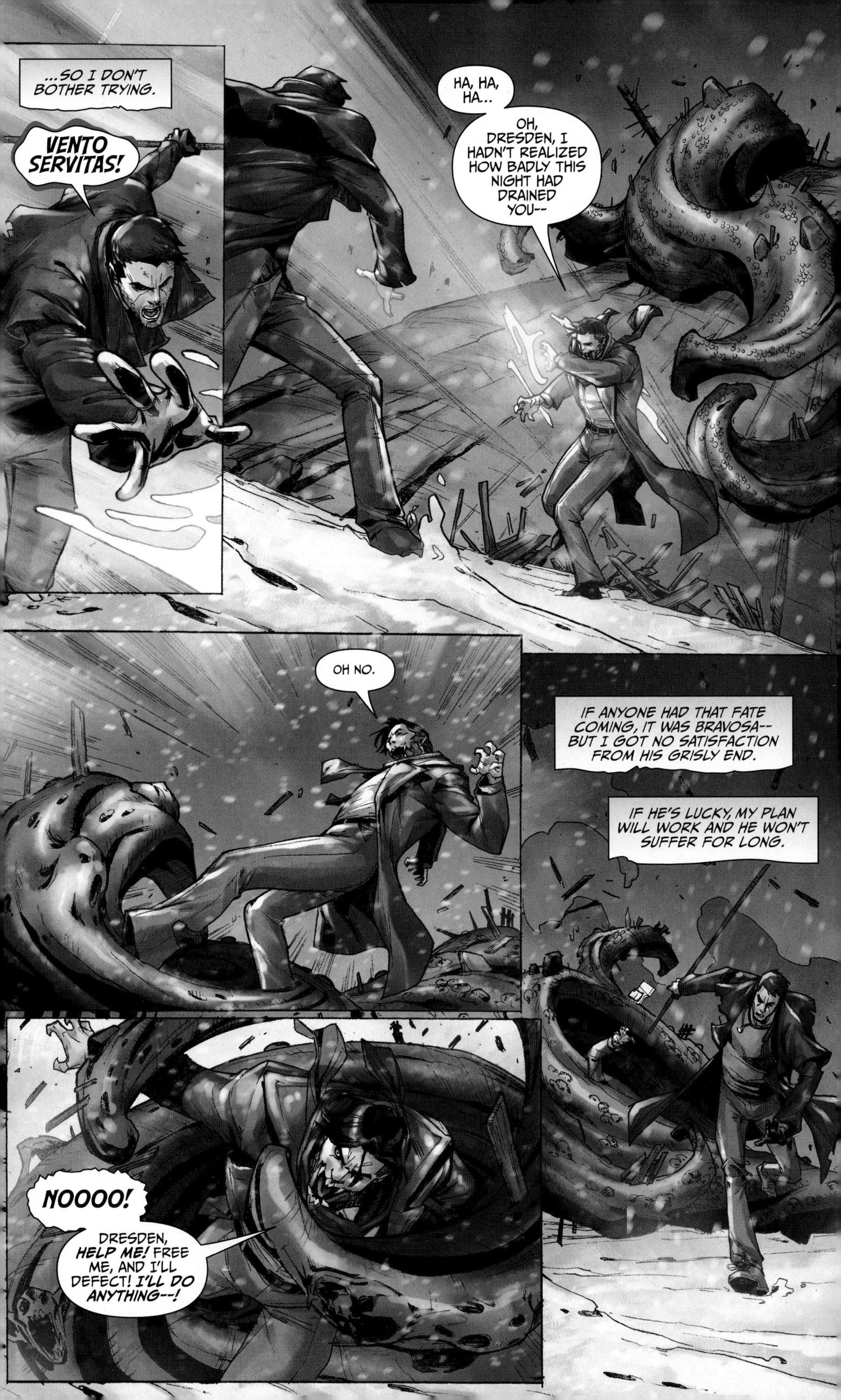

...SO I DON'T BOTHER TRYING.
VENTO SERVITAS!
HA, HA, HA...
OH, DRESDEN, I HADN'T REALIZED HOW BADLY THIS NIGHT HAD DRAINED YOU--
OH NO.
IF ANYONE HAD THAT FATE COMING, IT WAS BRAVOSA-- BUT I GOT NO SATISFACTION FROM HIS GRISLY END.
IF HE'S LUCKY, MY PLAN WILL WORK AND HE WON'T SUFFER FOR LONG.
NOOOO!
DRESDEN, HELP ME! FREE ME, AND I'LL DEFECT! I'LL DO ANYTHING--!

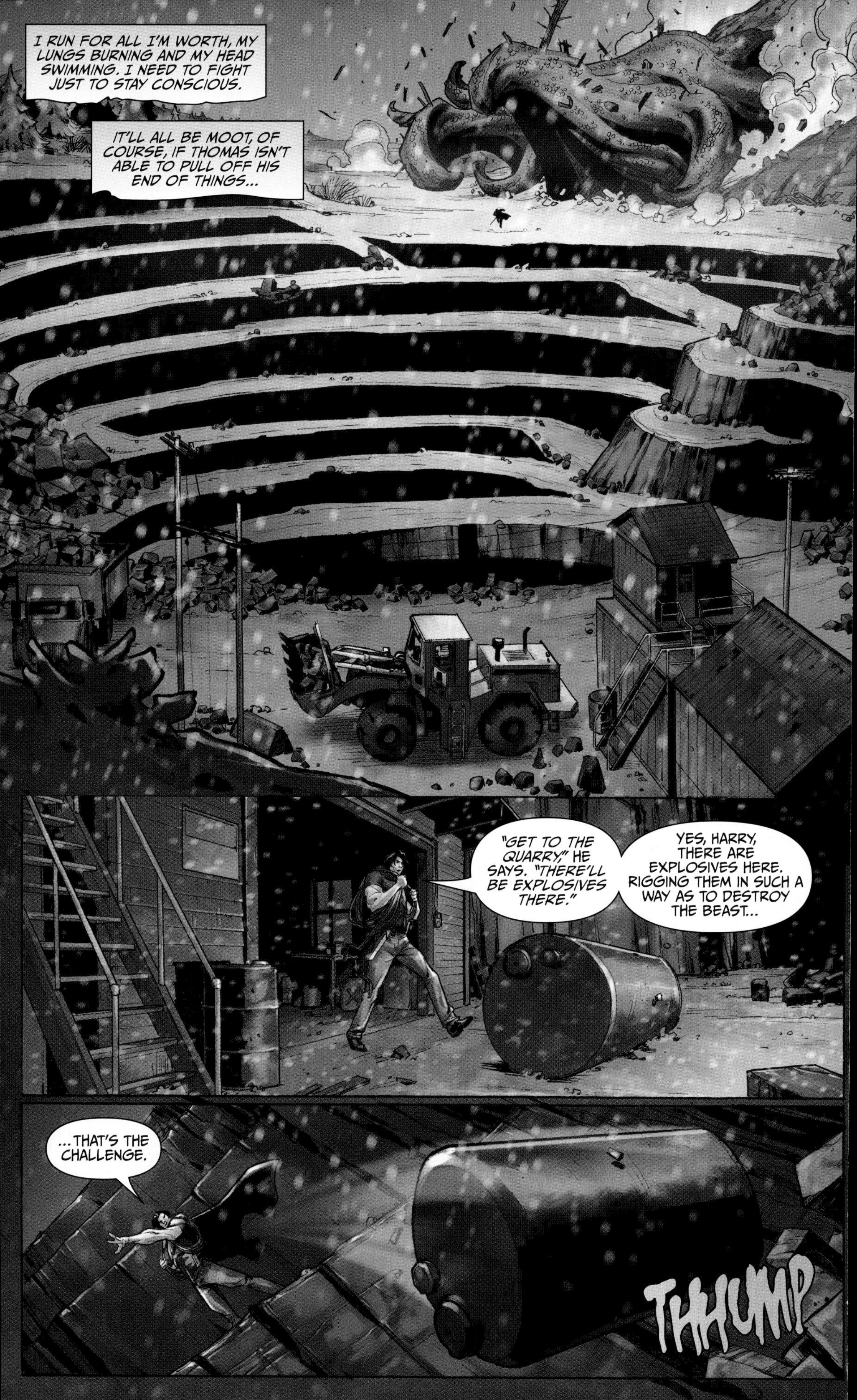

I RUN FOR ALL I'M WORTH, MY LUNGS BURNING AND MY HEAD SWIMMING. I NEED TO FIGHT JUST TO STAY CONSCIOUS.
IT'LL ALL BE MOOT, OF COURSE, IF THOMAS ISN'T ABLE TO PULL OFF HIS END OF THINGS...
"GET TO THE QUARRY," HE SAYS. "THERE'LL BE EXPLOSIVES THERE."
YES, HARRY, THERE ARE EXPLOSIVES HERE. RIGGING THEM IN SUCH A WAY AS TO DESTROY THE BEAST...
...THAT'S THE CHALLENGE.
THHUMP

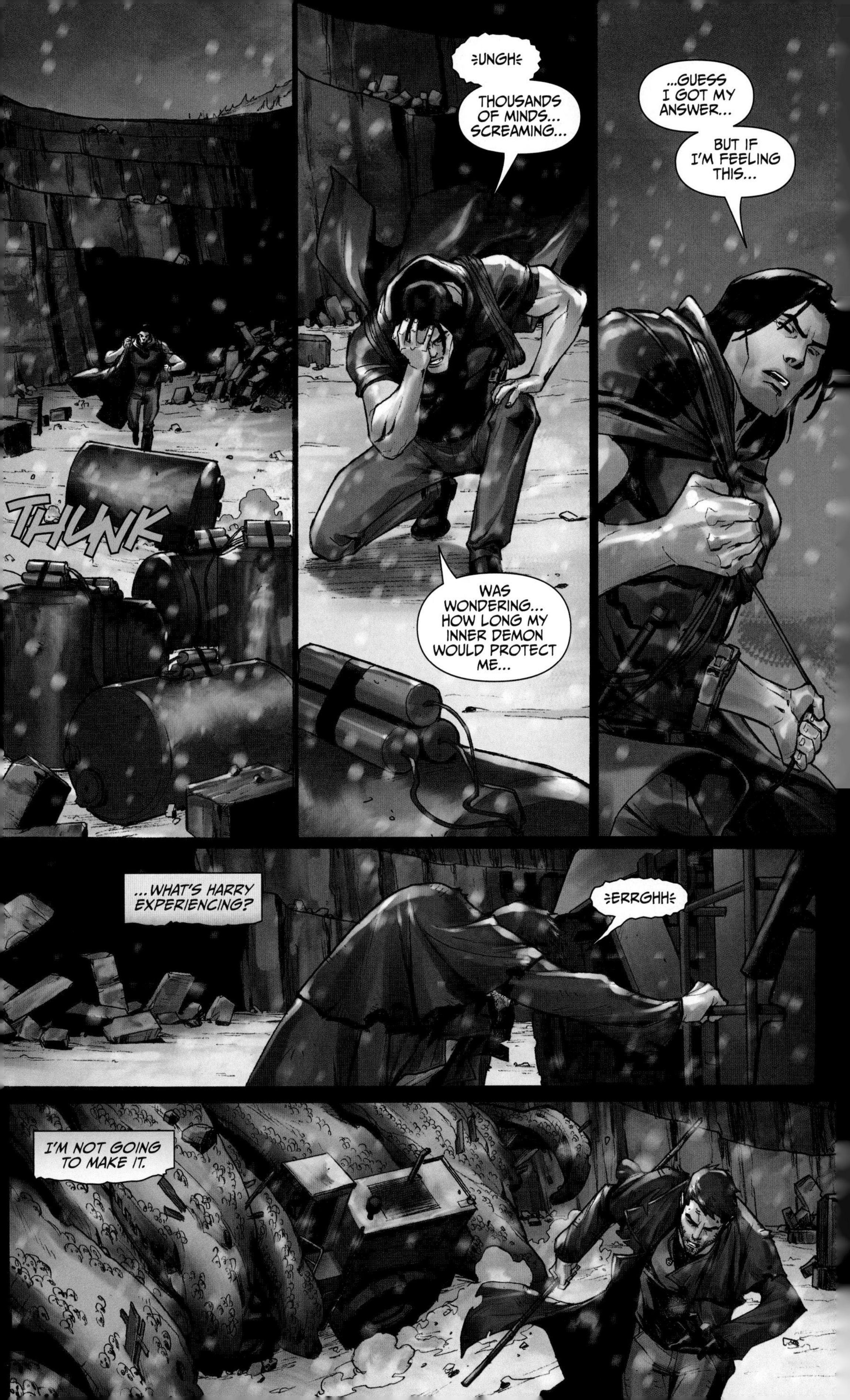
THUNK
UNGH
THOUSANDS OF MINDS... SCREAMING...
WAS WONDERING... HOW LONG MY INNER DEMON WOULD PROTECT ME...
...GUESS I GOT MY ANSWER...
BUT IF I'M FEELING THIS...
...WHAT'S HARRY EXPERIENCING?
ERRGHH
I'M NOT GOING TO MAKE IT.

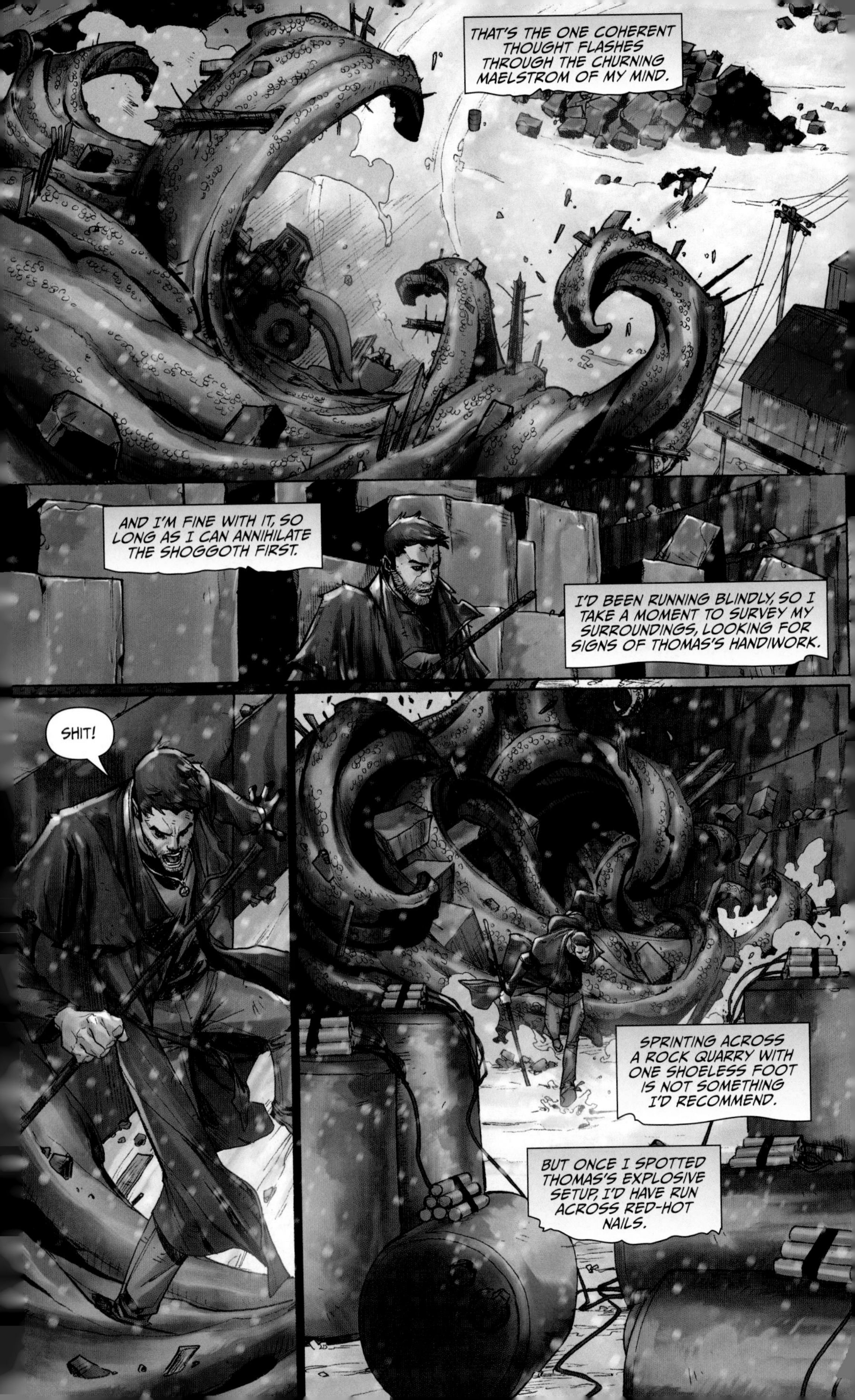
THAT'S THE ONE COHERENT THOUGHT FLASHES THROUGH THE CHURNING MAELSTROM OF MY MIND.
AND I'M FINE WITH IT, SO LONG AS I CAN ANNIHILATE THE SHOGGOTH FIRST.
I'D BEEN RUNNING BLINDLY, SO I TAKE A MOMENT TO SURVEY MY SURROUNDINGS, LOOKING FOR SIGNS OF THOMAS'S HANDIWORK.
SHIT!
SPRINTING ACROSS A ROCK QUARRY WITH ONE SHOELESS FOOT IS NOT SOMETHING I'D RECOMMEND.
BUT ONCE I SPOTTED THOMAS'S EXPLOSIVE SETUP, I'D HAVE RUN ACROSS RED-HOT NAILS.

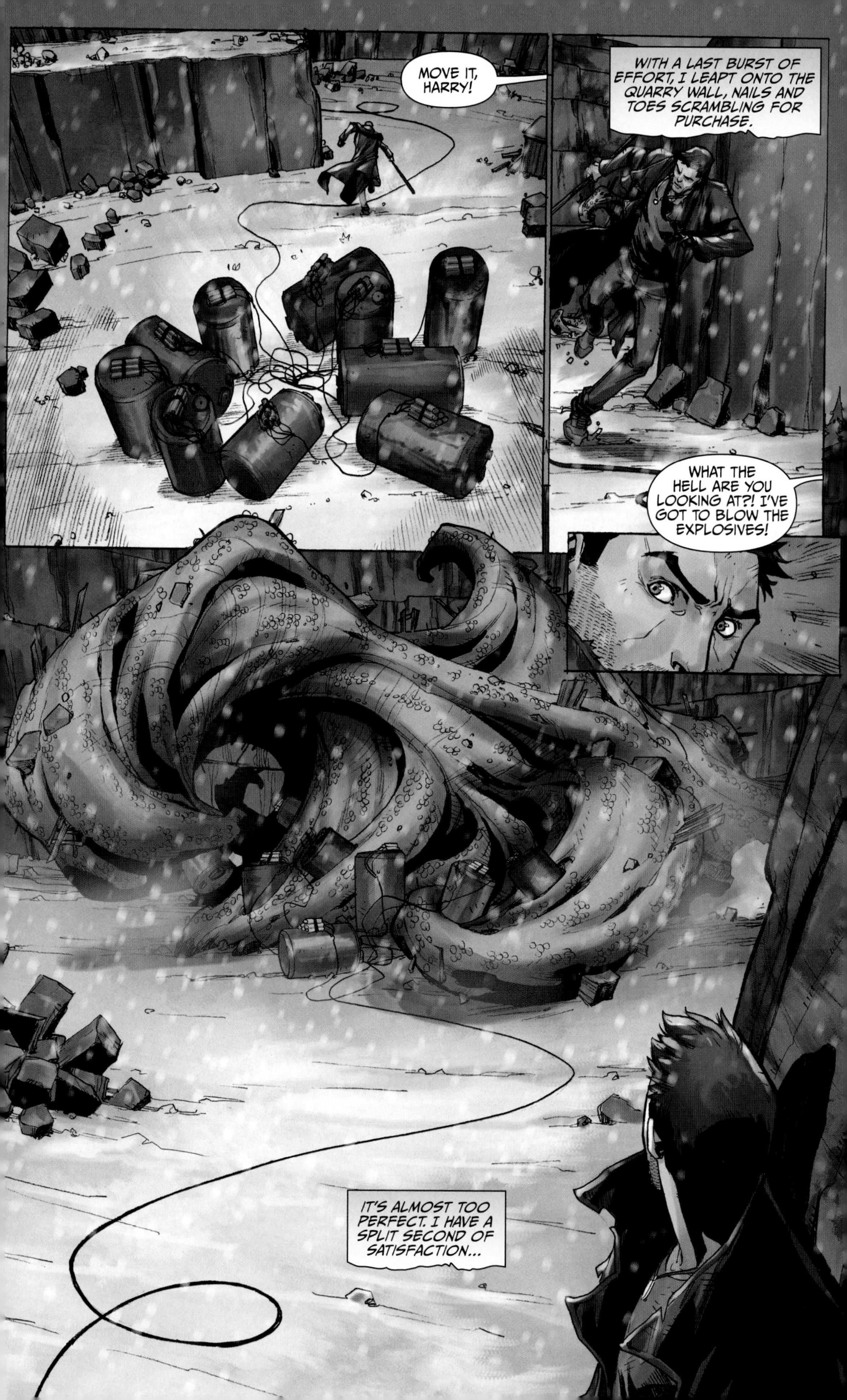
MOVE IT, HARRY!
WITH A LAST BURST OF EFFORT, I LEAPT ONTO THE QUARRY WALL, NAILS AND TOES SCRAMBLING FOR PURCHASE.
WHAT THE HELL ARE YOU LOOKING AT?! I'VE GOT TO BLOW THE EXPLOSIVES!
IT'S ALMOST TOO PERFECT. I HAVE A SPLIT SECOND OF SATISFACTION...

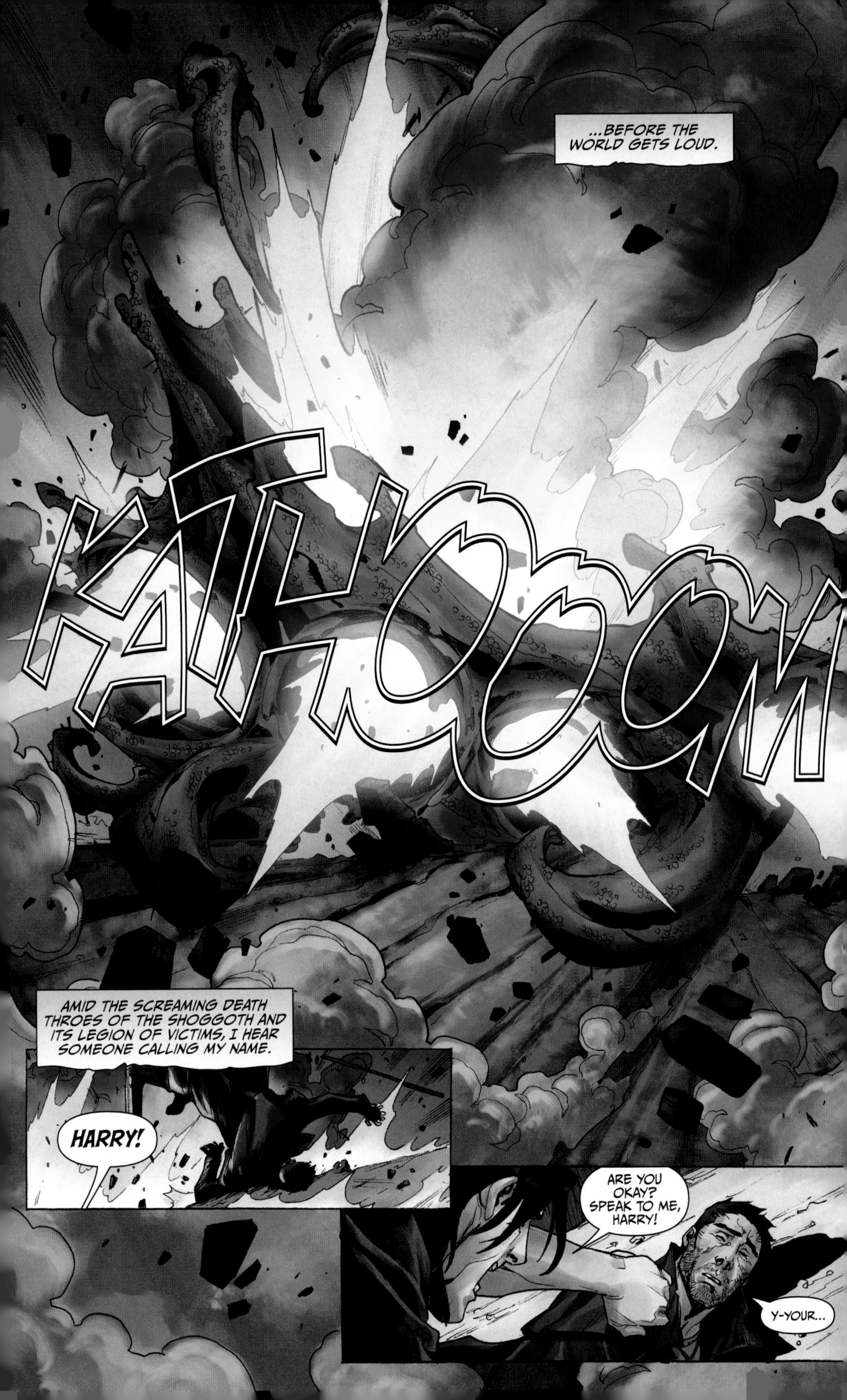
...BEFORE THE WORLD GETS LOUD.
KATHOOOM
AMID THE SCREAMING DEATH THROES OF THE SHOGGOTH AND ITS LEGION OF VICTIMS, I HEAR SOMEONE CALLING MY NAME.
HARRY!
ARE YOU OKAY? SPEAK TO ME, HARRY!
Y-YOUR...

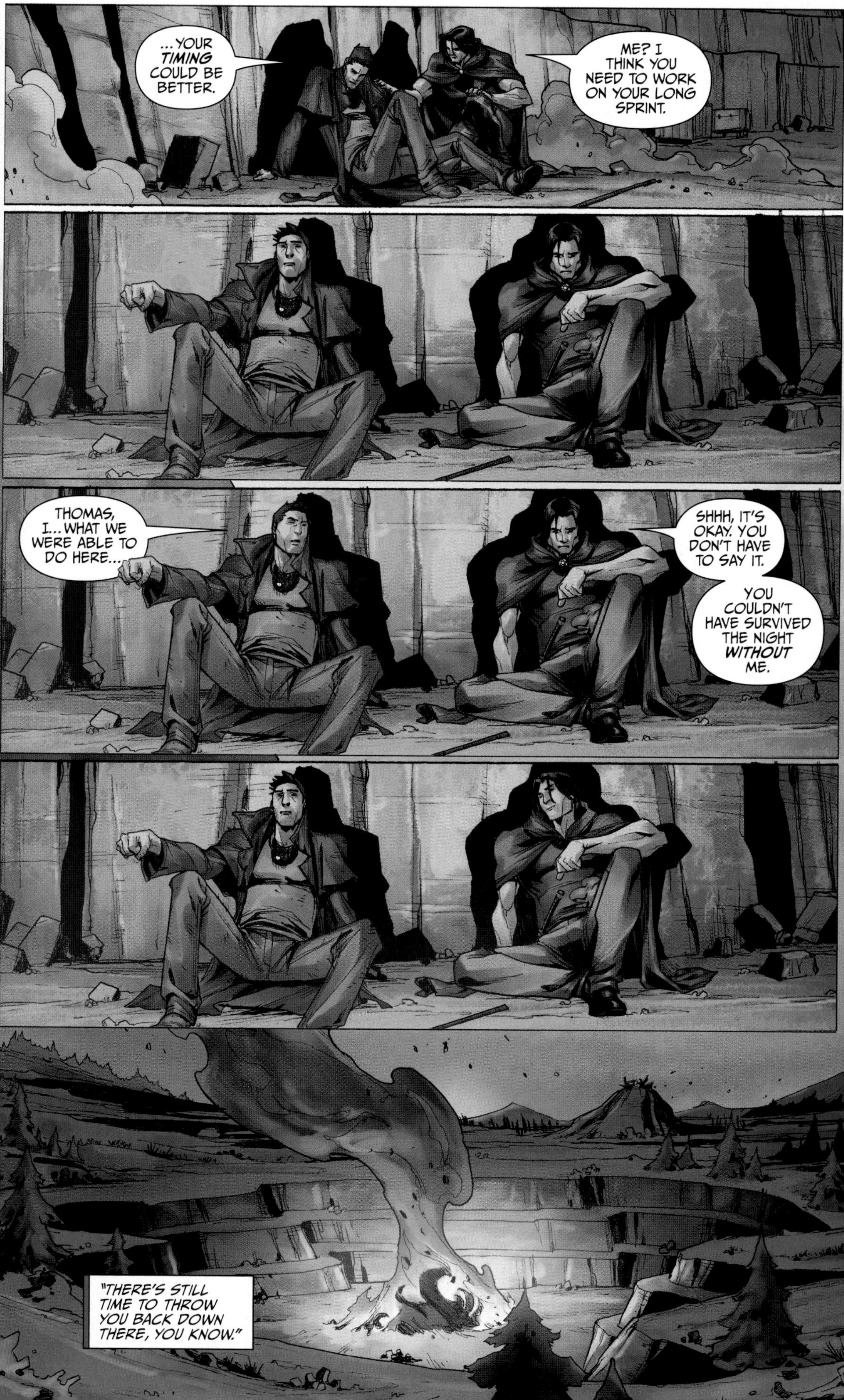

...YOUR *TIMING* COULD BE BETTER.
ME? I THINK YOU NEED TO WORK ON YOUR LONG SPRINT.
THOMAS, I...WHAT WE WERE ABLE TO DO HERE...
SHHH, IT'S OKAY. YOU DON'T HAVE TO SAY IT.
YOU COULDN'T HAVE SURVIVED THE NIGHT *WITHOUT* ME.
"THERE'S STILL TIME TO THROW YOU BACK DOWN THERE, YOU KNOW."

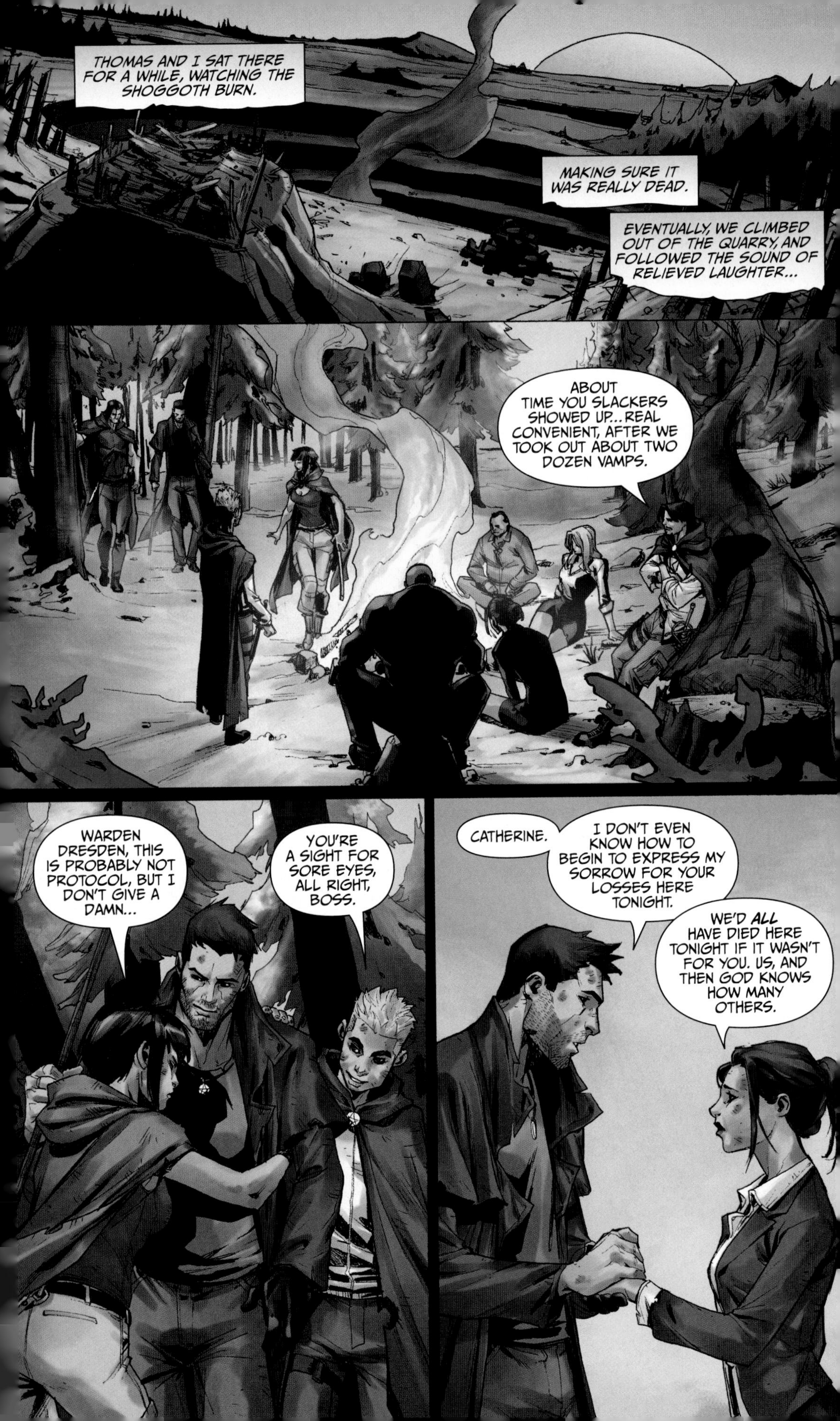
THOMAS AND I SAT THERE FOR A WHILE, WATCHING THE SHOGGOTH BURN.
MAKING SURE IT WAS REALLY DEAD.
EVENTUALLY, WE CLIMBED OUT OF THE QUARRY, AND FOLLOWED THE SOUND OF RELIEVED LAUGHTER...
ABOUT TIME YOU SLACKERS SHOWED UP... REAL CONVENIENT, AFTER WE TOOK OUT ABOUT TWO DOZEN VAMPS.
WARDEN DRESDEN, THIS IS PROBABLY NOT PROTOCOL, BUT I DON'T GIVE A DAMN...
YOU'RE A SIGHT FOR SORE EYES, ALL RIGHT, BOSS.
CATHERINE.
I DON'T EVEN KNOW HOW TO BEGIN TO EXPRESS MY SORROW FOR YOUR LOSSES HERE TONIGHT.
WE'D ALL HAVE DIED HERE TONIGHT IF IT WASN'T FOR YOU. US, AND THEN GOD KNOWS HOW MANY OTHERS.

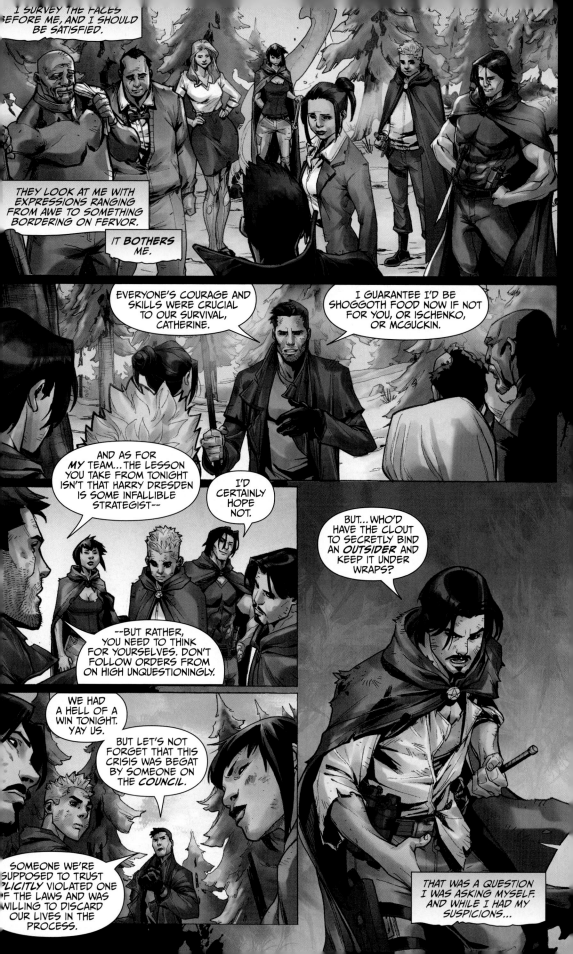

I SURVEY THE FACES BEFORE ME, AND I SHOULD BE SATISFIED.

THEY LOOK AT ME WITH EXPRESSIONS RANGING FROM AWE TO SOMETHING BORDERING ON FERVOR.

IT BOTHERS ME.

EVERYONE'S COURAGE AND SKILLS WERE CRUCIAL TO OUR SURVIVAL, CATHERINE.

I GUARANTEE I'D BE SHOGGOTH FOOD NOW IF NOT FOR YOU, OR ISCHENKO, OR MCGUCKIN.

AND AS FOR MY TEAM... THE LESSON YOU TAKE FROM TONIGHT ISN'T THAT HARRY DRESDEN IS SOME INFALLIBLE STRATEGIST--

I'D CERTAINLY HOPE NOT.

BUT... WHO'D HAVE THE CLOUT TO SECRETLY BIND AN OUTSIDER AND KEEP IT UNDER WRAPS?

--BUT RATHER, YOU NEED TO THINK FOR YOURSELVES. DON'T FOLLOW ORDERS FROM ON HIGH UNQUESTIONINGLY.

WE HAD A HELL OF A WIN TONIGHT. YAY US.

BUT LET'S NOT FORGET THAT THIS CRISIS WAS BEGAT BY SOMEONE ON THE COUNCIL.

SOMEONE WE'RE SUPPOSED TO TRUST ʼPLICITLY VIOLATED ONE ʼF THE LAWS AND WAS WILLING TO DISCARD OUR LIVES IN THE PROCESS.

THAT WAS A QUESTION I WAS ASKING MYSELF. AND WHILE I HAD MY SUSPICIONS...

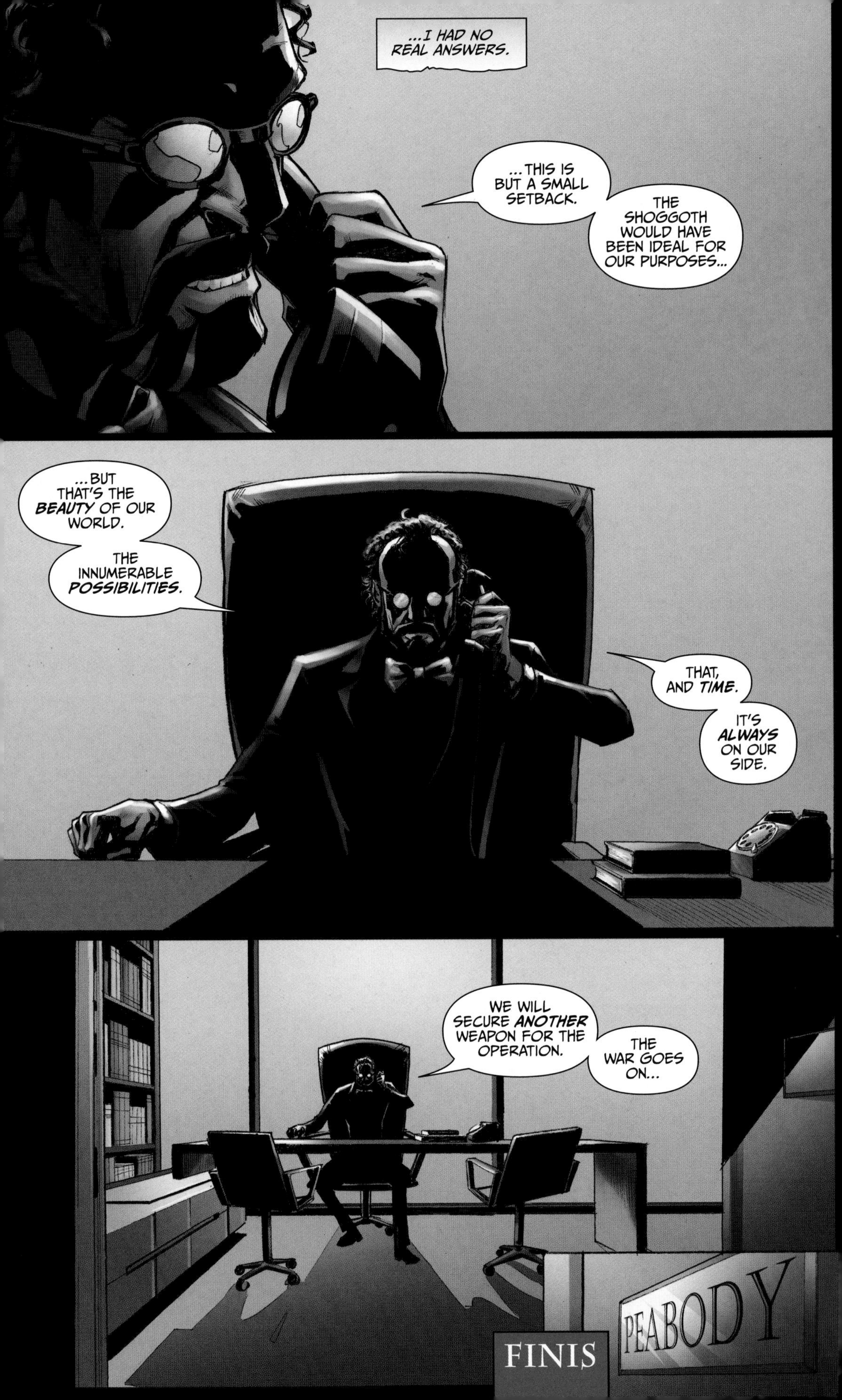
...I HAD NO REAL ANSWERS.
...THIS IS BUT A SMALL SETBACK.
THE SHOGGOTH WOULD HAVE BEEN IDEAL FOR OUR PURPOSES...
...BUT THAT'S THE BEAUTY OF OUR WORLD.
THE INNUMERABLE POSSIBILITIES.
THAT, AND TIME.
IT'S ALWAYS ON OUR SIDE.
WE WILL SECURE ANOTHER WEAPON FOR THE OPERATION.
THE WAR GOES ON...
PEABODY
FINIS

VARIANT COVERS

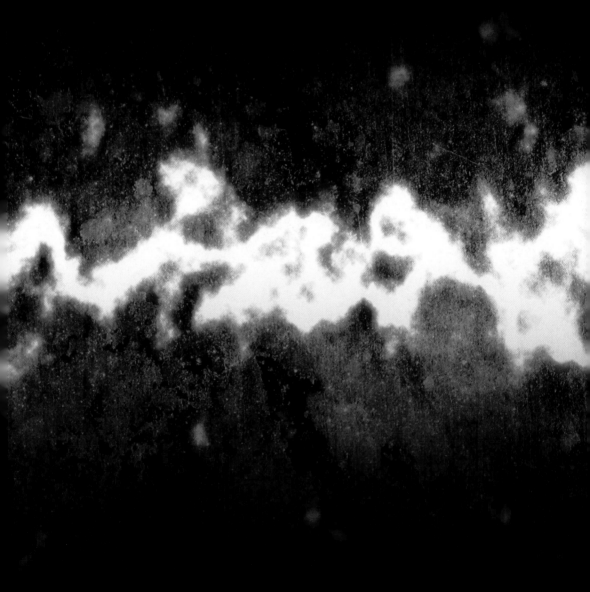

ISSUE ONE "STEAMPUNK" VARIANT COVER BY
CARLOS GOMEZ AND MOHAN

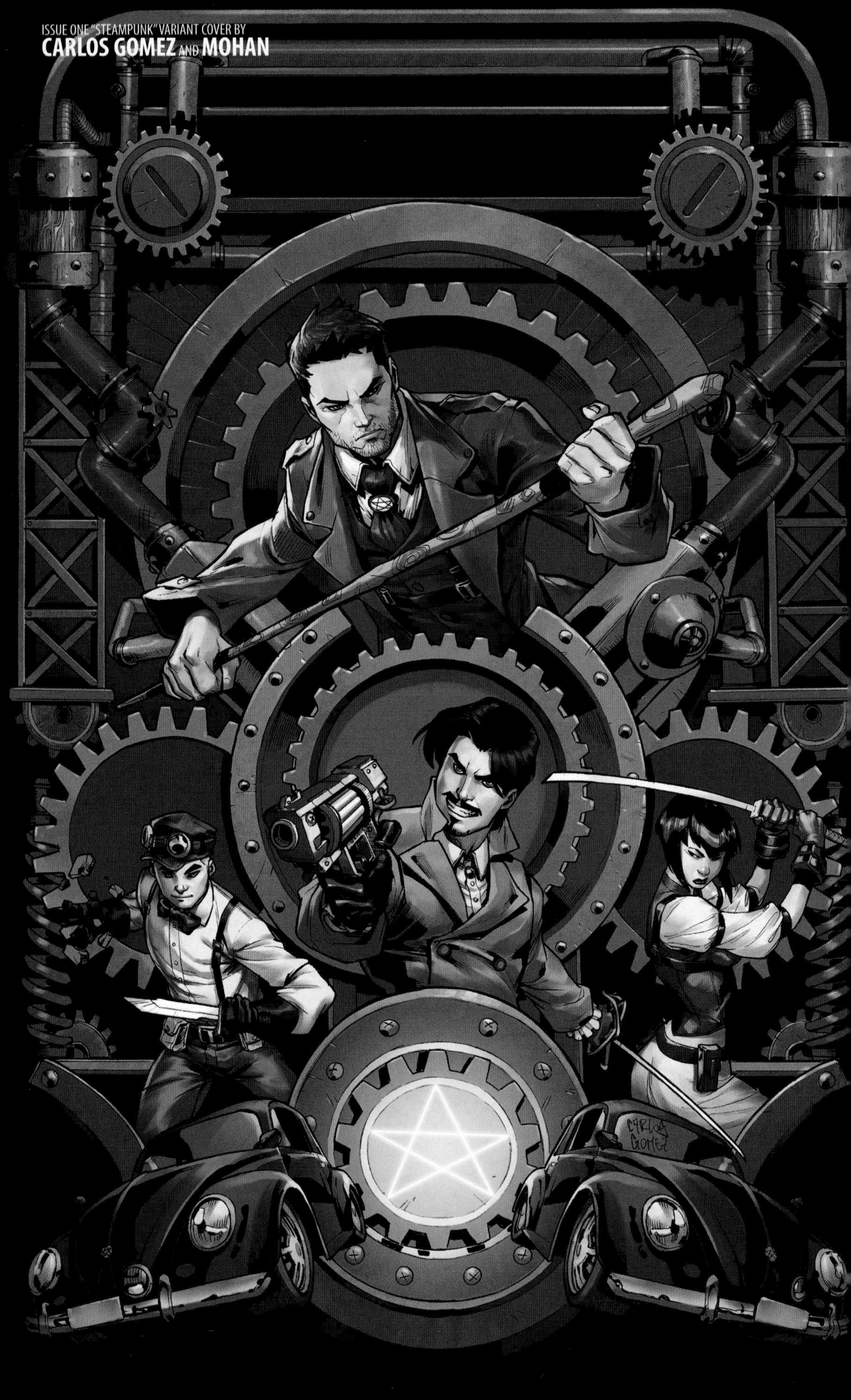

CARLOS GOMEZ AND MOHAN

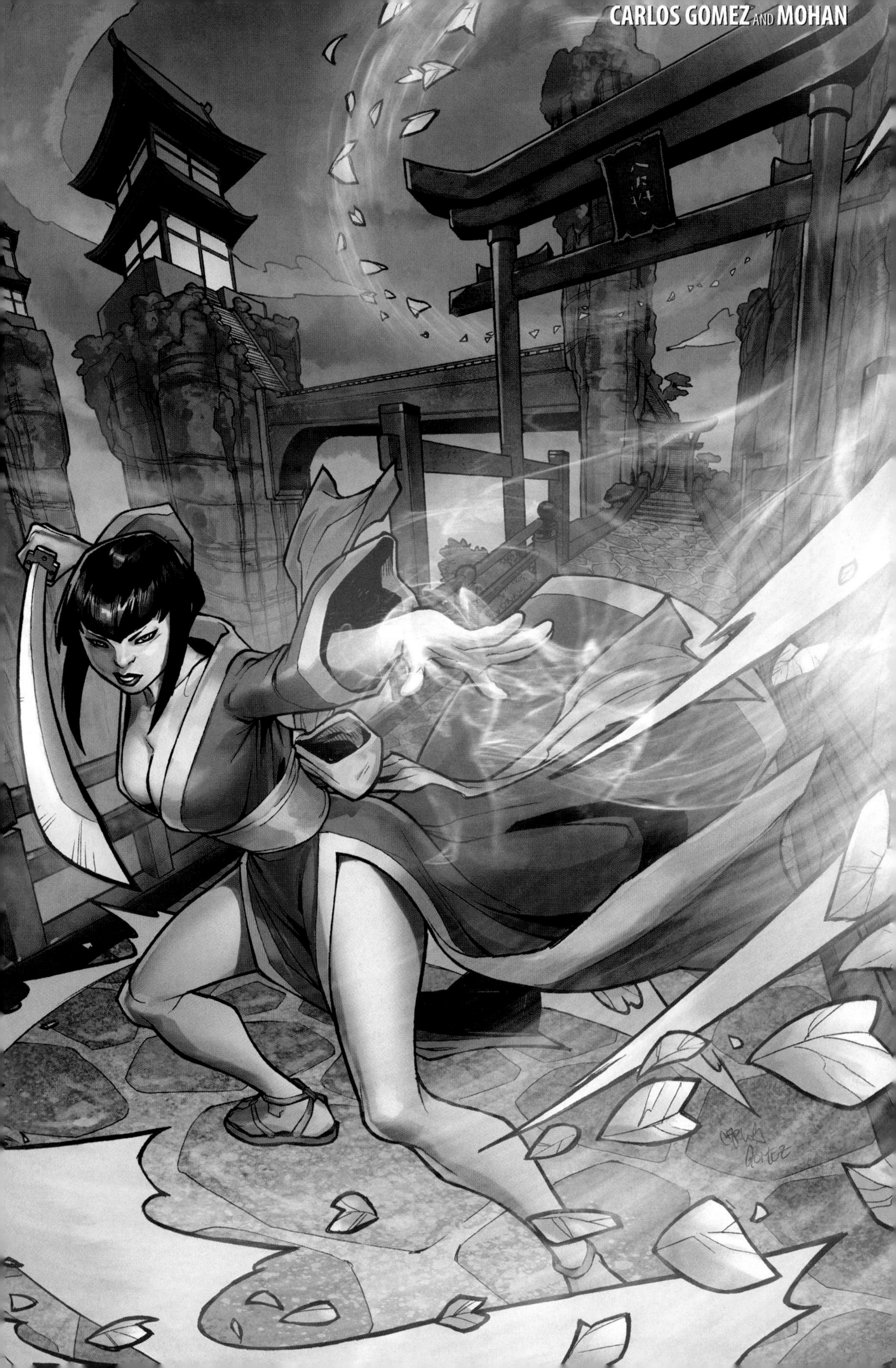

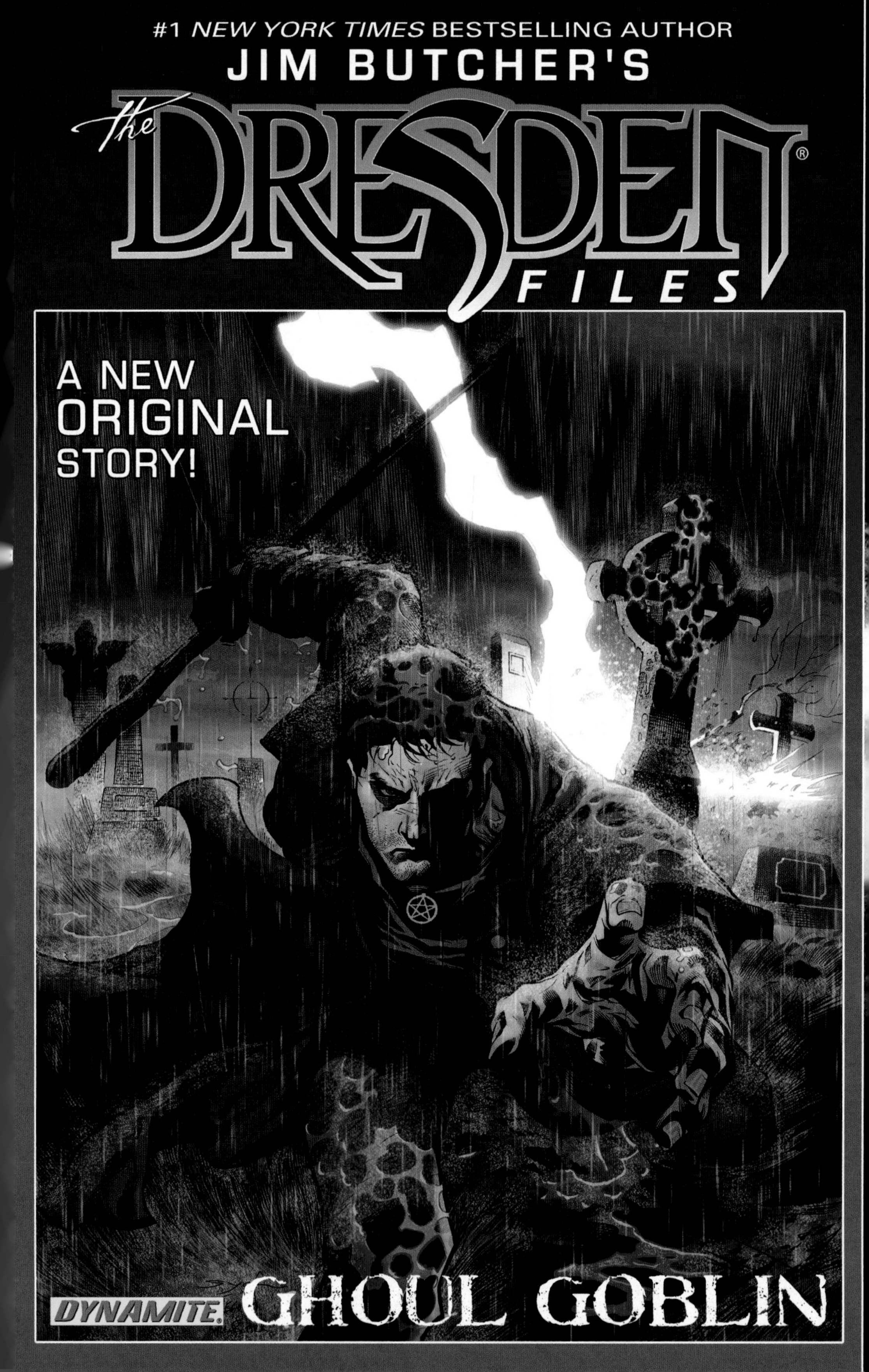

#1 NEW YORK TIMES BESTSELLING AUTHOR
JIM BUTCHER'S
the DRESDEN FILES
A NEW ORIGINAL STORY!
DYNAMITE
GHOUL GOBLIN

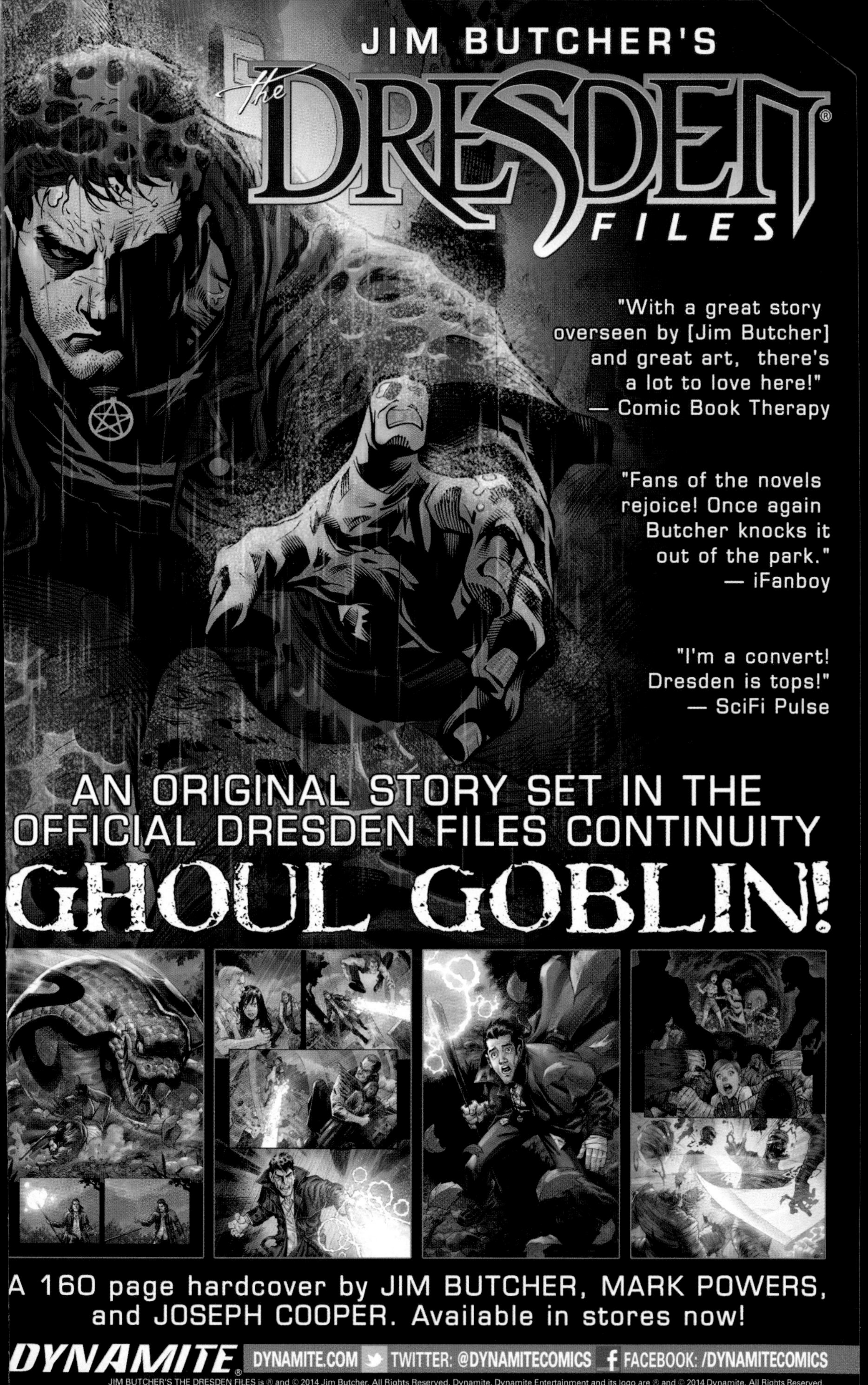
JIM BUTCHER'S
The DRESDEN® FILES
"With a great story overseen by [Jim Butcher] and great art, there's a lot to love here!" — Comic Book Therapy
"Fans of the novels rejoice! Once again Butcher knocks it out of the park." — iFanboy
"I'm a convert! Dresden is tops!" — SciFi Pulse
AN ORIGINAL STORY SET IN THE OFFICIAL DRESDEN FILES CONTINUITY
GHOUL GOBLIN!
A 160 page hardcover by JIM BUTCHER, MARK POWERS, and JOSEPH COOPER. Available in stores now!
DYNAMITE®
DYNAMITE.COM
TWITTER: @DYNAMITECOMICS
FACEBOOK: /DYNAMITECOMICS
JIM BUTCHER'S THE DRESDEN FILES is ® and © 2014 Jim Butcher. All Rights Reserved. Dynamite, Dynamite Entertainment and its logo are ® and © 2014 Dynamite. All Rights Reserved.

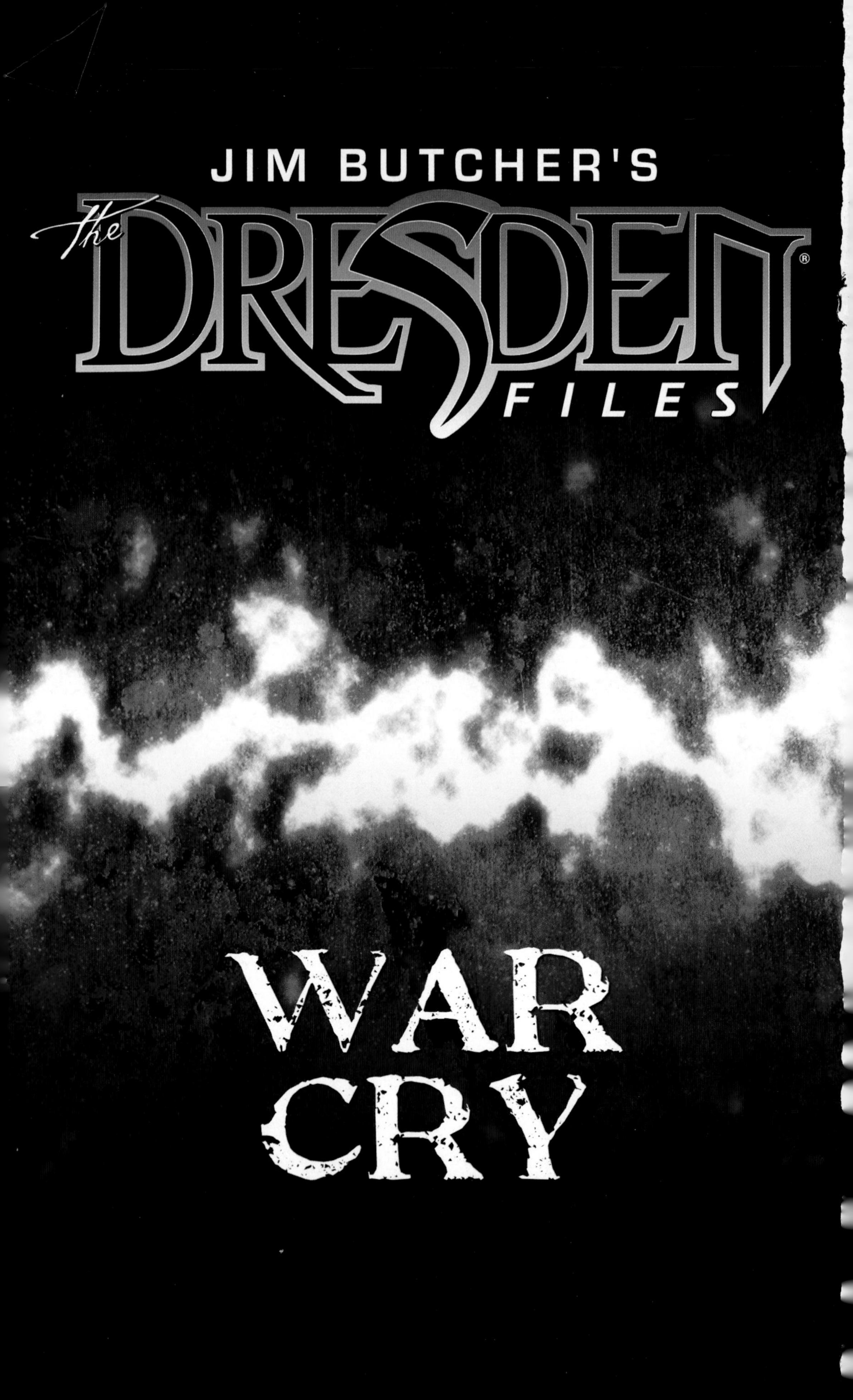
JIM BUTCHER'S
The DRESDEN FILES®
WAR
CRY